Combinatorial Algorithms

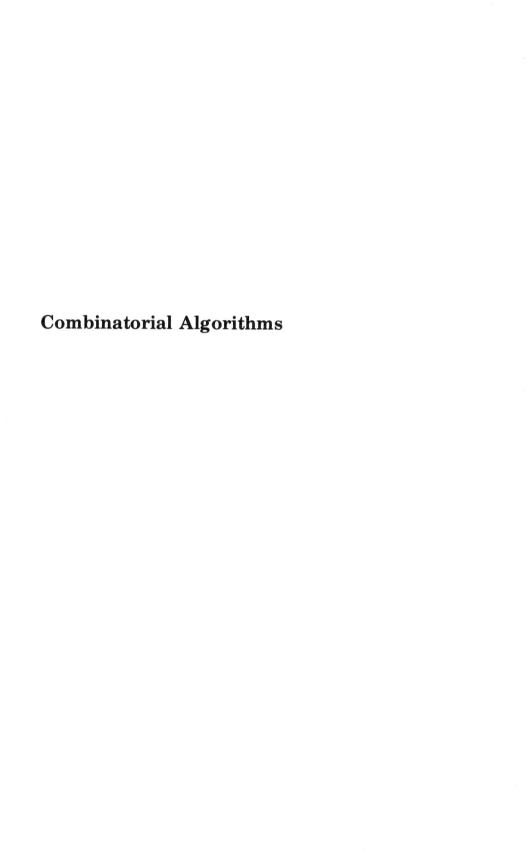

Combinatorial Algorithms

ALBERT NIJENHUIS and HERBERT S. WILF

ACADEMIC PRESS   New York   San Francisco   London   1975

A Subsidiary of Harcourt Brace Jovanovich, Publishers

ACADEMIC PRESS, INC.
111 Fifth Avenue, New York, New York 10003

United Kingdom Edition published by
ACADEMIC PRESS, INC. (LONDON) LTD.
24/28 Oval Road, London NW1

Library of Congress Cataloging in Publication Data

Nijenhuis, Albert.
    Combinatorial algorithms.

    (Computer science and applied mathematics)
    Bibliography: p.
    Includes index.
    1.   Combinatorial analysis–Computer programs.
I.   Wilf, Herbert S., (date)   II.   Title.
QA164.N54   511'.6'0285425   74-17976
ISBN 0–12–519250–9

AMS (MOS) 1970 Subject Classifications: 68A10, 05-04,
05A05, 05A17, 05C15, 06A10, 90B10

To

P. G. J. Vredenduin, for his early inspiration and support,

Henry and *Bernice Tumen,* with affection and esteem.

Contents

Preface

In the course of our combinatorial work over the past several years, we have been fond of going to the computer from time to time in order to see some examples of the things we were studying. We have built up a fairly extensive library of programs, and we feel that others might be interested in learning about the methods and/or use of the programs. This book is the result.

It can be read as a collection of mathematical algorithms, and as such we hope the reader will find much that is new and interesting. Yet to do so would be to miss something that to us seems essential: the interchange between the computer programs per se, the computer, the algorithms, and ultimately the mathematics. To capture the complete spirit of this work, we urge the reader to study the programs themselves. The extra dimension that the computer and the mathematics bestow on each other is, we believe worth the effort. Above all, we hope we have placed in the reader's hands a kit of building blocks with which the reader can construct more elaborate structures of his or her own.

The second-named author expresses his appreciation to the John Simon Guggenheim Memorial Foundation for its support during the writing of this book, and to Rockefeller University of New York for its hospitality during the same period. Much of the original research described herein was supported by the National Science Foundation.

We wish to thank Donald E. Knuth for reading the manuscript and for making a number of extremely valuable suggestions that resulted in improvements.

Introduction

AIMS

This book can be read at several levels. Those whose only need is to use one of the computer programs can turn immediately to those pages and satisfy their wants. Thus, on one level, this is a collection of subroutines, in FORTRAN, for the solution of combinatorial problems.

At the other extreme, pure mathematicians with no need of computer programs will find much that is new and hopefully interesting in these pages. For example, in the special section *Deus ex Machina* (pp. 77–80), the random selection algorithms of Chapters 10, 12, and 25 are shown to be manifestations of a general phenomenon which sheds light on a number of seemingly unrelated threads of research in combinatorial analysis.

Our hope, however, is that most readers will want to follow the entire road from general mathematics to particular mathematics to informal algorithm to formal algorithm to computer program and back again, which occurs in virtually every chapter of the book.

Our other hope is that readers will view these methods and programs as a beginning set of building blocks for their own kit of tools and will go on to add to these tools to meet their own needs, so that the contents of this book will be not a collection of pretty artifacts to be looked at but basic elements of the growing and working equipment of scientific investigation and learning.

HIGHLIGHTS

We preview some of the novel features which lie ahead. First, concerning the random choice algorithms previously mentioned, in Chapter 10 there is an algorithm for selecting, at random, a partition of an integer n, so that all are equally likely to occur. This seems to work for a special reason, but actually it works for a very general reason described in the section *Deus ex Machina* which follows Chapter 10. Another outcropping of the same idea is found in Chapter 25 where we can select, at random, an unlabeled rooted tree on n vertices so that all are equally likely, and, in Chapter 12, a closely related idea results in the selection of a random partition of an n-set. These methods are all new.

In Chapter 16 is a new algorithm for the computation of the chromatic polynomial of a graph. Its conceptual basis has been known for years, but between that basis and an efficient algorithm lie a considerable number of additional ingredients. That chapter makes use of Chapter 14 which finds a spanning forest of a graph and so, in particular, finds its connectivity. The spanning forest problem is central to many combinatorial calculations, and the method of Chapter 14 is also new.

Another method which appears for the first time in these pages is the calculation of the permanent function in Chapter 19 which for an $n \times n$ matrix is about $n/2$ times faster than standard algorithms at no cost in storage. It is in essence a variation of a known method in which subsets of a set are processed in a special sequence. The sequence is provided by the program in Chapter 1.

Further algorithms which have not previously been published are the revolving-door method of Chapter 3, which extends the spirit of Chapter 1 into the realm of fixed cardinality, the sequential generation of compositions, permutations, and partitions of Chapters 5, 8, and 9, the random selection of k-subsets (Chapter 4) and compositions (Chapter 6), and the logarithmic–derivative-based composition of power series (Chapter 17).

Chapter 18 on network flows uses a new implementation of a standard algorithm and works very smoothly on graphs whose edges have positive capacities in both directions (e.g., undirected graphs). Applications include graph connectivity and various matching problems. The Möbius sequence (Chapters 20–22) is also elementary but minimizes storage space and computing time by suitable relabeling of elements.

The backtrack method of Chapter 23 is well known, and we have added nothing new except for the specific implementation and applications. The renumbering method of Chapter 13 is curiously arresting. The problem it solves is nonexistent within the scope of mathematics, which does not concern itself with duplication of storage requirements. Yet, in computation, such questions as this thrust themselves to the fore time and time again.

CATEGORIES OF USAGE

We distinguish two kinds of usage, and try to deal with them both: the exhaustive search and the random sampling. In algorithms of search type, we have before us a list of combinatorial objects and we want to search the entire list, or perhaps to search sequentially until we find an object which meets certain conditions. For example, we may wish to hunt through the list of all 3,628,800 permutations of 10 letters in order to find the distribution of their largest cycles.

Random sampling, on the other hand, is done when we want to get the order of magnitude of a quantity of interest, but the exact determination of the quantity by exhaustive search would be so time consuming as to be impracticable. Thus, if we wanted to search through the 87,178,291,200 permutations of 14 letters to examine their largest cycles, it might be advisable to consider random sampling techniques.

These two categories of use call for different kinds of algorithms. For a search, we want a subprogram which, each time we call upon it, will present us with one of the objects on our list. We can then process the object and call the subprogram again to get the next object, etc. In broad outline, such a subprogram must (a) realize when it is being called for the first time, (b) remember enough about its previous output so that it can construct the next member of the list, (c) realize, at the end, that there are no more objects left, and (d) inform the calling program that the end has been reached. The algorithms in this work which are of the above type, and the lists of objects which they search sequentially are

(1)	NEXSUB	All subsets of a set of n elements (n given).
(3)	NEXKSB	All k-subsets of a set of n elements (n, k given).
(5)	NEXCOM	All compositions of n into k parts (n, k given).
(7)	NEXPER	All permutations of a set of n elements (n given).
(9)	NEXPAR	All partitions of an integer n (n given).
(11)	NEXEQU	All partitions of a set of n elements (n given).

The prefix NEX suggests "next," because these routines deliver the next subset, the next k-subset, etc.

In each case the routines are written in such a way as to minimize, if not actually to eliminate, the bookkeeping responsibilities of the calling program of the user. The detailed plan of construction of the programs will be discussed overall in the next section and individually in each chapter.

The logic of a random sampling subroutine is much simpler. Given the input parameters, the subprogram is expected to select at random just one object from the list specified by the input parameter. Here, "at random" has the strict and consistently followed interpretation that *each object on the list has equal a priori probability of being selected.* If the list is short, of course, one might consider constructing the whole list and selecting a member from it at random. The need for random selection methods, however, expresses itself at exactly the point where the above naïve approach fails, namely, when the lists are too long to deal with *in toto.* What are needed, therefore, are methods of *constructing* objects of desired type (the construction depending on the choices of random numbers) in such a way that all objects of the desired type are equally likely to result.

In some cases, these algorithms are trivial (Chapters 2 and 8); in other cases, a simple application of known theorems yields the algorithm (Chapter 24); and in still other cases, new methods are needed and the algorithms appear here for the first time (Chapters 10, 12, and 25). The complete list of algorithms in this work which are of this "random" type and the lists of objects from which they select are

(2) RANSUB All subsets of an n-set (n given).
(4) RANKSB All k-subsets of an n-set (n, k given).
(6) RANCOM All compositions of n into k parts (n, k given).
(8) RANPER All permutations of a set of n elements (n given).
(10) RANPAR All partitions of the integer n (n given).
(12) RANEQU All partitions of an n-set (n given).
(24) RANTRE All labeled trees on n vertices (n given).
(25) RANRUT All rooted unlabeled trees on n vertices (n given).

STRUCTURE OF THE CHAPTERS

Each chapter follows roughly the same format as detailed on page 5.

(a) The mathematical basis of the problem is examined and the chosen algorithm is informally described.

(b) A formal algorithm is stated.

(c) Where appropriate, a complete computer flow diagram is shown in which the numbering of boxes mirrors the numbering of instructions in the actual computer program.

(d) The flow chart, if present, is described.

(e) Just prior to the FORTRAN program itself there appears a "Subroutine Specifications" list. Readers who want only to use a certain program should turn first to this page in the chapter, for it contains complete descriptions of the variables of the subroutine as a user would need to know them. This Specifications list is described in detail in the next section below.

(f) The FORTRAN program. All programs are written in SUBROU-TINE form. While we have attempted to speak least-common-denominator FORTRAN, it cannot be expected that every program will always work with every compiler without slight changes. We believe that such changes will be minimal, and usually nonexistent.

(g) A sample problem, described in detail, followed by output reproduced from an actual machine run of the program.

THE SPECIFICATIONS LIST

Each computer program is immediately preceded by a specifications list which shows the name of the program and then the exact form of its calling statement. Next is a capsule statement of what the program does, and then there is a list which shows, for *each variable which is named in the calling statement*, the following information:

(a) The name of the variable.

(b) The type of the variable; e.g. INTEGER, REAL(N), IN-TEGER(K),DOUBLE PRECISION(M,N), etc. If a parenthesis is present, the variable is an array, and the quantities inside the parentheses indicate the maximum size of the array, expressed in terms of SUBROUTINE parameters.

(c) The column headed *I/O/W/B* describes the role which is played by the variable in the interaction between the subroutine and the "outside world." In this column, opposite each variable, will be found one of the five designations: *I* (input), *O* (output), *I/O* (input-output), *W* (working), *B* (bookkeeping). We have found it desirable to give quite precise meanings to these designations according to the truth or falsity of the following three propositions:

P1: The value(s) of this variable at the time the subroutine is called affects the operation of the subroutine.

P2: The value(s) of this variable is changed by the operation of the subroutine.

P3: The computation of this variable is one of the main purposes of the subroutine.

Then, our precise definitions of the five designations of variable are these:

$$I = (P1) \text{ and } (not \ P2) \text{ and } (not \ P3)$$
$$O = (not \ P1) \text{ and } (P2) \text{ and } (P3)$$
$$I/O = (P1) \text{ and } (P2) \text{ and } (P3)$$
$$W = (not \ P1) \text{ and } (P2) \text{ and } (not \ P3)$$
$$B = (P1) \text{ and } (P2) \text{ and } (not \ P3)$$

In particular, the user must be careful not to change inadvertently the values of variables designated I/O or B between calls of the subroutine, whereas variables of designation O,W may freely be used for any purposes by the calling program. The user need not concern himself otherwise with B variables as they are generated by the subroutine itself.

(d) The last column of the Specifications list gives a brief description of the variable as it appears in the program.

STRUCTURE OF THE "NEXT" PROGRAMS

The six programs of NEX... type are alike in their bookkeeping relationships to the calling program. It was thought desirable for the subroutines to do as much of the bookkeeping as possible, and, to achieve that end, the following programming format has been observed:

(a) There is a subroutine variable MTC (mnemonic: "More To Come"). This variable is LOGICAL, and is named in the calling statements of the six "next" routines. When the subroutine returns to the main program, MTC will be set to either .TRUE. or .FALSE. If .TRUE., then the output which is being returned by the subroutine is not the last object in the collection of objects which is being searched (there are "More To Come"). If .FALSE., then current output is the last. Thus the calling program need only test MTC in order to determine if the search is complete. The subroutine itself carries the burden of knowing when the last object has been produced.

(b)   There are internal subroutine variables (i.e., variables which are not named in the calling statement) such as NLAST, KLAST, which remember the parameter values from the last time the subroutine was called, e.g., when searching the list of subsets of an n-set in NEXSUB, NLAST holds the value of n from the last call.

Whenever the subroutine observes that one or more calling parameters in the current call differ from those of the previous call, it assumes that the previous search is to be terminated and a new search begun on the family of objects corresponding to the new parameters. It therefore "rewinds" itself to the beginning of the new list. No effort on the part of the user (calling program) is necessary to achieve this.

(c)   Finally, it is possible that the user will want to terminate a search and start a new search even though the parameter values are the same. In this case, or when for any reason the user wants to restart the subroutine from the beginning of its list of objects, it is only necessary for the user to set MTC=.FALSE. himself prior to the call. The subroutines test MTC on entry, and if it is .FALSE., they reset themselves back to the first object corresponding to the current parameter values.

A typical use of a NEXT subroutine will look like this in the calling program:

```
        {Set parameters N,K, . . .}
   10   CALL NEX. . .
        {Process output object}
        IF (MTC) GO TO 10
        . . .
```

STRUCTURE OF THE "RANDOM" PROGRAMS

The eight programs of random type listed above require a random number generator. A random number is a sample ξ drawn from a population which is uniformly distributed on the interval $0 < \xi < 1$. The preparation of such generators is discussed fully in several standard references. Also, on many computers, random number generators are built-in. The programs in this book expect that a compiled FUNCTION subprogram is available of the form

```
FUNCTION RAND(I)
   . . .
   . . .
RAND=. . .
RETURN
END
```

to be supplied by the user. We refrain from showing one here because such subprograms tend to be strongly machine-dependent. We follow the convention that each appearance of the letter ξ in a flow chart calls for the selection of a new random number.

ARRAYS AND SPECIFICATIONS

One of the main problems which must be confronted in the preparation of a collection of combinatorial subroutines is that of the organization of array storage. The choice of the correct array can often save considerable computing time, and in most of our applications this is very important. Yet the proliferation of large numbers of arrays may lead to insuperable storage problems when several subroutines are compiled together for some large application. We have been very conscious of these problems, and we have made certain policy decisions regarding the handling of arrays, which we now describe.

First, suppose a subroutine makes use of several arrays *in addition to* those which are of primary interest to the user. In FORTRAN, arrays which are not named in the calling statement must receive fixed dimensions in the subroutine itself, whereas the arrays which are named in the calling statement can have dimensions inherited from the main program.

Every such assignment of fixed dimension to an array whose actual length varies from one call of the subroutine to the next introduces a limitation on the capacity of the program. It is true that for different applications the user could change the DIMENSION statements to suit his needs, but at considerable inconvenience. This would lead to potentially frustrating problems for the user, and so (rightly or not!) we have almost invariably followed

Policy 1: No subroutine in this book contains any hidden arrays. More positively, every array used by a subroutine is named in its calling statement.

(A few short arrays have been excepted from this rule.)

This policy has several corollaries, some pleasant and some not so. For example, two arrays of the same type which appear in two independent subroutines used for working storage only can be given the same name, thereby saving space.

As regards dimensioning, there are two main types of compilers. In one type, a dimension statement of the form

(∗)   DIMENSION A(1), B(1, 1),...

appears in the subroutine and causes it to use the fixed dimensions assigned in the main program. In the second type, dimension statements like

(†)   DIMENSION A(N), B(M,N), C(K),...

appear, where K,M,N, . . . are calling variables, and these may cause array space to be assigned according to the values of K,M,N, . . . at execution time. We have, quite arbitrarily, selected the second alternative here and followed it.

Policy 2: All arrays used by subroutines in this book carry dimension statements of the type (†) above.

One of the effects of Policy 1 is that calling statements are somewhat larger than they would be if hidden arrays were used. This is rarely troublesome since most subroutines have fewer than 6 variables in their parentheses, and only two subroutines have as many as 10 such variables. In order to achieve this economy we have been very aware of the need to avoid the use of unnecessary arrays, and we have not shrunk from doing even a small amount of extra computing toward that end.

An extreme example is Chapter 13, a subroutine whose sole raison d'etre is to avoid the use of an extra matrix array, and which, as a result, poses some very entertaining problems of programming and mathematics. Another small illustration is in Chapter 14 where an output array NV, after being computed, is taken apart and put back together again because the cost of so doing was very slight and an array of storage was thereby saved. We state this, in summary, as

Policy 3: When confronted with the choice of a small amount of extra computation versus an extra array, save the array and do the computation.

We are under no illusions that these policies are ideal in all circumstances, but we do feel that they have been generally quite successful, and we should at this time take the opportunity to make the reader aware of them.

1

Next Subset of an *n*-Set (NEXSUB)

A number of straightforward methods for generating the 2^n subsets of an n-set exist. We might, for example, represent a subset S by a 0–1 vector $(a_1, \ldots, a_n)$ where $a_i = 1$ if $i \in S$, $= 0$ if $i \notin S$. The 2^n distinct vectors could be constructed, then, by finding the n binary digits of an integer m, $m = 0, 1, \ldots, 2^n - 1$. To go from one subset to the next, we would just increase m by 1 and read off its bit sequence.

We shall adopt, however, a less straightforward method (known as the Gray Code) because of its importance in applications such as the following: Suppose that, after each subset S is produced, we want to perform a certain computation depending on S and then to return to get the next subset. If the next subset S' differs only slightly from S then the computation that we do for S' may differ only slightly from the one for S, and *we may be able to preserve many of our partial computations for S to use in the case of S'*. A very important application of this idea appears in Chapter 19 where we can save large amounts of calculation by the correct sequencing of subsets, which we now discuss.

Our problem, then, is to arrange the subsets of $\{1, 2, \ldots, n\}$ in a sequence such that each one differs from its predecessor only slightly. In Chapter 3, we discuss a variant in which the cardinality of the subset is to be kept fixed. In the list below, we show the 8 subsets of $\{1, 2, 3\}$ arranged in order so that each one is obtained

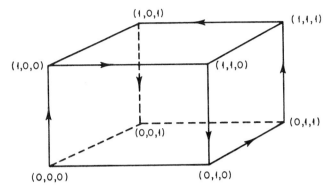

Figure 1.1 A Hamilton walk on the cube.

from its predecessor by the insertion or deletion of a *single element:*

$$\varnothing, \quad \{1\}, \quad \{1, 2\}, \quad \{2\}, \quad \{2, 3\}, \quad \{1, 2, 3\}, \quad \{1, 3\}, \quad \{3\}$$

Pictorially, consider the cube in 3-space whose vertices are the vectors of 0's and 1's. A sequence of sets such as the above corresponds to a walk along the edges of the cube, which starts from the origin and which visits each vertex exactly once. The list above corresponds to the walk shown in Fig. 1.1.

A walk which visits every vertex of a graph exactly once is called a Hamilton walk on the graph. Hence, a sequence of subsets of the desired type corresponds to a Hamilton walk on the n-cube, and our problem now is to describe such a walk algorithmically. What we need is a rule of the following type: Suppose at the $(m - 1)$th step of our walk we have arrived at a certain vertex $(a_1, \ldots, a_n)$ of the cube. Determine (somehow) the index j of the single coordinate a_j which is to be changed in order to go to the mth step of the walk $(m = 1, 2, \ldots, 2^n)$.

Table 1.1

m	$Q(m) + 1$	$(m - 1)$th subset	mth subset
1	1	(0, 0, 0)	(1, 0, 0)
2	2	(1, 0, 0)	(1, 1, 0)
3	1	(1, 1, 0)	(0, 1, 0)
4	3	(0, 1, 0)	(0, 1, 1)
5	1	(0, 1, 1)	(1, 1, 1)
6	2	(1, 1, 1)	(1, 0, 1)
7	1	(1, 0, 1)	(0, 0, 1)
8	4	(0, 0, 1)	—

We claim that the following rule for finding the index j will work: Define $Q(m)$ to be the highest power of 2 which divides m ($m = 1$, $2, \ldots$). Then, take $j = Q(m) + 1$. Table 1.1 illustrates the method.

To prove that the rule works in general, observe first that it does so when $n = 1$. Assuming that it is true for $1, 2, \ldots, n$, consider the 2^{n+1} vectors generated by applying the rule to the $(n + 1)$-cube. The first 2^n of these vectors all have the $(n + 1)$th coordinate $= 0$, and, inductively, they constitute a Hamilton walk on the n-cube. The remaining 2^n of these $(n + 1)$-vectors all have the $(n + 1)$th coordinate $= 1$. Furthermore, the sequence of n-vectors formed by their first n coordinates follows exactly the *reversed* sequence of steps of the walk taken in the first 2^n vectors. To see why this is so, note that the two integers m and $2^{n+1} - m$ have sum 2^{n+1}, whose first n bits vanish. The first nonvanishing bit of m and of $2^{n+1} - m$ must therefore be in the same location, i.e., $Q(m) = Q(2^{n+1} - m)$, QED.

The algorithm for generating these sets follows the procedure outlined above, with one or two modifications. A set S is represented by a vector of 0's and 1's: `IN(I),I=1,N`, where `IN(I)=1` if $I \in S$, `IN(I)=0` if $I \notin S$. The cardinality of the output set is `NCARD`, and it is easy to keep track of because it changes by `2*IN(J)-1` at each step.

ALGORITHM NEXSUB

(A) [*First entry*] M←0; IN(I)←0 (I=1,N); NCARD←0; Exit.
(B) [*Later entries*] M←M+1; J←Q(M)+1; IN(J)←1-IN(J); NCARD←NCARD+2*IN(J)-1; If NCARD=1 and IN(N) > 0, final exit; Exit ■

In many applications, the subsets themselves are not needed. Instead, the values of $j = 1 + Q(m)$ and of a parameter $z = \pm 1$ are sufficient where $z = +1$, if element j was just *entered into* the mth subset, and where $z = -1$, if j was just *deleted from* the mth subset.

If just the pair (j, z) is wanted, it can be obtained without the array `IN(I)` (I=1,N) which describes the subset and, indeed, without any arrays at all. Suppose we have found j and we need z. In other words, the jth coordinate is to be changed in order to get the $(m + 1)$th subset from the mth, but is it to be changed from 0 to 1 or from 1 to 0?

To answer this question, ask how many times prior to the $(m + 1)$th subset the same coordinate j has been changed. This was done as often as $j - 1$ was the highest power of 2 which divides some integer $\leqq m$. Hence, for each $l \leqq m$ such that

$$l = 2^{j-1}(2p - 1) \quad (p \geqq 1)$$

the jth coordinate was changed. The number of times is therefore the number of integers $p \geqq 1$ such that

$$(2p - 1)2^{j-1} \leqq m$$

i.e.,

$$t = \frac{1}{2}\left(\frac{m}{2^{j-1}} + 1\right)$$

times altogether. Now $m/2^{j-1}$ is the odd number which is obtained from m by dividing out all of its 2's; hence, t is an integer, and $z = (-1)^t$.

A complete algorithm which supplies the pairs (j, z) corresponding to a Hamilton walk on the cube, using no array storage, is given below.

ALGORITHM NS

(A) [*First entry*] $m \leftarrow 1$; $j \leftarrow 1$; $z \leftarrow 1$; Exit.
(B) [*Later entries*] $m \leftarrow m + 1$; $x \leftarrow m$; $j \leftarrow 0$.
(C) $j \leftarrow j + 1$; $x \leftarrow x/2$; If x is an integer, to (C).
(D) $z \leftarrow (-1)^{x + 1/2}$; If $m = 2^n$, final exit; Exit ■

Our FORTRAN program is of Algorithm NEXSUB.

DESCRIPTION OF FLOW CHART

Box 10   If N≠NLAST or MTC is .FALSE., the current call starts a new series.

Box 20   On first call of a new sequence, initialize all variables, then exit.

Box 30   On later calls, increase M and start search for highest power of two which divides M. Set J=1.

Box 40   If M1 is now odd, we have found J, go to Box 60.

Box 50   If not, increase J, divide M1 by 2, and return to 40.

Box 60   Change IN(J) and NCARD, set MTC, and exit.

FLOW CHART NEXSUB

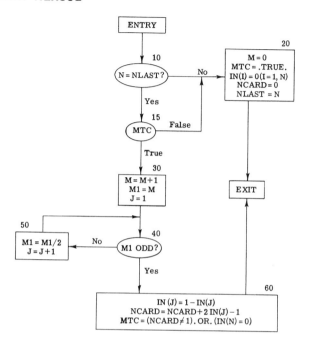

SUBROUTINE SPECIFICATIONS

(1) *Name of subroutine:* NEXSUB.
(2) *Calling statement:* CALL NEXSUB(N,IN,MTC,NCARD,J).
(3) *Purpose of subroutine:* Generate subsets of $\{1, 2, \ldots, n\}$.
(4) *Descriptions of variables in calling statement:*

Name	Type	I/O/W/B	Description
N	INTEGER	I	Number of elements in universe.
IN	INTEGER(N)	I/O	IN(I) = 1 if I is in output set; 0 if I is not in output set (I=1,N).
MTC	LOGICAL	I/O	.TRUE. if current output set is not the last one; .FALSE. if no more sets remain after current output.
NCARD	INTEGER	I/O	Cardinality of output set.
J	INTEGER	O	Index of coordinate changed to create current output set from previous (not available on first output).

(5) *Other routines which are called by this one:*   None.

(6) *Approximate number of* FORTRAN *instructions:*   25.

(7) *Remarks:*   First output set is the empty set.

```
      SUBROUTINE NEXSUB(N,IN,MTC,NCARD,J)
      LOGICAL MTC
      DIMENSION IN(N)
      DATA NLAST/0/
10    IF(N.EQ.NLAST) GO TO 15
20    M=0
      MTC=.TRUE.
      DO 21  I=1,N
21    IN(I)=0
      NCARD=0
      NLAST=N
      RETURN
15    IF(.NOT.MTC) GO TO 20
30    M=M+1
      M1=M
      J=0
39    J=J+1
40    IF(MOD(M1,2).EQ.1) GO TO 60
50    M1=M1/2
      GO TO 39
60    L=IN(J)
      IN(J)=1-L
      NCARD=NCARD+1-2*L
      MTC=NCARD.NE.1.OR.IN(N).EQ.0
      RETURN
      END
```

SAMPLE OUTPUT

In the listing below are the 32 subsets of $\{1, 2, \ldots, 5\}$, one on each line, as produced by NEXSUB. On a line are IN(1), IN(2), ..., IN(5), followed by J, the index of the coordinate which was changed, and NCARD. Note how each line agrees with its predecessor except in the Jth entry.

0	0	0	0	0	0	0
1	0	0	0	0	1	1
1	1	0	0	0	2	2
0	1	0	0	0	1	1
0	1	1	0	0	3	2
1	1	1	0	0	1	3
1	0	1	0	0	2	2
0	0	1	0	0	1	1
0	0	1	1	0	4	2
1	0	1	1	0	1	3
1	1	1	1	0	2	4
0	1	1	1	0	1	3
0	1	0	1	0	3	2
1	1	0	1	0	1	3
1	0	0	1	0	2	2
0	0	0	1	0	1	1
0	0	0	1	1	5	2
1	0	0	1	1	1	3
1	1	0	1	1	2	4
0	1	0	1	1	1	3
0	1	1	1	1	3	4
1	1	1	1	1	1	5
1	0	1	1	1	2	4
0	0	1	1	1	1	3
0	0	1	0	1	4	2
1	0	1	0	1	1	3
1	1	1	0	1	2	4
0	1	1	0	1	1	3
0	1	0	0	1	3	2
1	1	0	0	1	1	3
1	0	0	0	1	2	2
0	0	0	0	1	1	1

2

Random Subset of an *n*-Set (RANSUB)

It is quite trivial to select a random subset of $\{1, 2, \ldots, n\}$: We flip a coin n times. If the ith toss is heads, then letter i belongs to the subset, otherwise it does not belong. If $A(I)$ ($I=1,N$) is a random variable such that $A(I)=1$ or 0, depending on whether I belongs or does not belong to our set, then the algorithm is as follows:

ALGORITHM RANSUB

(A) $A(I) \leftarrow \lfloor 2\xi \rfloor$ ($I=1,N$); Exit ■

FLOW CHART RANSUB

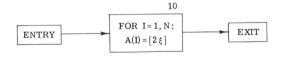

DESCRIPTION OF FLOW CHART

Box 10 For each $I=1,N$ we select a random number ξ (a new one for each I), and set $A(I)$ equal to the greatest integer contained in 2ξ, i.e., $A(I)=0$ if $\xi < \frac{1}{2}$, $=1$ if $\xi \geq \frac{1}{2}$.

SUBROUTINE SPECIFICATIONS

(1) *Name of subroutine:* RANSUB.
(2) *Calling statement:* CALL RANSUB(N,A).
(3) *Purpose of subroutine:* Generate random subset of an *n*-set.
(4) *Descriptions of variables in calling statement:*

Name	Type	I/O/W/B	Description
N	INTEGER	I	Number of elements in set.
A	INTEGER(N)	O	A(I)=1 if I is in output set; 0 otherwise (I=1,N).

(5) *Other routines which are called by this one:* FUNCTION RAND(I) (random numbers).
(6) *Approximate number of* FORTRAN *instructions:* 6.

```
      SUBROUTINE RANSUB(N,A)
      INTEGER A(N)
      DO 10  I=1,N
   10 A(I)=2.*RAND(1)
      RETURN
      END
```

SAMPLE OUTPUT

The program RANSUB was called 1280 times with N=5. The following output shows the frequency with which each of the 32 subsets were selected, e.g., the empty set 43 times, etc. The value $\chi^2 = 21.35$ is computed, as usual, from

$$\chi^2 = \sum_S \frac{(\phi(S) - 40)^2}{40}$$

where $\phi(S)$ is the frequency of the subset S and the sum is over all 32 subsets. In 95% of such experiments, the observed value of χ^2 would lie between 17.5 and 48.2 if, indeed, all subsets were equally likely to be chosen.

```
0  0  0  0  0    43
1  0  0  0  0    33
0  1  0  0  0    41
1  1  0  0  0    53
0  0  1  0  0    38
1  0  1  0  0    35
0  1  1  0  0    40
1  1  1  0  0    37
0  0  0  1  0    39
1  0  0  1  0    44
0  1  0  1  0    42
1  1  0  1  0    41
0  0  1  1  0    44
1  0  1  1  0    38
0  1  1  1  0    47
1  1  1  1  0    39
0  0  0  0  1    47
1  0  0  0  1    39
0  1  0  0  1    32
1  1  0  0  1    34
0  0  1  0  1    30
1  0  1  0  1    48
0  1  1  0  1    37
1  1  1  0  1    43
0  0  0  1  1    38
1  0  0  1  1    44
0  1  0  1  1    35
1  1  0  1  1    37
0  0  1  1  1    34
1  0  1  1  1    44
0  1  1  1  1    37
1  1  1  1  1    47
```

CHI SQ IS 21.35 WITH 31 DEG FREEDOM

3

Next k-Subset of an n-Set (NEXKSB/NXKSRD)

We consider here the combinations of n things taken k at a time. There are $\binom{n}{k}$ k-subsets of an n-set altogether, and in this chapter we give two different methods for generating them all, sequentially. In the first method we construct them in "alphabetical order," yielding a very simple algorithm. Following that, we describe a "revolving-door" method which generates each subset from its immediate predecessor by deleting some single element and adjoining some other single element. The list of the ten 3-subsets of $\{1, 2, 3, 4, 5\}$ in lexicographic order is

$$
\begin{array}{ccc}
1 & 2 & 3 \\
1 & 2 & 4 \\
1 & 2 & 5 \\
1 & 3 & 4 \\
1 & 3 & 5 \\
1 & 4 & 5 \\
2 & 3 & 4 \\
2 & 3 & 5 \\
2 & 4 & 5 \\
3 & 4 & 5
\end{array}
$$

while the same list in revolving-door order is

$$
\begin{array}{l}
1\ 2\ 3 \\
1\ 3\ 4 \\
2\ 3\ 4 \\
1\ 2\ 4 \\
1\ 4\ 5 \\
2\ 4\ 5 \\
3\ 4\ 5 \\
1\ 3\ 5 \\
2\ 3\ 5 \\
1\ 2\ 5
\end{array}
$$

First, as regards the lexicographic algorithm, suppose that

$$\{a_1, \ldots, a_k\}$$

is a given k-subset. Then these are generated by

ALGORITHM NEXKSB (LEXICOGRAPHIC)

(A) [*First entry*] $a_j \leftarrow j$ $(j = 1, k)$; Exit.
(B) [*All later entries*] $h \leftarrow \min \{j | a_{k+1-j} \neq n + 1 - j\}$; $m_1 \leftarrow a_{k+1-h}$; $a_{k+j-h} \leftarrow m_1 + j$ $(j = 1, h)$; If $a_1 = n - k + 1$, final exit; Exit ∎

It is interesting to measure the average amount of computational labor per subset generated. We claim that less than two units of labor are required, on the average. The index h measures the amount of labor per subset. For a fixed l, the number of k-subsets with $h = l$, i.e., with

$$a_k = n,\ a_{k-1} = n - 1,\ \ldots,\ a_{k-l+1} = n - l + 1 \qquad \text{and} \qquad a_{k-l} < n - l$$

is exactly

$$\binom{n - l - 1}{k - l}$$

since $a_1, \ldots, a_{k-l}$ can be any $(k - l)$-subset of $\{1, 2, \ldots, n - l - 1\}$. It follows that

$$\sum_{l=0}^{k} \binom{n - l - 1}{k - l} = \binom{n}{k}$$

since every k-subset contributes exactly once to the left side, and furthermore, the average value of h is

$$\bar{h} = \binom{n}{k}^{-1} \sum_{l=0}^{k} \binom{n-l-1}{k-l} l$$

$$= \binom{n}{k}^{-1} \left\{ \binom{n-k-1}{0} + \left[\binom{n-k}{1} + \binom{n-k-1}{0} \right] \right.$$

$$+ \left[\binom{n-k+1}{2} + \binom{n-k}{1} + \binom{n-k-1}{0} \right] + \cdots \right\}$$

$$= \binom{n}{k}^{-1} \left\{ \binom{n-k}{0} + \binom{n-k+1}{1} + \binom{n-k+2}{2} + \cdots + \binom{n-1}{k-1} \right\}$$

$$= \binom{n}{k}^{-1} \binom{n}{k-1}$$

$$= k/(n-k+1)$$

Thus, if $k < (n/2)$, we do *less than two units of labor* per k-subset, on the average.

If we average $\bar{h}$ again over all 2^n subsets, we find that the average amount of labor per subset of an n-set is

$$2 - 2^{-n}$$

as claimed. A request for a subset is therefore quite inexpensive!

We turn now to the revolving-door (RD) algorithm. The motivation for this is similar to that in Chapter 1, namely, if we want to do a calculation for each subset, then if a subset differs only slightly from its predecessor we may be able to save much of the calculation from the predecessor, thereby saving time. Since the cardinality k is fixed, to differ only slightly means that each subset is obtained by ejecting one element and adjoining another. An additional feature of RD is that the last k-subset on the list is next to the first one on the list in that one more "turn of the door" will return us to the beginning.

It is very easy to prove that such an algorithm exists for each n, k $(n = 1, 2, \ldots ; 0 \leq k \leq n)$. Indeed, let $A(m, l)$ denote a list of all of the l-subsets of $\{1, 2, \ldots, m\}$ *arranged in RD order, beginning with*‡

$$\{1, 2, \ldots, l\}$$

and ending with

$$\{1, 2, \ldots, l-1, m\}$$

‡ There are other possibilities which, however, do not lead to much simpler algorithms.

Then we have (the bar means reverse order)

(1) $A(n, k) =$
$A(n - 1, k),$ $\overline{A(n - 2, k - 2) \cup \{n - 1, n\}},$ $A(n - 2, k - 1) \cup \{n\}$

In other words, we construct $A(n, k)$ by first forming the list $A(n - 1, k)$, then following with the list $A(n - 2, k - 2)$ in which each subset has had the pair $\{n - 1, n\}$ adjoined, then finally the list $A(n - 2, k - 1)$, in reverse order, with the singleton $\{n\}$ adjoined to each subset. It is then simple to check that if $A(n - 1, k)$, $A(n - 2, k - 2)$, and $A(n - 2, k - 1)$ are in RD order, then so is $A(n, k)$. It follows, by induction, that a list $A(n, k)$ exists for each n, k ■

The next question is much harder: How do we make an algorithm out of this existence proof? Let $\{a_1, \ldots, a_k\} = S$ be a subset $(1 \leqq a_1 < a_2 < \cdots < a_k \leqq n)$. By a "block" of length h, we mean a maximal subsequence $a_i, a_{i+1}, \ldots, a_{i+h-1}$ in which each element is 1 more than its predecessor. The first block is the block which contains a_1, etc. Let n_1, n_2 denote the lengths of the first and second blocks in S.

We claim that the successor of S in the RD list is completely determined by the first two blocks of S (or one, if it has only one). Consider the 10-subset of 37 elements

(2) $S = \{4, 5, 6, 7, 12, 13, 14, 25, 33, 34\}$

Here $n = 37$, so S does not contain n or $n - 1$. From (1) we see that we must be going forward through the list $A(n - 1, k) = A(36, 10)$, and after two more such deletions we are going forward in $A(34, 10)$. Now S contains n and $n - 1$. Therefore, from Eq. (1), we are in the second of the three phases of the list, going forward through $A(32, 8) \cup \{33, 34\}$. Thus we need the successor of $S - \{33, 34\}$ in the list $A(32, 8)$. After further reductions of the first type, we want the successor of $S - \{33, 34\}$ in the list $A(25, 8)$. Now our set contains n but not $n - 1$, so we are in the third of the three phases of (1), going backward through the list $A(23, 7) \cup \{25\}$. We now delete the 25 and continue to the left in this fashion. Each block of odd length in the original set S contributes a reversal of direction; blocks of even length can be simply removed.

When just two blocks remain, we have

$$S' = \{4, 5, 6, 7, 12, 13, 14\}$$

and since an odd number of odd blocks occur to the right of these two, we are going backward through $A(14, 7)$. The general proposition is that the successor of any k-subset S is the successor or predecessor of the first two blocks of S in their universe, depending on whether an even or an odd number of odd blocks lie to the right of the first two. But, the number of odd blocks to the right of the first two is even or odd with the number of elements of $\{1, 2, \ldots, n\}$ which are in blocks to the right of the first two, which is even or odd with $k + n_1 + n_2$. Thus, *the successor of S is completely determined by the first two blocks of S*, as claimed.

To describe the RD algorithm, then, we need only describe the predecessor and successor of a set S of the special form

$$\{a_1, a_1 + 1, a_1 + 2, \ldots, a_1 + n_1 - 1, b_1, b_1 + 1, \ldots, b_1 + n_2 - 1\}$$

At this point, the analysis splits into a large number of cases, each of which can be handled directly from the recurrence (1) and which we will not derive here. It turns out that some one of exactly six basic operations is applied to a given subset in order to find its successor on the RD list. We tabulate these six operations in Table 3.1, each operation being uniquely described by the two integers OUT, the element which the operation deletes from the input set, and IN, the element which the operation adjoins to the input set.

In detail, suppose we are given S:

$$1 \leq A(1) < A(2) < \ldots < A(K) \leq N$$

a K-subset whose first two blocks are of sizes N1, N2, respectively (N2=0 if just one block exists.) The successor of S is found by selecting one of the six operations A, B, C, D, E, F given in Table 3.1.

Table 3.1

	A	B	C	D	E	F
IN	A(N1)+1	A(1)−1	A(N1)+1	A(N1+1)+1	A(1)+1	1
OUT	A(N1−1)	A(1)	A(N1+2)	A(N1)	A(1)	A(2)

The selection of one of the six operations is, in each case, made according to Flow Chart NXKSRD.

FLOW CHART NXKSRD

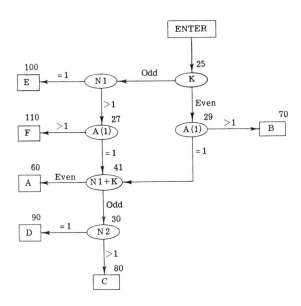

It is not hard to estimate the labor involved in the revolving-door method. The only loop of uncertain length which may be involved in a typical step of the algorithm is where the length N1 of the first block of the input set is calculated. The work in this step is estimated by deriving the average length of the first block of a k-subset of n elements. Now, the number of such subsets whose first block is

$$m, m + 1, \ldots, m + h - 1$$

is exactly

$$\binom{n - m - h}{k - h}$$

Hence the number of k-subsets of n elements whose first block has exactly h elements is

$$\sum_{m=1}^{n-k} \binom{n - m - h}{k - h} = \binom{n - h}{k - h + 1}$$

The average length of the first block is therefore

$$\bar{h} = \binom{n}{k}^{-1} \sum_{h=1}^{k} h \binom{n - h}{k - h + 1} = \left(1 - \frac{k}{n + 1}\right)^{-1} - \binom{n}{k}^{-1}$$

which varies from 1 when $k = 1$ to $2 + o(1)$ when $k = n/2$. It follows that the average per-step labor in the revolving-door algorithm is *uniformly bounded in n, k* for $k \le n/2$.

The two programs and sample outputs from each appear following Flow Chart NEXKSB (Lexicographic Order).

FLOW CHART NEXKSB (LEXICOGRAPHIC ORDER)

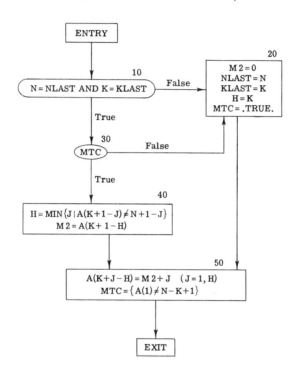

DESCRIPTION OF FLOW CHART (LEXICOGRAPHIC ORDER)

Box 10   If N≠NLAST or K≠KLAST, this is a first entry.

Box 20   Set MTC to .TRUE. and initialize output subset to {1, 2, . . . , k}.

Box 30   If MTC=.FALSE., this is a first entry.

Box 40   Find index *h*, as described in text.

Box 50   Modify elements of output subset A(K+1−H),....,A(K). Reset MTC to .FALSE. if A(1)=N−K+1.

SUBROUTINE SPECIFICATIONS

(1) *Name of subroutine:* NEXKSB.

(2) *Calling statement:* CALL NEXKSB(N,K,A,MTC).

(3) *Purpose of subroutine:* Next k-subset of an n-set, in lexicographic order.

(4) *Descriptions of variables in calling statement:*

Name	Type	I/O/W/B	Description
N	INTEGER	I	Number of elements in universe.
K	INTEGER	I	Number of elements in desired subset.
A	INTEGER(K)	I/O	A(I) is the Ith element of the output subset (I=1,K).
MTC	LOGICAL	I/O	=.TRUE. if current output is not the last subset; =.FALSE. if current output is the last.

(5) *Other routines which are called by this one:* None.

(6) *Approximate number of* FORTRAN *instructions:* 21.

(7) *Remarks:* $1 \leq A(1) < A(2) < \ldots < A(K) \leq N$.

```
      SUBROUTINE NEXKSB(N,K,A,MTC)
      INTEGER A(K),H
      LOGICAL MTC
      DATA NLAST/0/,KLAST/0/
10    IF(K.NE.KLAST.OR.N.NE.NLAST)GO TO 20
30    IF(MTC) GO TO 40
20    M2=0
      H=K
      NLAST=N
      KLAST=K
      MTC=.TRUE.
      GO TO 50
40    DO 41  H=1,K
      M2=A(K+1-H)
      IF(M2.NE.N+1-H) GO TO 50
41    CONTINUE
50    DO 51 J=1,H
51    A(K+J-H)=M2+J
      MTC=(A(1).NE.N-K+1)
      RETURN
      END
```

SAMPLE OUTPUT

The program NEXKSB (in lexicographic order) was called, repeatedly, with N=7, K=4, until termination. The 35 output vectors A(1),A(2),A(3),A(4) are now shown.

```
1   2   3   4
1   2   3   5
1   2   3   6
1   2   3   7
1   2   4   5
1   2   4   6
1   2   4   7
1   2   5   6
1   2   5   7
1   2   6   7
1   3   4   5
1   3   4   6
1   3   4   7
1   3   5   6
1   3   5   7
1   3   6   7
1   4   5   6
1   4   5   7
1   4   6   7
1   5   6   7
2   3   4   5
2   3   4   6
2   3   4   7
2   3   5   6
2   3   5   7
2   3   6   7
2   4   5   6
2   4   5   7
2   4   6   7
2   5   6   7
3   4   5   6
3   4   5   7
3   4   6   7
3   5   6   7
4   5   6   7
```

SUBROUTINE SPECIFICATIONS

(1) *Name of subroutine:* NXKSRD.

(2) *Calling statement:* CALL NXKSRD(N,K,A,MTC,IN,OUT).

(3) *Purpose of subroutine:* List k-subsets of an n-set, in RD order.

(4) *Descriptions of variables in calling statement:*

Name	Type	I/O/W/B	Description
N	INTEGER	I	Number of elements in universe.
K	INTEGER	I	Number of elements in desired subset.
A	INTEGER(K)	I/O	A(I) is the Ith element of the output subset (I=1,K).
MTC	LOGICAL	I/O	=.TRUE. if current output is not the last; =.FALSE. if no more subsets remain after current one.
IN	INTEGER	O	Element of output set which was not in input set.
OUT	INTEGER	O	Element of input set which is not in output set.

(5) *Other routines which are called by this one:* None.

(6) *Approximate number of* FORTRAN *instructions:* 57.

```
      SUBROUTINE NXKSRD(N,K,A,MTC,IN,OUT)
      IMPLICIT INTEGER(A-Z)
      LOGICAL MTC
      DIMENSION A(K)
      DATA NLAST,KLAST/0,0/
5     IF(N.EQ.NLAST.AND.K.EQ.KLAST) GO TO 20
      NLAST=N
      KLAST=K
6     MTC=.TRUE.
10    DO 11  I=1,K
11    A(I)=I
      IN=0
      OUT=0
      GO TO 120
20    IF(.NOT.MTC)  GO TO 6
25    IF(MOD(K,2).EQ.0) GO TO 29
26    IF(K.EQ.1.OR.A(2)-A(1).GT.1)  GO TO 100
```

```
27    IF(A(1).GT.1) GO TO 110
28    KM1=K-1
      DO 40  N1=1,KM1
      IF(A(N1+1).GT.A(N1)+1)  GO TO 41
40    CONTINUE
      N1=K
41    IF(MOD(N1+K,2).EQ.0)  GO TO 60
30    IF(N1.EQ.KM1.OR.(N1.LT.KM1.AND.A(N1+2).GT.A(N1+1)
     *+1)) GO TO 90
      GO TO 80
      29 IF(A(1)-1) 29,28,70
60    OUT=A(N1-1)
      IN=OUT+2
      A(N1-1)=A(N1)
      A(N1)=OUT+2
      GO TO 120
70    IN=A(1)-1
      OUT=A(1)
      A(1)=IN
      GO TO 120
80    IN=A(N1)+1
      OUT=A(N1+2)
      A(N1+2)=A(N1+1)
      A(N1+1)=IN
      GO TO 120
90    IN=A(N1+1)+1
      OUT=A(N1)
      A(N1)=IN-1
      A(N1+1)=IN
      GO TO 120
100   IN=A(1)+1
      OUT=A(1)
      A(1)=IN
      GO TO 120
110   IN=1
      OUT=A(2)
      A(2)=A(1)
      A(1)=1
120   MTC=A(K).NE.N.OR.(K.NE.1.AND.A(K-1).NE.K-1)
      RETURN
      END
```

SAMPLE OUTPUT

Below there appear the 4-subsets of $\{1, \ldots, 7\}$ and the 5-subsets of $\{1, \ldots, 8\}$ as output by the revolving-door subroutine. On each line, we show first the elements of the set, then the two elements IN, OUT which have just been exchanged.

```
1   2   3   4       0   0
1   2   4   5       5   3
2   3   4   5       3   1
1   3   4   5       1   2
1   2   3   5       2   4
1   2   5   6       6   3
2   3   5   6       3   1
1   3   5   6       1   2
3   4   5   6       4   1
2   4   5   6       2   3
1   4   5   6       1   2
1   2   4   6       2   5
2   3   4   6       3   1
1   3   4   6       1   2
1   2   3   6       2   4
1   2   6   7       7   3
2   3   6   7       3   1
1   3   6   7       1   2
3   4   6   7       4   1
2   4   6   7       2   3
1   4   6   7       1   2
4   5   6   7       5   1
3   5   6   7       3   4
2   5   6   7       2   3
1   5   6   7       1   2
1   2   5   7       2   6
2   3   5   7       3   1
1   3   5   7       1   2
3   4   5   7       4   1
2   4   5   7       2   3
1   4   5   7       1   2
1   2   4   7       2   5
2   3   4   7       3   1
1   3   4   7       1   2
1   2   3   7       2   4
```

1	2	3	4	5	0	0
1	2	3	5	6	6	4
1	3	4	5	6	4	2
2	3	4	5	6	2	1
1	2	4	5	6	1	3
1	2	3	4	6	3	5
1	2	3	6	7	7	4
1	3	4	6	7	4	2
2	3	4	6	7	2	1
1	2	4	6	7	1	3
1	4	5	6	7	5	2
2	4	5	6	7	2	1
3	4	5	6	7	3	2
1	3	5	6	7	1	4
2	3	5	6	7	2	1
1	2	5	6	7	1	3
1	2	3	5	7	3	6
1	3	4	5	7	4	2
2	3	4	5	7	2	1
1	2	4	5	7	1	3
1	2	3	4	7	3	5
1	2	3	7	8	8	4
1	3	4	7	8	4	2
2	3	4	7	8	2	1
1	2	4	7	8	1	3
1	4	5	7	8	5	2
2	4	5	7	8	2	1
3	4	5	7	8	3	2
1	3	5	7	8	1	4
2	3	5	7	8	2	1
1	2	5	7	8	1	3
1	5	6	7	8	6	2
2	5	6	7	8	2	1
3	5	6	7	8	3	2
4	5	6	7	8	4	3
1	4	6	7	8	1	5
2	4	6	7	8	2	1
3	4	6	7	8	3	2
1	3	6	7	8	1	4
2	3	6	7	8	2	1
1	2	6	7	8	1	3
1	2	3	6	8	3	7

```
1   3   4   6   8       4   2
2   3   4   6   8       2   1
1   2   4   6   8       1   3
1   4   5   6   8       5   2
2   4   5   6   8       2   1
3   4   5   6   8       3   2
1   3   5   6   8       1   4
2   3   5   6   8       2   1
1   2   5   6   8       1   3
1   2   3   5   8       3   6
1   3   4   5   8       4   2
2   3   4   5   8       2   1
1   2   4   5   8       1   3
1   2   3   4   8       3   5
```

4

Random k-Subset of an n-Set (RANKSB)

Integers n, k are given, $1 \leq k \leq n$, and we want to select k distinct elements from $\{1, 2, \ldots, n\}$. This is easy to do if we are willing to allow either the amount of array storage used or the amount of calculation to depend on n. On the other hand, some delicacy is needed if we should insist that no more than k words of array storage and $O(k)$ computations be done.

Intuitively speaking, our problem is just to reach into a bag of n labeled balls and select k at random. It seems that just k operations should be needed, until we realize that someone had to fill the bag first! Before proceeding, the reader may wish to try his hand at solving the problem within the constraints mentioned above. The desirability of having these constraints will be recognized if we consider the question of selecting three distinct integers from $\{1, 2, \ldots, 10000\}$ in which we want the speed and storage of the algorithm to depend on the "three" and not on the "10000."

In broad outline, what we plan to do is the following: (a) Choose an integer m at random in $\{1, 2, \ldots, n\}$. (b) Attempt to insert m into our partially constructed subset $\{a_1, \ldots, a_j\}$. (c) If m is not already present, set $a_{j+1} \leftarrow m$ and repeat from (a); if m is already present, repeat from (a).

First, let us analyze the number of choices of the integer m which must be made in order to obtain k distinct integers. It is well-known [Kn1, Vol. II, p. 470] that the expected number of independent random drawings from $\{1, 2, \ldots, n\}$ which must be made in order to obtain k *distinct* samples is

(1)
$$\Delta = n \left\{ \frac{1}{n - k + 1} + \cdots + \frac{1}{n} \right\}$$

If $k = n$, for example, we need $\Delta \sim n \log n$ such drawings, on the average. If $k/n \leqq \theta < 1$, then the number of such drawings needed is

$$\Delta \leqq \left\{ \frac{1}{\theta} \log \frac{1}{1 - \theta} \right\} k$$

The first component of the labor required to execute our algorithm, namely, the work needed to select k distinct integers from $\{1, 2, \ldots, n\}$ by independent random samples, is therefore $O(k)$, provided $k \leqq n/2$, say, and is $O(k \log k)$ in any case.

Next we consider the insertion of a newly selected integer m into the partial list $a_1, \ldots, a_j$. This is easy to do in $O(j)$ operations (compare m with each of $a_1, \ldots, a_j$, and if different, insert it). It is also easy to do in an average of only $O(\log j)$ steps if we are willing to store the elements in a binary search tree with two link-field arrays of length k. We propose, in fact, to insert m in just $O(1)$ operations, on the average, while paying the price of only a single link-field array.

The idea is a simple application of a general "hashing" procedure due to F. A. Williams. If $m \in [1, n]$ has been chosen at random, we calculate $i \equiv m$ (modulo k). In the ith one of the k array locations $a_1, \ldots, a_k$ which ultimately will hold our subset, we examine a_i. If a_i is empty, we immediately set $a_i \leftarrow m$, and exit. Most of the time this is all that happens. Sometimes, however, we will find that position a_i is occupied.

If, at that moment, we discover that $m = a_i$, we exit to get a new m. Otherwise, we examine the ith element of the link array (whose creation we discuss below) and if j is its content, we repeat the process with a_j, etc., stopping when we encounter either an element a_s in this chain, whose link field is empty, or an element equal to m. In the former case, m has passed all of its entrance examinations, and so it will be inserted into the list.

For this purpose, we will have maintained a counter r which is initially set to $k + 1$. To insert m, we set $a_t \leftarrow m$, where t is the index of the first empty array location below the rth, set t into the link field of a_s, set the link of a_t to "empty," and reduce r to t.

This procedure involves two kinds of searches, each with its own cost: the search for the end a_s of the linked chain which begins at a_i and the search for a vacant array location in which to insert m. The latter one of these is easy to analyze: since the pointer r moves monotonically downward, the total labor involved in finding all homes for new integers m is $O(k)$.

It is a good deal harder to study the average lengths of the chains, but it turns out [Kn1, Vol. III, pp. 513–518] that fewer than two and a half links need be explored, on the average, per arrival of a new integer m, before its fate has been decided, independent of how full the list was when m arrived and of the size of k relative to n.

Observe, for example, that when $k = n$, no links are ever created, and this whole portion of the algorithm is never used! (Why?) When k is near n, then, this will be nearly true, and when k is small compared to n, only few integers are being selected so there will not be many conflicts of position. The formal algorithm follows.

ALGORITHM RANKSB

n and k are given. Output is $a_1, \ldots, a_k$, a randomly chosen k-subset of $\{1, 2, \ldots, n\}$, not in sorted order.

(A) [*Initialize*] $r \leftarrow k + 1$; $a_i \leftarrow 0$ $(i = 1, k)$
(B) [*Choose m*] $m \leftarrow 1 + \lfloor \xi n \rfloor$; $i \leftarrow m$ (mod k); If $a_i = 0$, to **(E)**.
(C) [*Compare and move down*] If $m = a_i$, to **(B)**; If link$(i) = 0$, to **(D)**; $i \leftarrow$ link(i); to **(C)**.
(D) [*Find home for m*] $r \leftarrow r - 1$; If $r = 0$, exit; If $a_r \neq 0$, to **(D)**; link$(i) \leftarrow r$; $i \leftarrow r$.
(E) [*Insert m*] $a_i \leftarrow m$; link$(i) \leftarrow 0$; to **(B)** ■

The output subset is not delivered in ascending order. If that order is desirable in a particular application, a call to HPSORT, the program of Chapter 27, will sort it at a cost of $O(k \log k)$ additional operations.

The required labor could have been held to $O(k)$ uniformly for $1 \leq k \leq n$ by using a different method when $k \geq n/2$. The following algorithm, for example, uses just k memory locations, operates in $O(k)$ steps when $n/2 \leq k \leq n$, and it even produces sorted output.

ALGORITHM RKS2

(A) $c_1 \leftarrow k$; $c_2 \leftarrow n$; $k_0 \leftarrow 0$; $i \leftarrow 0$.
(B) $i \leftarrow i + 1$; If $\xi > c_1/c_2$, to **(C)**; $c_1 \leftarrow c_1 - 1$; $k_0 \leftarrow k_0 + 1$; $a_{k_0} \leftarrow i$; If $c_1 \leq 0$, exit.
(C) $c_2 \leftarrow c_2 - 1$; To **(B)** ■

In the interest of programming simplicity, we have chosen not to include this algorithm in our program.

In the program RANKSB we store a_i and link(i) in the same word; precisely, the contents of register A(I) is $(k + 1)a_i + \text{link}(i)$ ($i = 1, k$). The restriction which this imposes on the sizes of n and k is that $(n + 1)(k + 1)$ fits into one machine word. The links are removed on output.

This restriction due to the link field can be almost entirely eliminated by a somewhat more elaborate insertion scheme [Kn1, Vol. III, ex. 6.4(13), pp. 543,689] in which we would store only $\lfloor m/k \rfloor$ and the link in the same word instead of m and the link. We have chosen the simpler method to keep the program short and the ideas clear together with virtually optimum storage and speed characteristics.

SUBROUTINE SPECIFICATIONS

(1) *Name of subroutine:* RANKSB.
(2) *Calling statement:* CALL RANKSB(N,K,A).
(3) *Purpose of subroutine:* Choose a random k-subset of $\{1, 2, \ldots, n\}$.
(4) *Description of variables in calling statement:*

Name	Type	I/O/W/B	Description
N	INTEGER	I	Number of elements in universe.
K	INTEGER	I	Number of elements in desired subset.
A	INTEGER(K)	O	A(I) is the Ith element of the output subset (I=1,K).

(5) *Other routines which are called by this one:* Random number generator FUNCTION RAND(I).
(6) *Number of FORTRAN instructions:* 25.
(7) *Remarks:* A(1),...,A(K) are not in sorted sequence; $(n + 1)(k + 1)$ must fit into one machine word; output is *not* a random *ordered* k-tuple of elements from $\{1, 2, \ldots, n\}$.

```
SUBROUTINE RANKSB(N,K,A)
INTEGER R,A(K)
L2=K+1
R=L2
DO 15 I=1,K
```

```
15   A(I)=0
     GO TO 20
45   A(I)=A(I)+R
     I=R
50   A(I)=L2*M
20   M=1+RAND(1)*N
     I=1+MOD(M-1,K)
     IF (A(I).EQ.0) GO TO 50
30   IF (M.EQ.A(I)/L2) GO TO 20
     LINK=MOD(A(I),L2)
     IF (LINK.EQ.0) GO TO 40
     I=LINK
     GO TO 30
40   R=R-1
     IF (R.EQ.0) GO TO 55
     IF (A(R)) 45,45,40
55   DO 60   I=1,K
60   A(I)=A(I)/L2
     RETURN
     END
```

SAMPLE OUTPUT

The program RANKSB was called 200 times with $n = 5$, $k = 3$. The frequencies with which each of the ten subsets were obtained are shown below. Thus {1, 2, 3} occurred 20 times, etc. The value of χ^2 is 14.2 with 9 degrees of freedom. In 95% of such experiments, the observed value of χ^2 would lie between 2.6 and 19.6 if all 3-subsets were equally likely to occur.

1	2	3	20
1	2	4	14
1	2	5	20
1	3	4	12
1	3	5	15
1	4	5	25
2	3	4	24
2	3	5	23
2	4	5	25
3	4	5	22

5

Next Composition of n into k Parts (NEXCOM)

Let n and k be fixed positive integers. By a *composition* of n into k parts, we mean a representation of the form

$$(1) \qquad n = r_1 + r_2 + \cdots + r_k$$

in which $r_i \geqq 0$ $(i = 1, k)$ and the order of the summands is important.

For example, there are exactly 28 compositions of 6 into 3 parts, namely,

$$
\begin{aligned}
6 = 6 + 0 + 0 &= 0 + 6 + 0 = 0 + 0 + 6 = 1 + 2 + 3 \\
&= 5 + 1 + 0 = 5 + 0 + 1 = 1 + 5 + 0 = 2 + 1 + 3 \\
&= 1 + 0 + 5 = 0 + 1 + 5 = 0 + 5 + 1 = 2 + 2 + 2 \\
&= 4 + 2 + 0 = 4 + 0 + 2 = 0 + 4 + 2 = 2 + 4 + 0 \\
&= 2 + 0 + 4 = 0 + 2 + 4 = 4 + 1 + 1 = 1 + 4 + 1 \\
&= 1 + 1 + 4 = 3 + 3 + 0 = 3 + 0 + 3 = 0 + 3 + 3 \\
&= 3 + 2 + 1 = 3 + 1 + 2 = 1 + 3 + 2 = 2 + 3 + 1
\end{aligned}
$$

We now derive a formula for $J(n, k)$, the number of compositions of n into k parts. The derivation will show, also, how to construct a simple algorithm for generating all of them.

Suppose that n indistinguishable balls are to be arranged in k labeled cells. There are evidently exactly $J(n, k)$ ways to do the arranging because, if we have such an arrangement, let r_i be the number of balls in the ith cell for $i = 1, k$. Then we have a composition (1), and the converse is also true. Hence, we can find $J(n, k)$ if we can count these arrangements of n balls in k cells.

Let $n + k + 1$ spaces be marked on a sheet of paper, and suppose that in the first space and the last space we mark a vertical bar, as

$$
\begin{array}{ccccccccc}
| & - & - & - & - & - & - & - & | \\
1 & 2 & 3 & 4 & . & . & . & . & (n+k+1)
\end{array}
$$

Figure 5.1

shown in Fig. 5.1. In the remaining $n + k - 1$ spaces, distribute the n balls with no more than one ball occupying any space. There are obviously

$$
\binom{n + k - 1}{n}
$$

ways of doing this. In each of the other $k - 1$ spaces which remain, place a vertical bar. We now have a pattern like the one shown in Fig. 5.2.

$$
\begin{array}{cccccccccccc}
| & 0 & 0 & | & | & 0 & | & 0 & 0 & 0 & | & 0 & | \\
1 & 2 & 3 & 4 & 5 & 6 & 7 & . & . & . & . & (n+k+1)
\end{array}
$$

Figure 5.2

Now we think of the vertical bars as representing cell boundaries. Hence, in Fig. 5.2 there are 5 cells containing, respectively, 2, 0, 1, 3, 1 balls. It is now clear that there are precisely

(2)
$$
J(n, k) = \binom{n + k - 1}{n}
$$

compositions of n into k parts. For example, the

$$
\binom{6 + 3 - 1}{6} = \binom{8}{6} = 28
$$

compositions of 6 into 3 parts have been listed above.

Another proof of the same result can be given, which, while it does not help with the design of an algorithm, shows an important area of applications. Indeed, suppose we are given a number of power series and we want to multiply them together. How can we calculate the coefficients of the product series? For instance, if

$$\left(\sum a_i x^i\right)\left(\sum b_j x^j\right)\left(\sum c_k x^k\right) = \sum d_m x^m$$

how can we express d_m in terms of a_i, b_j, c_k? Clearly,

(3)
$$d_m = \sum_{i+j+k=m} a_i b_j c_k$$

On the right side of (3) there is a term corresponding to each composition of m into three parts.

Consider the power series $f(x) = 1 + x + x^2 + \cdots$. If we raise it to the kth power, we get

(4)
$$f(x)^k = \sum_{r_1=0}^{\infty} \sum_{r_2=0}^{\infty} \cdots \sum_{r_k=0}^{\infty} x^{r_1+r_2+\cdots+r_k}$$

Collecting terms with equal exponents, we see that x^m appears exactly as often as there are compositions of m; hence,

(5)
$$f(x)^k = \sum_{n=0}^{\infty} J(n, k) x^n$$

On the other hand, $f(x)^k = (1 - x)^{-k}$ but by Taylor's theorem,

(6)
$$\frac{1}{(1-x)^k} = \sum \binom{n+k-1}{n} x^n$$

and comparison of (5) and (6) yields (2) again.

The algorithm for generating compositions of n into k parts sequentially is suggested by our first proof, above, of the relation (2). What we must do in order to generate all of the compositions of n into k parts is to generate all of the $(k-1)$-subsets of $n+k-1$ objects and to interpret each such subset as the set of locations of the interior vertical bars in Fig. 5.2. From the bar locations we can, by subtraction or otherwise, determine the number of balls between each consecutive pair of bars and thereby determine the composition which corresponds to the given subset.

Instead of generating the subsets and from each subset computing the composition, we can do both together by going back to our lexicographic algorithm NEXKSB and translating it into a direct algorithm for compositions. Recall that in that algorithm, if

(7)
$$\{a_1, a_2, \ldots, a_{k-1}\}$$

is a $(k-1)$-subset, we go to the next one by finding the smallest h for which

(8) $\quad a_{k-1} = n, \, a_{k-2} = n-1, \, \ldots, \, a_{k-h} = n-h+1; \, a_{k-h-1} < n-h$

We then increase a_{k-h-1} by 1 and set each succeeding a_{r+1} equal to one more than its predecessor a_r $(r = k-h-1, \ldots, k-2)$.

In terms of the composition associated with the subset (7)

(9) $\qquad\qquad\qquad n = r_1 + r_2 + \cdots + r_k$

the relations (8) imply that $r_k = r_{k-1} = \cdots = r_{k+1-h} = 0$ and $r_{k-h} > 0$. The act of increasing a_{k-h-1} by 1 and setting each following a_r equal to one more than its predecessor, will (a) increase r_{k-h-1} by 1, (b) set $r_k = r_{k-h} - 1$, and (c) set $r_{k-h} = 0$. The reader can easily follow this by watching what happens to the moving vertical bars in Fig. 5.2 and noticing that the end bars remain fixed.

The language of subsets can therefore be removed, and the entire algorithm can be stated directly in terms of compositions. It is also convenient to search for the first nonzero part of the composition starting from the left rather than from the right-hand side.

ALGORITHM NEXCOM

(A) [*First entry*] $r_1 \leftarrow n$; $r_i \leftarrow 0$ $(i = 2, k)$; Exit.

(B) [*Later entries*] $h \leftarrow \min \{i \,|\, r_i \neq 0\}$; $t \leftarrow r_h$; $r_h \leftarrow 0$; $r_1 \leftarrow t-1$; $r_{h+1} \leftarrow r_{h+1} + 1$; If $r_k = n$, final exit; Exit ∎

FLOW CHART NEXCOM

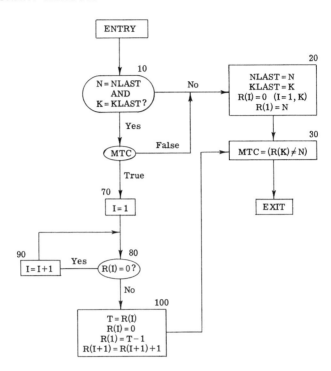

DESCRIPTION OF FLOW CHART

Box 10   If N≠NLAST or K≠KLAST, this is a first entry.

Box 20   Prepare for first entry. Set first composition, remember N, K.

Box 30   MTC is .TRUE. if and only if R(K)≠N.

Box 60   If MTC is .FALSE., this is a first entry by demand of the calling program.

Boxes 70–90   Find first I such that R(I)≠0.

Box 100   Change to next composition and go to Box 30 for exit.

SUBROUTINE SPECIFICATIONS

(1) *Name of subroutine:* NEXCOM.
(2) *Calling statement:* CALL NEXCOM(N,K,R,MTC).
(3) *Purpose of subroutine:* Next composition of *n* into *k* parts.
(4) *Descriptions of variables in calling statement:*

Name	Type	I/O/W/B	Description
N	INTEGER	I	Number whose compositions are desired.
K	INTEGER	I	Number of parts of desired composition.
R	INTEGER(K)	I/O	R(I) is the Ith part of the output composition (I=1,K).
MTC	LOGICAL	I/O	=.TRUE. if this is not the last composition; =.FALSE. if the current output is the last.

(5) *Other routines which are called by this one:* None.
(6) *Approximate number of* FORTRAN *instructions:* 22.

```
         SUBROUTINE NEXCOM(N,K,R,MTC)
         INTEGER R(K),T
         LOGICAL MTC
         DATA KLAST,NLAST/0,0/
10       IF (N.EQ.NLAST.AND.K.EQ.KLAST) GO TO 60
20       NLAST=N
         KLAST=K
         DO 21  I=1,K
21       R(I)=0
         R(1)=N
30       MTC=(R(K).NE.N)
         RETURN
60       IF(.NOT.MTC) GO TO 20
70       DO 71  I=1,K
         IF(R(I).NE.0) GO TO 100
71       CONTINUE
100      T=R(I)
         R(I)=0
         R(1)=T-1
         R(I+1)=R(I+1)+1
         GO TO 30
         END
```

SAMPLE OUTPUT

The program NEXCOM was called, repeatedly, with N=6, K=3, until termination. The 28 output vectors R(1), R(2), R(3) are shown below.

```
6  0  0
5  1  0
4  2  0
3  3  0
2  4  0
1  5  0
0  6  0
5  0  1
4  1  1
3  2  1
2  3  1
1  4  1
0  5  1
4  0  2
3  1  2
2  2  2
1  3  2
0  4  2
3  0  3
2  1  3
1  2  3
0  3  3
2  0  4
1  1  4
0  2  4
1  0  5
0  1  5
0  0  6
```

6

Random Composition of n into k Parts (RANCOM)

Our algorithm for random compositions is based on the "balls-in-cells" model which was described in the previous chapter. Briefly, we choose the positions of the cell boundaries at random, then by differencing we find out how many balls are in each cell. Since our RANKSB routine of Chapter 4 delivers unsorted output, it is necessary to sort the output set prior to the differencing. We do this by a call to HPSORT, the program of Chapter 27.

The algorithm is quite fast, requiring just $O(k \log k)$ operations per composition, on the average.

ALGORITHM RANCOM

(A) Choose $a_1, \ldots, a_{k-1}$, a random $(k-1)$-subset of $\{1, 2, \ldots, n+k-1\}$.

(B) Sort, so that $a_1 < a_2 < \cdots < a_{k-1}$.

(C) Set $r_1 \leftarrow a_1 - 1; r_j \leftarrow a_j - a_{j-1} - 1 \ (j = 2, k-1); r_k \leftarrow n+k-1-a_{k-1}$; Exit ∎

SUBROUTINE SPECIFICATIONS

(1) *Name of subroutine:* RANCOM.

(2) *Calling statement:* CALL RANCOM(N,K,R).

(3) *Purpose of subroutine:* Random composition of *n* into *k* parts.

(4) *Description of variables in calling statement:*

Name	Type	I/O/W/B	Description
N	INTEGER	I	Number whose compositions are desired.
K	INTEGER	I	Number of parts in desired composition.
R	INTEGER(K)	O	R(I) is the Ith part in the output composition (I=1,K).

(5) *Other routines which are called by this one:* RANKSB (Chapter 4), HPSORT (Chapter 27), FUNCTION RAND(I) (random numbers).

(6) *Approximate number of* FORTRAN *instructions:* 12.

```
      SUBROUTINE RANCOM(N,K,R)
      INTEGER R(K)
      CALL RANKSB(N+K-1,K-1,R)
      CALL HPSORT(K-1,R)
      R(K)=N+K
      L=0
      DO 10 I=1,K
      M=R(I)
      R(I)=M-L-1
   10 L=M
      RETURN
      END
```

7

Next Permutation of n Letters (NEXPER)

There are many methods of sequentially producing all $n!$ permutations of n letters. Some of these methods require the construction of the next permutation ab initio while others produce it by a small modification of the previous permutation. Our inclination here is toward the latter approach because of its computational simplicity and elegance.

One knows, for example, that the transpositions generate the full permutation group, i.e., that each permutation σ of n letters is a product

$$\sigma = t_1 t_2 \cdot \cdot \cdot t_m$$

of transpositions. The question of algorithmic importance is this: can the $n!$ permutations be arranged in order in such a way that each one is obtainable from its predecessor by a single transposition?

For example, when $n = 3$ we have the list

$$
\begin{array}{ccc}
1 & 2 & 3 \\
1 & 3 & 2 \\
3 & 1 & 2 \\
3 & 2 & 1 \\
2 & 3 & 1 \\
2 & 1 & 3 \\
\end{array}
$$

in which each of the six permutations of three letters is obtained from its predecessor by a single exchange of two letters (transposition).

The same question can be asked in terms of graphs. Consider a graph of $n!$ vertices, one corresponding to each permutation of n letters. Let T_n denote the set of all transpositions. We construct a directed edge, in our graph, from vertex σ_1 to vertex σ_2 if there is a transposition $t \in T_n$ such that

$$\sigma_2 = t\sigma_1$$

For instance, in the case $n = 3$, the graph G has 6 vertices and looks like that shown in Fig. 7.1.

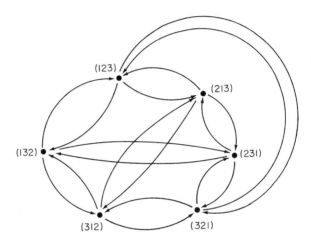

Figure 7.1

In terms of this graph, our question is just this: Is there a Hamilton path in the graph G? (A Hamilton path is a walk on the edges of G, following the "one-way" signs, which visits each vertex exactly once.) The question can also be asked about an arbitrary finite group G and set T of generators, and the answer is unknown in general,‡ although some partial results have been found.

Problem 1 Given a finite group G and set T of generators of G. When can we conclude that all of the elements of G can be arranged in a sequence so that each one is obtainable from its immediate predecessor by the application of a single generator?

---

‡ It is not always true! See Exercise 6.

Problem 2 For which groups G can this be done for *every* set of generators of G?

In the case at hand, the answer is always affirmative, i.e., the permutations of n letters can be arranged so that each is obtained by a single transposition from its predecessor on the list. In fact, several methods for doing this are known. An algorithm due to Wells [W1] accomplishes this in a nice way in that the amount of computational labor needed to decide which pair of letters to transpose at each stage is quite small. We mention also an elegant method of Trotter [Tr1] which sequences the transpositions so that at each step the two letters which are to be transposed are *adjacent* to each other. Trotter's method can be implemented by the following algorithm, which clearly reveals its inductive nature:

(A) [*First entry*] $a_j \leftarrow j (j = 1, n)$; $m \leftarrow 1$; Exit.
(B) [*Later entries*] $n' \leftarrow n$; $m' \leftarrow m$; $s \leftarrow n$.
(C) [*Find n', the active letter*] $q \leftarrow m' \pmod{n'}$; $t \leftarrow m' \pmod{2n'}$; If $q \neq 0$, to (D); If $t = 0$, set $s \leftarrow s - 1$; $m' \leftarrow m'/n$; $n' \leftarrow n' - 1$; To (C).
(D) [*n' at left or right?*] If $q = t$, to (E); $s \leftarrow s + q - n'$; To (F).
(E) [*Right end moves*] $s \leftarrow s - q$.
(F) Exchange a_s, a_{s+1}; $m \leftarrow m + 1$; If $m = n!$, final exit; Exit ■

We present, in this chapter, another algorithm, which has its own inductive structure. This algorithm is not loop-free, but nevertheless we show that an average of less than two operations is needed to find the pair which is to be exchanged. The mathematical basis of the method is, we believe, very simple. To motivate the discussion, Table 7.1 presents the list of permutations of four letters in the order in which our method will produce them.

Table 7.1

1	1234	7	4321	13	1342	19	1423
2	2134	8	3421	14	3142	20	4123
3	2314	9	2431	15	3412	21	2143
4	3214	10	4231	16	4312	22	1243
5	3124	11	3241	17	4132	23	4213
6	1324	12	2341	18	1432	24	2413

Observe that

(a) The first two letters go through both of their possible arrangements.

(b) The third letter is exchanged with one of the first two.

(c) The first two letters go through both of their possible arrangements.

(d) The third letter is exchanged with one of the first two.

(e) The first two letters go through both of their possible arrangements.

(f) The fourth letter is exchanged with one of the first three, etc.

In general, the first k letters will appear in all $k!$ possible arrangements; then the $(k+1)$th letter will be exchanged with one of the first k; then the first k letters will appear in all $k!$ possible arrangements; etc.

We now confront the two questions which must be answered in order to have a precise statement of the algorithm: Suppose that the mth permutation of n letters is

$$a_1, a_2, a_3, \ldots, a_n$$

To find the $(m+1)$th permutation, we exchange exactly two letters, say a_r and a_h $(r < h)$.

Question 1 How do we determine the index h of the rightmost one of the two elements to be exchanged?

Question 2 How do we determine the index r of the leftmost one of the two elements to be exchanged?

Table 7.2

m	h	m	h	m	h	m	h
1	2	7	2	13	2	19	2
2	3	8	3	14	3	20	3
3	2	9	2	15	2	21	2
4	3	10	3	16	3	22	3
5	2	11	2	17	2	23	2
6	4	12	4	18	4	24	5

As regards Question 1, let us refer to Table 7.1 again, and from it we construct a new table of the index h (Table 7.2). The general rule which is illustrated in Table 7.2 is that h *is the smallest value of j* $(j = 1, 2, 3, \cdots)$ *with the property that $j!$ is not a divisor of m.*

We have answered Question 1. Now suppose that we are given the mth permutation in the list and that the index h of the rightmost element to be transposed has been determined as above. With which element a_r to the left of a_h shall we exchange a_h? To motivate our choice, here is a rule which does *not* work: "Exchange a_h with the element immediately to its left (a_{h-1})." If we were to follow this procedure, then with $n = 4$ we would get the sequence

1234	1342	1423	1234
2134	3142	4123	?
2314	3412	4213	
3214	4312	4213	
3124	4132	2143	
1324	1432	1243	

We would have returned to the identity permutation after having visited only 18 of the 24 permutations of 4 letters.‡

To illustrate the method, suppose we have arrived at the permutation

$$8 \quad 2 \quad 4 \quad 7 \quad 1 \quad 5 \cdots$$

of n letters, and suppose it has been found that $h = 6$, i.e., that the letter 5 is about to be exchanged with one of the letters to its left. Among the letters to its left, we choose the smallest one which is larger that 5, i.e., 7. The occupant of the 6th place will then be 7, and the first five places will then run through all 120 permutations of the letters 1, 2, 4, 5, 8 at which time, 120 permutations later, we will have arrived at a permutation

$$(1 \quad 2 \quad 4 \quad 5 \quad 8) \, \underline{7} \cdots$$

where the parenthesis denotes some arrangement of the letters inside. (Note that all letters to the right of the 6th place remain fixed throughout.) We now have $h = 6$ again, so the 7 must be exchanged with a letter to its left. We again choose the smallest letter which is larger than 7, in this case 8. The occupant of the sixth place is now 8, and the first five places run through all 120 permutations of 1, 2, 4, 5, 7, arriving at

$$(1 \quad 2 \quad 4 \quad 5 \quad 7) \, \underline{8} \cdots$$

Again we exchange 8 with the smallest letter to its left which is larger than 8. No such letter exists, so we slightly modify the formulation of the rule, by adding the condition that if there are no letters larger than a_h to the left of the hth position, we choose the *smallest of*

---

‡ Wells's method is a small modification of this rule, which does work!

the letters to its left. In the above example, we would continue by exchanging the 8 with the 1. Thus, the successive occupants of the sixth place would be

$$5, 7, 8, 1, 2, 4$$

If we think of the letters in the first five places as being arranged in numerical order around a *circle* (Fig. 7.2), then the rule in this example is simply that whenever $h = 6$, the current occupant a_6 of the

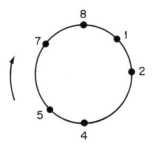

Figure 7.2

6th place is exchanged with its clockwise successor on the above circle. The reason for the rule is just to insure that each of the six letters gets a chance to occupy the sixth place before the seventh letter has to move. The insurance results from the fact that the circle introduces a natural clockwise ordering among the six candidates which guarantees that none will be selected twice.

Our answer to Question 2, in general, is precisely this: Given a permutation of n letters and the value of h found from the answer to Question 1, *exchange a_h with a_r, the smallest of the letters $a_1, \ldots, a_{h-1}$ which exceeds a_h, or, if no such letter exists, the smallest of the letters $a_1, \ldots, a_{h-1}$.*

At first glance it appears that a good deal of labor is involved in the search for a_r. It is remarkable that an average of *less than* one unit of labor suffices to determine the index r (!!!).

Remark 1 In *half* of the cases there is no search at all because places 1 and 2 are exchanged whenever m is odd. In the program flow chart, this fact is exploited by bypassing the search loop completely on every other entry.

Remark 2 In *two-thirds* of the remaining cases, we search exactly two elements, i.e., a single comparison is made. So far, then, the average labor per search looks like

$$\tfrac{1}{2} \cdot 0 + \tfrac{1}{3} \cdot 1 + \cdots$$

It is not hard to write down the whole series which represents the number of comparisons required to determine the index r. Indeed, the number of permutations of n letters which require exactly j comparisons is

$$\frac{n!}{j! \, (j+2)} \quad (j = 0, 1, 2, \ldots)$$

whence the average number of comparisons is

$$\begin{aligned} &\leqq \frac{1}{n!} \sum_{j=0}^{\infty} \frac{n!}{j! \, (j+2)} \cdot j \\ &= e - 2 \\ &= 0.718 \cdots \end{aligned}$$

We see here the justification of the statement that, on the average, less than one comparison is needed to determine r. The flow chart which follows utilizes this feature of the method by means of a variable exit V which flip-flops between 1 and 2 on successive entries to the program.

ALGORITHM NEXPER

(A) [*First entry*] $a_j \leftarrow j \ (j = 1, n); \ m \leftarrow 1$; Exit. (Next entry to (B).)

(B) Interchange $a_1, a_2; \ m \leftarrow m + 1$; If $m = n!$, final exit; Exit. (Next entry to (C).)

(C) $h \leftarrow \min \{j \geqq 1 \,|\, j! + m\}; \ j_1 \leftarrow \{j \,|\, 1 \leqq j \leqq h - 1 \text{ and } a_j - a_h \pmod{n} \text{ is minimal}\}$; Interchange $a_h, a_{j_1}; \ m \leftarrow m + 1$; Exit (Next entry to (B).) ∎

FLOW CHART NEXPER

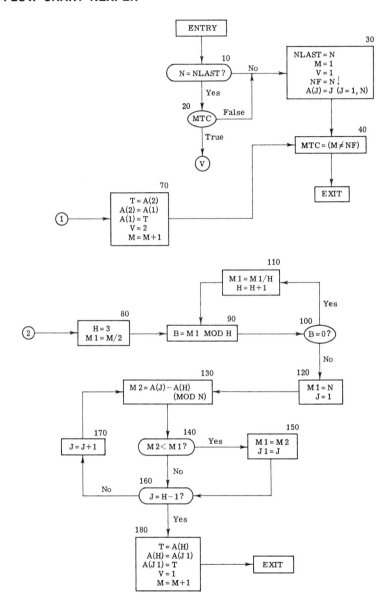

DESCRIPTION OF FLOW CHART

Box 10 If N≠NLAST, this is a first entry.

Box 20 If MTC=.FALSE., this is a first entry by request of the calling program.

Box 30   Initialize to first permutation. V is a variable exit parameter which flip-flops between 1 and 2 on alternate calls.

Box 40   Reset MTC to .FALSE. if M=NF.

Box 70   Enter here if variable exit V = 1. Interchange A(1), A(2) and exit.

Boxes 80–110   Enter here if variable exit V = 2. Find least H such that H! does not divide M.

Boxes 120–170   Find index J1 such that A(J1)−A(H) (mod N) is minimal.

Box 180   Exchange A(H), A(J1), reset V, increase M, and exit.

SUBROUTINE SPECIFICATIONS

(1) *Name of subroutine:*   NEXPER.
(2) *Calling statement:*   CALL NEXPER(N,A,MTC).
(3) *Purpose of subroutine:*   Give next permutation of 1, 2, . . . ,n.
(4) *Descriptions of variables in calling statement:*

Name	Type	I/O/W/B	Description
N	INTEGER	I	Number of letters being permuted.
A	INTEGER(N)	I/O	A(I) is the value of the output permutation at I (I=1,N).
MTC	LOGICAL	I/O	=.TRUE., if current output is not the last permutation; =.FALSE., if no more permutations of *n* letters exist.

(5) *Other routines which are called by this one:*   None.
(6) *Approximate number of* FORTRAN *instructions:*   46.
(7) *Remarks:* Permutations produced are alternately even and odd.


```
      SUBROUTINE NEXPER(N,A,MTC)
      IMPLICIT INTEGER(A-Z)
      LOGICAL MTC
      DIMENSION A(N)
      DATA NLAST/0/
10    IF(N.EQ.NLAST) GO TO 20
30    NLAST=N
      M=1
      V=1
      NF=1
```

```
      DO 31  J=1,N
      NF=NF*J
31    A(J)=J
40    MTC=(M.NE.NF)
      RETURN
20    IF(.NOT.MTC) GO TO 30
      GO TO (70,80),V
70    T=A(2)
      A(2)=A(1)
      A(1)=T
      V=2
      M=M+1
      GO TO 40
80    H=3
      M1=M/2
90    B=MOD(M1,H)
100   IF(B.NE.0) GO TO 120
110   M1=M1/H
      H=H+1
      GO TO 90
120   M1=N
      H1=H-1
      DO 160  J=1,H1
130   M2=A(J)-A(H)
      IF(M2.LT.0)  M2=M2+N
140   IF(M2.GE.M1) GO TO 160
150   M1=M2
      J1=J
160   CONTINUE
180   T=A(H)
      A(H)=A(J1)
      A(J1)=T
      V=1
      M=M+1
      RETURN
      END
```

SAMPLE OUTPUT

The subprogram NEXPER was called repeatedly with N=5, until termination. The 120 output vectors $A(1), A(2), \ldots, A(5)$ follow.

```
1  2  3  4  5        2  3  4  5  1        2  5  4  1  3
2  1  3  4  5        3  2  4  5  1        5  2  4  1  3
2  3  1  4  5        3  5  4  2  1        4  2  5  1  3
3  2  1  4  5        5  3  4  2  1        2  4  5  1  3
3  1  2  4  5        4  3  5  2  1        1  4  5  2  3
1  3  2  4  5        3  4  5  2  1        4  1  5  2  3
4  3  2  1  5        5  4  3  2  1        4  5  1  2  3
3  4  2  1  5        4  5  3  2  1        5  4  1  2  3
2  4  3  1  5        4  5  3  1  2        5  1  4  2  3
4  2  3  1  5        5  4  3  1  2        1  5  4  2  3
3  2  4  1  5        5  3  4  1  2        1  5  2  4  3
2  3  4  1  5        3  5  4  1  2        5  1  2  4  3
1  3  4  2  5        3  4  5  1  2        2  1  5  4  3
3  1  4  2  5        4  3  5  1  2        1  2  5  4  3
3  4  1  2  5        4  1  5  3  2        5  2  1  4  3
4  3  1  2  5        1  4  5  3  2        2  5  1  4  3
4  1  3  2  5        5  4  1  3  2        2  5  1  3  4
1  4  3  2  5        4  5  1  3  2        5  2  1  3  4
1  4  2  3  5        1  5  4  3  2        5  1  2  3  4
4  1  2  3  5        5  1  4  3  2        1  5  2  3  4
2  1  4  3  5        5  1  3  4  2        1  2  5  3  4
1  2  4  3  5        1  5  3  4  2        2  1  5  3  4
4  2  1  3  5        1  3  5  4  2        2  1  3  5  4
2  4  1  3  5        3  1  5  4  2        1  2  3  5  4
2  4  5  3  1        3  5  1  4  2        3  2  1  5  4
4  2  5  3  1        5  3  1  4  2        2  3  1  5  4
4  5  2  3  1        4  3  1  5  2        1  3  2  5  4
5  4  2  3  1        3  4  1  5  2        3  1  2  5  4
5  2  4  3  1        1  4  3  5  2        3  5  2  1  4
2  5  4  3  1        4  1  3  5  2        5  3  2  1  4
2  5  3  4  1        3  1  4  5  2        5  2  3  1  4
5  2  3  4  1        1  3  4  5  2        2  5  3  1  4
3  2  5  4  1        1  2  4  5  3        2  3  5  1  4
2  3  5  4  1        2  1  4  5  3        3  2  5  1  4
5  3  2  4  1        2  4  1  5  3        3  1  5  2  4
3  5  2  4  1        4  2  1  5  3        1  3  5  2  4
3  4  2  5  1        4  1  2  5  3        5  3  1  2  4
4  3  2  5  1        1  4  2  5  3        3  5  1  2  4
4  2  3  5  1        5  4  2  1  3        1  5  3  2  4
2  4  3  5  1        4  5  2  1  3        5  1  3  2  4
```

8

Random Permutation of n Letters (RANPER)

We produce a random permutation by a sequence of random interchanges, as follows:

ALGORITHM RANPER

(A) $a_i \leftarrow i \ (i = 1, n)$.
(B)   For $m = 1, n : \{l \leftarrow m + \lfloor \xi(n + 1 - m) \rfloor$; Exchange $a_l, a_m\}$.
(C)   Exit ■

DESCRIPTION OF FLOW CHART

Box 10   Initialize output locations to 1, 2, . . . , N.

Boxes 20–50   For each M=1, N we exchange A(M) with A(L), where L is randomly chosen in the range M≤L≤N.

FLOW CHART RANPER

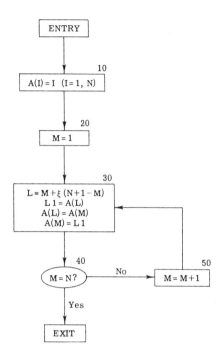

SUBROUTINE SPECIFICATIONS

(1) *Name of subroutine:* RANPER.

(2) *Calling statement:* CALL RANPER(N,A).

(3) *Purpose of subroutine:* Generate random permutation of n letters.

(4) *Descriptions of variables in calling statement:*

Name	Type	I/O/W/B	Description
N	INTEGER	I	Number of letters to be permuted.
A	INTEGER(N)	O	A(I) is the value of the output permutation at I (I=1,N).

(5) *Other routines which are called by this one:* Random number generator FUNCTION RAND(I).

(6) *Approximate number of* FORTRAN *instructions:* 11.

```
      SUBROUTINE RANPER(N,A)
      INTEGER A(N)
      DO 10   I=1,N
10    A(I)=I
20    DO 40   M=1,N
30    L=M+RAND(1)*(N+1-M)
      L1=A(L)
      A(L)=A(M)
40    A(M)=L1
      RETURN
      END
```

SAMPLE OUTPUT

For each $n = 3, \ldots, 8$, a set of 50 random permutations of n letters was chosen, and the number of cycles of each of these 50 permutations was found. In Table 8.1, we tabulate the average number

Table 8.1

n	(a)	(b)
3	1.78	1.83
4	2.04	2.08
5	2.28	2.28
6	2.50	2.45
7	2.52	2.59
8	2.58	2.72

of cycles in a permutation of n letters (a) estimated as described above and (b) calculated exactly, using the NEXPER subroutine (and well known to be equal to $1 + \frac{1}{2} + \cdots + 1/n$).

9

Next Partition of Integer n (NEXPAR)

If n is a positive integer, then a representation

$$n = r_1 + r_2 + \cdots + r_k \quad (r_1 \geqq r_2 \geqq \cdots \geqq r_k)$$

is called a *partition of n*, where it is understood that the "parts" $r_1, \ldots, r_k$ are strictly positive numbers. Thus, in Chapter 5, we saw that there are 28 *compositions* of 6 into 3 parts, but there are only 3 *partitions* of 6 into 3 parts, viz.,

$$
\begin{aligned}
6 &= 4 + 1 + 1 \\
&= 3 + 2 + 1 \\
&= 2 + 2 + 2
\end{aligned}
$$

Indeed, if we do not restrict the number of parts, then for a fixed n there are infinitely many *compositions* of n, but only a finite number of *partitions* of n. We let $p(n)$ denote the number of partitions of n. Then, for example, $p(6) = 11$ and the eleven partitions of 6 are

(1)
$$
\begin{aligned}
6 &= 6 \\
6 &= 5 + 1 \\
6 &= 4 + 2 \\
6 &= 4 + 1 + 1 \\
6 &= 3 + 3 \\
6 &= 3 + 2 + 1 \\
6 &= 3 + 1 + 1 + 1 \\
6 &= 2 + 2 + 2 \\
6 &= 2 + 2 + 1 + 1 \\
6 &= 2 + 1 + 1 + 1 + 1 \\
6 &= 1 + 1 + 1 + 1 + 1 + 1
\end{aligned}
$$

In the above list of partitions of 6, the arrangement of the partitions is in antilexicographic (reversed dictionary) order. More precisely, a partition

$$n = r_1 + r_2 + \cdots + r_k$$

occurs in the list above a partition

$$n = s_1 + s_2 + \cdots + s_q$$

if for some integer $t \geqq 0$ we have

(2) $\qquad r_i = s_i \quad (i = 1, \ldots, t) \qquad$ and $\qquad r_{t+1} > s_{t+1}$

The algorithm which we will now discuss generates from a given partition

(3) $\qquad\qquad n = r_1 + r_2 + \cdots + r_k$

its immediate successor on the list of all partitions of n, ordered antilexicographically. Suppose

(4) $\qquad\qquad n = \bar{r}_1 + \bar{r}_2 + \cdots + \bar{r}_l$

is the immediate successor. How can we determine the $\bar{r}_i$ from the r_i?

Suppose first that $r_k > 1$, e.g.,

(5) $\qquad\qquad 59 = 22 + 21 + 10 + 3 + 3$

What is the immediate successor of (5) in the list of partitions of 59? It is found by decreasing the last part r_k by 1 and adjoining a new part $= 1$:

(6) $\qquad\qquad 59 = 22 + 21 + 10 + 3 + 2 + 1$

Indeed, it is clear that (6) occurs *somewhere* after (5) on the list. If some third partition of 59 lies between (5) and (6), then it is easy to deduce a contradiction from the definition (2) of the ordering.

Hence, our first rule for obtaining (4) from (3) is:

(I) If $r_k > 1$,

$\qquad$ set $\bar{r}_1 = r_1, \bar{r}_2 = r_2, \ldots, \bar{r}_{k-1} = r_{k-1}, \bar{r}_k = r_k - 1, \bar{r}_{k+1} = 1$;

$\qquad$ Exit.

Now we need to deal with the case where $r_k = 1$. Suppose, in fact, that

$$r_k = r_{k-1} = \cdots = r_{j+1} = 1, \quad r_j > 1$$

as in the example

(7) $59 = 19 + 16 + 14 + 3 + 1 + 1 + 1 + 1 + 1 + 1 + 1$

If the first part, 19, were to change to 18, say

(8) $59 = 18 + \cdots$

we would not have the immediate successor of (7) because any partition

(9) $59 = 19 + 15 + \cdots$

would lie between (7) and (8). Similarly, the 16 and the 14 must both remain fixed. Hence the immediate successor of (7) is of the form

(10) $59 = 19 + 16 + 14 + \cdots$

and the dots in (10) constitute a partition of 10, namely, the one which is the successor of

$$10 = 3 + 1 + 1 + 1 + 1 + 1 + 1 + 1$$

in the list of partitions of 10. We need to go from the "last" partition of 10 whose largest part is 3 to the "first" partition of 10 whose largest part is 2

$$10 = 2 + 2 + 2 + 2 + 2$$

The successor of (7) is then

$$59 = 19 + 16 + 14 + 2 + 2 + 2 + 2 + 2$$

If we return now to the general case, suppose we have a partition

$$n = r_1 + r_2 + \cdots + r_j + 1 + 1 + 1 + \cdots + 1$$

In the successor partition, none of the first $j - 1$ parts will change, so that

$$\bar{r}_i = r_i \quad (i < j)$$

What remains is the last partition of the number

$$n' = r_j + (k - j)$$

whose largest part is r_j, and we must go to the first partition of n' whose largest part is

$$m = r_j - 1$$

This first partition is made by repeating the part m as often as it will "fit" into n', namely

$$\lfloor n'/m \rfloor$$

times, and if there is a positive remainder

$$s = n' - m\lfloor n'/m \rfloor$$

then we adjoin one additional part equal to s.

The complete formulation of the transition from (3) to (4) in the case where

$$r_{j+1} = \cdots = r_k = 1, \quad r_j > 1$$

is

(11)
$$
\begin{aligned}
\bar{r}_i &= r_i \quad (i = 1, \ldots, j - 1) \\
\bar{r}_j &= \bar{r}_{j+1} = \cdots = \bar{r}_{j+q-1} = m \\
\bar{r}_{j+q} &= s \quad (\text{if } s > 0)
\end{aligned}
$$

where $m = r_j - 1$, $\quad q = \lfloor (r_j + (k - j))/m \rfloor$, $\quad s = r_j + (k - j) - mq$.

The algorithm avoids the repeated listing of equal parts by maintaining a list $r_1 > r_2 > \cdots > r_d > 0$ of distinct parts, and a list $m_1, \ldots, m_d$ of their respective (positive) multiplicities. This economy results in a running time for each call to the subroutine which is independent of the value of n, and the program is loop-free.

ALGORITHM NEXPAR

(A) [*First entry*] $r_1 \leftarrow n$; $m_1 \leftarrow 1$; $d \leftarrow 1$; Exit.

(B) [*Later entries*] (Set σ equal to the sum of all parts of size one, plus the part preceding them.) If $r_d = 1$, set $\sigma \leftarrow m_d + 1$, $d \leftarrow d - 1$; Otherwise, $\sigma \leftarrow 1$.

(C) [*Remove one part of size r_d*] $f \leftarrow r_d - 1$; If $m_d = 1$, to (D); $m_d \leftarrow m_d - 1$; $d \leftarrow d + 1$.

(D) [*Add new parts of size f*] $r_d \leftarrow f$; $m_d \leftarrow \lfloor \sigma/f \rfloor + 1$.

(E) [*Add positive remainder*] $s \leftarrow \sigma \pmod{f}$; If $s = 0$, to (F); Otherwise, $d \leftarrow d + 1$; $r_d \leftarrow s$; $m_d \leftarrow 1$.

(F) [*Exit*] If $m_d = n$, final exit; Exit ■

SUBROUTINE SPECIFICATIONS

(1) *Name of subroutine:*   NEXPAR.

(2) *Calling statement:*   CALL NEXPAR(N,R,M,D,MTC).

(3) *Purpose of subroutine:*   Find next partition of *n*.
(4) *Descriptions of variables in calling statement:*

Name	Type	I/O/W/B	Description
N	INTEGER	I	Integer whose partitions are desired.
R	INTEGER(N)	I/O	R(I) is the Ith distinct part of the output partition (I=1,D).
M	INTEGER(N)	I/O	M(I) is the multiplicity of R(I) in the output partition (I=1,D).
D	INTEGER	I/O	Number of distinct parts in output partition.
MTC	LOGICAL	I/O	=.TRUE. if more partitions of N remain after this one. =.FALSE. if this is the last partition of N.

(5) *Other routines which are called by this one:*   None.
(6) *Approximate number of* FORTRAN *instructions:*   28.

```
      SUBROUTINE NEXPAR(N,R,M,D,MTC)
      IMPLICIT INTEGER (A-Z)
      LOGICAL MTC
      DIMENSION R(N),M(N)
      DATA NLAST/0/
10    IF(N.EQ.NLAST) GO TO 20
      NLAST=N
30    S=N
      D=0
50    D=D+1
      R(D)=S
      M(D)=1
40    MTC=M(D).NE.N
      RETURN
20    IF(.NOT.MTC) GO TO 30
      SUM=1
      IF(R(D).GT.1) GO TO 60
      SUM=M(D)+1
      D=D-1
60    F=R(D)-1
      IF(M(D).EQ.1) GO TO 70
      M(D)=M(D)-1
      D=D+1
70    R(D)=F
      M(D)=1+SUM/F
      S=MOD(SUM,F)
```

```
IF(S) 40,40,50
END
```

SAMPLE OUTPUT

The subprogram NEXPAR was called repeatedly with N=10, until termination. The 42 output partitions are shown below where, for clarity, we have shown multiple parts repeated.

```
10
 9  1
 8  2
 8  1  1
 7  3
 7  2  1
 7  1  1  1
 6  4
 6  3  1
 6  2  2
 6  2  1  1
 6  1  1  1  1
 5  5
 5  4  1
 5  3  2
 5  3  1  1
 5  2  2  1
 5  2  1  1  1
 5  1  1  1  1  1
 4  4  2
 4  4  1  1
 4  3  3
 4  3  2  1
 4  3  1  1  1
 4  2  2  2
 4  2  2  1  1
 4  2  1  1  1  1
 4  1  1  1  1  1  1
 3  3  3  1
 3  3  2  2
 3  3  2  1  1
```

```
3   3   1   1   1   1
3   2   2   2   1
3   2   2   1   1   1
3   2   1   1   1   1   1
3   1   1   1   1   1   1   1
2   2   2   2   2
2   2   2   2   1   1
2   2   2   1   1   1   1
2   2   1   1   1   1   1   1
2   1   1   1   1   1   1   1   1
1   1   1   1   1   1   1   1   1   1
```

10

Random Partition of Integer n (RANPAR)

The choice of a random partition of an integer n is a matter of some delicacy, the difficulty being, of course, that we insist on having all partitions of n with equal a priori probability $1/p(n)$, where $p(n)$ is the number of partitions of n (see Chapter 9).

One method which suggests itself quickly, although we shall not adopt it here, is to suppose that we have tabulated $p(n, k)$, the number of partitions of n whose largest part is exactly k, as well as $p(n)$. We then select the largest part r_1 according to the probabilities

$$(1) \qquad \text{Prob } \{r_1 = r\} = \frac{p(n, r)}{p(n)} \quad (r = 1, 2, \ldots , n)$$

Having chosen r_1 we replace n by $n - r_1$ and continue, using scaled probabilities. To tabulate $p(n, r)$, a moment's reflection shows that

$$(2) \qquad p(n, k) = \sum_{j=1}^{k} p(n - k, j)$$

We can replace n by $n - 1$ and k by $k - 1$ simultaneously to obtain

$$(3) \qquad p(n - 1, k - 1) = \sum_{j=1}^{k-1} p(n - k, j)$$

and if we subtract (3) from (2), we get the simple recurrence

$$(4) \qquad p(n, k) = p(n - 1, k - 1) + p(n - k, k)$$

from which it is easy to compute $p(n, k)$.

Despite the simplicity of the above algorithm, we can describe a new one which avoids any tabulation of a function of two indices, requiring only a linear array.

Let $\sigma(n)$ denote the sum of the divisors of the integer n, and consider the identity

$$(5) \qquad np(n) = \sum_{m<n} \sigma(n-m)p(m)$$

of Euler. We give two proofs of this identity, the classical proof, and a purely combinatorial one which forms the basis of the present algorithm.

The original proof depends on the generating function

$$(6) \qquad \prod_{j=1}^{\infty} (1-x^j)^{-1} = \sum_{n=0}^{\infty} p(n)x^n \quad (p(0)=1)$$

whose proof can be found in any standard text. If we take logarithms of both sides and differentiate with respect to x, we obtain

$$(7) \qquad \sum_{j=1}^{\infty} \frac{jx^j}{1-x^j} = \frac{\sum_n np(n)x^n}{\sum_n p(n)x^n}$$

If we develop the left side in a power series, we obtain

$$\sum_{j=1}^{\infty} jx^j(1+x^j+x^{2j}+\cdots) = \sum_{k=1}^{\infty} \sigma(k)x^k$$

and then (7) yields

$$(8) \qquad \left\{ \sum_{k=1}^{\infty} \sigma(k)x^k \right\} \left\{ \sum_{m=0}^{\infty} p(m)x^m \right\} = \sum_{n=0}^{\infty} np(n)x^n$$

Euler's identity now follows by equating the coefficients of x^n on both sides of (8).

Next we give a combinatorial proof of (5) which is based on a multiple counting of the partitions. Suppose π denotes a partition of some integer $m < n$ and d is a divisor of $n-m$; then the pair (π, d) gives rise to a partition of n. We simply adjoin to the partition π of m exactly $(n-m)/d$ copies of d, yielding a partition π' of n. We make d copies of the partition π'.

We claim that as d runs over all divisors of $n-m$ and π runs over partitions of m $(m=0, 1, \ldots, n-1)$, each partition of n is counted exactly n times by this process, which will prove (5). Indeed, if

$$(9) \qquad \pi' : n = \mu_1 r_1 + \cdots + \mu_k r_k$$

is a fixed partition of n where the r_i are the *distinct* parts of π' and the μ_i are their multiplicities, then for each t, $1 \leq t \leq \mu_i$, $1 \leq i \leq k$, π' is constructed by adjoining t copies of r_i to a partition of $n - tr_i$ and by replicating the resulting partition of n r_i times. This gives a total of

$$(10) \qquad \sum_{i=1}^{k} r_i \mu_i = n$$

copies of π' altogether, as required.

To obtain an algorithm for random partitions, we replace $n - m$ in (5) by jd, as we now describe. For simplicity of notation, we assume that $p(k) = 0$ for $k < 0$. Then

$$np(n) = \sum_{m=1}^{\infty} \sigma(m)p(n - m)$$

$$= \sum_{m=1}^{\infty} \sum_{d \mid m} dp(n - m)$$

$$= \sum_{j=1}^{\infty} \sum_{d=1}^{\infty} dp(n - jd)$$

or equivalently,

$$1 = \sum_{d=1}^{\infty} \sum_{j=1}^{\infty} \frac{dp(n - jd)}{np(n)}$$

and we interpret the terms on the right as probabilities which sum to 1.

ALGORITHM RANPAR

Given n.

(A) Set $\mathscr{P} \leftarrow$ empty partition; $m \leftarrow n$.

(B) Choose a pair of integers (d, j) according to the probabilities
$$\text{Prob}(d, j) = \frac{dp(m - jd)}{mp(m)} \qquad (d, j = 1, 2, \ldots).$$

(C) Adjoin j copies of d to $\mathscr{P}$.

(D) $m \leftarrow m - jd$.

(E) If $m = 0$, exit; Otherwise go to (B) ∎

FLOW CHART RANPAR

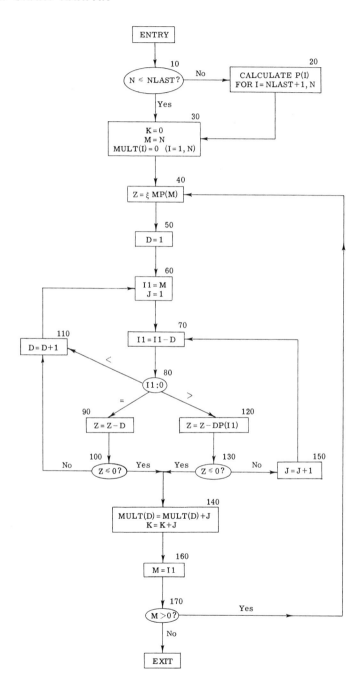

DESCRIPTION OF FLOW CHART

Box 10   If N≤NLAST we go to 30 because no further values of P(I) are needed.

Box 20   Otherwise we extend the table of P(I) to N, by use of (5).

Box 30   Initialize for obtaining random partition.

Box 40–130   A pair (J,D) is determined with the correct probability by reducing Z by amounts D·P(M−J·D) until negative. The current M−J·D is called I1. The case I1=0 is specially treated in Box 90.

Box 140   J copies of D are adjoined to the partition.

Boxes 160, 170   M is set to new value I1, and if still positive we return to Box 40 to select next parts. Otherwise, exit.

It is easy to see that all partitions of n have equal a priori probabilities of being chosen. Indeed, let

$$(11) \qquad n = \mu_1 d_1 + \mu_2 d_2 + \cdots + \mu_k d_k$$

be a fixed partition of n, where the $d_1, \ldots, d_k$ are distinct, and $\mu_1, \mu_2,$ are their multiplicities. This partition is chosen in $\mu_1 + \cdots + \mu_k$ ways by adjoining j copies of d_i to the partition of $n - jd_i$ given by

$$n - jd_i = \mu_1 d_1 + \cdots + (\mu_i - j)\, d_i + \cdots + \mu_k d_k$$
$$(1 \leqq j \leqq \mu_i; \; 1 \leqq i \leqq k)$$

Inductively, these latter partitions each have an a priori probability equal to $1/p(n - jd_i)$. The a priori probability of (11) is therefore

$$\sum_{i=1}^{k} \sum_{j=1}^{\mu_i} \frac{d_i p(n - d_i j)}{np(n)} \, \frac{1}{p(n - jd_i)} = \frac{1}{np(n)} \sum_{i=1}^{k} \sum_{j=1}^{\mu_i} d_i$$
$$= \frac{1}{np(n)} \sum_{i=1}^{k} \mu_i d_i$$
$$= \frac{1}{p(n)}$$

as required.

SUBROUTINE SPECIFICATIONS

(1) *Name of subroutine:* RANPAR
(2) *Calling statement:* CALL RANPAR(N,K,MULT,P).

(3) *Purpose of subroutine:* Generate a random partition of n.

(4) *Descriptions of variables in calling statement:*

Name	Type	I/O/W/B	Description
N	INTEGER	I	Number whose partitions are desired.
K	INTEGER	O	Number of parts in output partition.
MULT	INTEGER(N)	O	MULT(I) is the multiplicity of I in the output partition (I=1,2,...,N).
P	INTEGER(N)	B	P(I) is the number of partition of I (I=1,N).

(5) *Other routines which are called by this one:* FUNCTION RAND(I) (random numbers).

(6) *Approximate number of* FORTRAN *instructions:* 42.

```
      SUBROUTINE RANPAR(N,K,MULT,P)
      INTEGER P(N),D,MULT(N)
      DATA NLAST/0/
10    IF(N.LE.NLAST) GO TO 30
20    P(1)=1
      M=NLAST+1
      NLAST=N
      IF(N.EQ.1) GO TO 30
      DO 21  I=M,N
      ISUM=0
26    DO 22  D=1,I
      IS=0
      I1=I
24    I1=I1-D
      IF(I1) 22,25,23
23    IS=IS+P(I1)
      GO TO 24
25    IS=IS+1
22    ISUM=ISUM+IS*D
21    P(I)=ISUM/I
30    M=N
      K=0
      DO 31  I=1,N
31    MULT(I)=0
40    Z=RAND(1)*M*P(M)
      D=0
110   D=D+1
60    I1=M
      J=0
```

```
150    J=J+1
70     I1=I1-D
80     IF(I1)  110,90,120
120    Z=Z-D*P(I1)
130    IF(Z)  145,145,150
90     Z=Z-D
100    IF(Z)  145,145,110
145    MULT(D)=MULT(D)+J
       K=K+J
160    M=I1
170    IF(M.NE.0) GO TO 40
       RETURN
       END
```

SAMPLE OUTPUT

The subprogram RANPAR was called 880 times with N=6. The frequencies with which each of the 11 partitions of 6 were obtained are shown on the next page. Thus, $6 = 3 + 2 + 1$ occurred 83 times, etc. The value $\chi^2 = 13.475$ was calculated from

$$\chi^2 = \sum_{\pi} \frac{(\phi(\pi) - 80)^2}{80}$$

where $\phi(\pi)$ is the frequency of the partition π, and the sum is over the 11 partitions of 6. In 95% of such experiments, the observed value of χ^2 would lie between 3.247 and 20.483 if the partitions did indeed have equal a priori probabilities.

```
 80    6
 77    5  1
106    4  2
 73    4  1  1
 72    3  3
 83    3  2  1
 67    3  1  1  1
 75    2  2  2
 76    2  2  1  1
 86    2  1  1  1  1
 85    1  1  1  1  1  1
```

CHI SQ IS 13.475 WITH 10 DEG FREEDOM

Postscript: Deus ex Machina

There is, in the material of Chapter 10, an excellent example of how new pure mathematics can result from the use of computers. In this case, we asked a question about the proper way to generate partitions at random. The mere asking of such a question is itself a product of the existence of computers. The resulting answer was obtained by seeking the combinatorial meaning of a certain identity (cf. Eq. (6)) and following the construction thereby suggested.

The next question is, "Why did it work?" That is, does our construction apply only to this problem, or is it a manifestation of something more general? It turns out that the latter is the case, and many other applications of the same ideas can be made (see Chapters 12 and 25).

The situation as regards partitions of an integer is that every partition is uniquely constructed from a set of basic building blocks, namely, the special partitions $1 = 1$, $2 = 2$, $3 = 3$, $4 = 4$, . . . (which we abbreviate as (1), (2), (3), (4), . . .) and their multiplicities. Thus

$$8 = 4 + 2 + 2 = (4) + 2 \cdot (2)$$

can be regarded as exhibiting a partition of 8 in terms of the special partitions (4), (2).

We have then a family of combinatorial objects, namely, the set of all partitions of all integers, and in that family is a distinguished subset (1), (2), (3), . . . , called "primes," with the property that every partition in the large family is uniquely expressible as a synthesis of primes with multiplicities. We shall now abstract from this case to a more general setting, and we will see that the algorithms follow along.

Consider a system $\mathcal{S}$ which consists of

1. a set $\mathcal{T}$ of objects
2. a *synthesis* map $\otimes : \mathcal{T} \times \mathcal{T} \to \mathcal{T}$
3. an *order function* $\Omega : \mathcal{T} \to \mathbf{Z}^+$
4. a distinguished subset $\mathcal{P}$ of $\mathcal{T}$ of *primes*,

with the properties:

H1 Additivity of order under synthesis:

$$\Omega(t' \otimes t'') = \Omega(t') + \Omega(t'')$$

H2 Properties of synthesis: $\otimes$ is associative and commutative

H3 Unique factorization: There are no primes of order 0 and every $t \in \mathcal{T}$ is uniquely a synthesis of primes, i.e.,

$$t = p_1{}^{\mu_1} \otimes p_2{}^{\mu_2} \otimes \cdots$$

where $\forall_i : p_i \in \mathcal{P}$ and p^μ means $p \otimes p \otimes \cdots \otimes p$ (μ factors).

Let a_n denote the number of objects in $\mathcal{T}$ of order n, and let Π_n denote the number of *prime* objects of order n, for each $n = 1, 2, \ldots$. We seek the relationship between $\{a_n\}$ and $\{\Pi_n\}$.

Let $s \in \mathcal{T}$ be an object of order n, and let

$$(1) \qquad s = p_1{}^{\mu_1} \otimes p_2{}^{\mu_2} \otimes \cdots \otimes p_l{}^{\mu_l}$$

be the unique "prime factorization" of s. We shall construct the object s in all possible ways by a two-step process of synthesis and replication:

Step 1 (Synthesis) Let s' be any object of $\mathcal{T}$ whose prime decomposition is identical with Eq. (1) except that exactly *one* of the primes, say p_k, appears to a lower power, say $\mu_k - j$ ($1 \leqq j \leqq \mu_k$). Then

$$(2) \qquad s = s' \otimes p_k{}^j$$

The object s is uniquely determined by the object s' of lower order, and the integers j, p_k. Note that $\Omega(s') = \Omega(s) - j\Omega(p_k)$.

Step 2 (Replication) Make $d_k = \Omega(p_k)$ copies of the object s, after synthesizing it in Eq. (2).

Now, as s' runs over all objects of order $< n = \Omega(s)$, exactly how many copies of the object s will be made? For each j such that $1 \leq j \leq \mu_k$ we make $\Omega(p_k)$ copies of s, for a total of

$$\sum_{k=1}^{l} \mu_k \Omega(p_k) = \Omega(p_1^{\mu_1} \otimes p_2^{\mu_2} \otimes \cdots \otimes {}^{\prime}p_l^{\mu_l}) = \Omega(s) = n$$

copies of s altogether. Thus, *every object of order n is produced exactly n times*. It follows that

$$(3) \qquad na_n = \sum_{j \geq 1} \sum_{d \geq 1} a_{n-jd} d\Pi_d$$

because the right side is the total number of copies of all objects of order n which are made by our synthesis and replication. The fundamental relation (3) expresses the total number of objects of each order in our system $\mathscr{S}$ in terms of the number of prime objects of each order.

The identity (3) can also be written in the more familiar equivalent form

$$(4) \qquad na_n = \sum_{m<n} a_m \left\{ \sum_{d|(n-m)} d\Pi_d \right\}$$

The identity (6) of Chapter 10 appears as the analytic statement of unique factorization among the partitions of integers.

We can express (4) in terms of generating functions. Let

$$A(x) = \sum_{n \geq 0} a_n x^n, \qquad P(x) = \sum_{n \geq 1} \Pi_n x^n$$

be the counting functions for all objects and for prime objects, respectively, then

$$(5) \qquad A(x) = \exp\left\{ \sum_{r=1}^{\infty} \frac{P(x^r)}{r} \right\}$$

Indeed, logarithmic differentiation of (5), followed by matching coefficients of like powers of x yields (4) and conversely. (*Remark:* $a_0 = 1$; it counts the identity element whose prime decomposition is the "empty" product.)

In this general situation, an algorithm for selecting an object of order n uniformly at random can always be given. Suppose that we know how to select a prime object uniformly of given order; then

(A)   Choose a pair of integers (j, d) with probabilities

$$\text{Prob}(j, d) = \frac{da_{n-jd}\Pi_d}{na_n} \quad (j \geq 1, d \geq 1)$$

(B)   Choose an object $s' \in \mathscr{T}$ of order $n - jd$ and a prime object p of order d uniformly.

(C)   Synthesize s of order n from s' and j copies of p:

$$s = s' \otimes p^j$$

It is easy to check that every $s \in \mathscr{T}$, $\Omega(s) = n$, has a priori probability a_n^{-1} of being selected.

Aside from partitions of integers, there are many examples of such systems in the literature. If $\mathscr{T}$ is the set of all forests of rooted unlabeled trees, with $\Omega(t) = $ number of vertices of t, and if $\mathscr{P}$ is the subset of connected objects (i.e., rooted unlabeled trees), then we have the following interesting situation: Our algorithm will select a random forest on n vertices, given a knowledge of how to select a random tree of $m \leq n$ vertices. However, there is a 1–1 correspondence between forests of n vertices and trees of $n + 1$ vertices: just adjoin a new vertex $n + 1$, call it the new root, and connect it to each of the roots of the trees in the original forest. It follows that our algorithm will select a *tree* of $n + 1$ vertices if we know how to select a *tree* of $\leq n$ vertices, i.e., we have an *inductive* process for selecting random rooted, unlabeled trees! This is discussed in detail in Chapter 25.

The abstract structures which we have introduced here are a special case of a family of objects, called "prefabs," first studied by E. Bender and J. Goldman who also pointed out the interesting property of rooted forests noted above. What we have added to their work is first of all the constructive procedure of synthesis and replication, which gives direct combinatorial meaning to the logarithmic derivative (4) of the functional equation (5), and secondly the realization that such structures are invariably equipped with recurrent algorithms for randomly uniform selection of objects of given order.

11

Next Partition of an n-Set (NEXEQU)

From partitions of integers we turn to partitions of sets. If $S = \{1, 2, \ldots, n\}$, then by a *partition* of S we mean a family of sets $T_1, T_2, \ldots, T_k$ satisfying

(a) $$T_i \cap T_j = \varnothing \quad (i \neq j)$$

and

(b) $$\bigcup_{i=1}^{k} T_i = S$$

and

(c) $$T_i \neq \varnothing \quad (i = 1, \ldots, k)$$

It is assumed that no significance is attached to the order in which $T_1, \ldots, T_k$ are listed nor to the order of the listing of elements within these sets. For $n = 3$, therefore, we have the following 5 partitions:

$$
\begin{array}{cl}
1 & (123) \\
2 & (12)\ (3) \\
3 & (13)\ (2) \\
4 & (23)\ (1) \\
5 & (1)\ (2)\ (3)
\end{array}
$$

A partition of a set is evidently identical with an equivalence relation on the set, with the T_i as the equivalence classes, which accounts for the name NEXEQU of this routine.

Given a partition $\mathcal{P}$ of $\{1, 2, \ldots, n\}$ into k classes $T_1, \ldots, T_k$, we may associate with $\mathcal{P}$ exactly $k + 1$ different partitions of $\{1, 2, \ldots, n, n + 1\}$, namely —

$$\mathcal{P}_1 : T_1 \cup \{n + 1\}, T_2, T_3, \ldots, T_k$$
$$\mathcal{P}_2 : T_1, T_2 \cup \{n + 1\}, T_3, \ldots, T_k$$
$$\vdots$$
$$\mathcal{P}_k : T_1, T_2, T_3, \ldots, T_k \cup \{n + 1\}$$
$$\mathcal{P}_{k+1} : T_1, T_2, T_3, \ldots, T_k, \{n + 1\}$$

The first k of these descendants of $\mathcal{P}$ have k classes, and the last one has $k + 1$ classes in which the last class is just the singleton $\{n + 1\}$.

We can visualize all of the partitions of $\{1, 2, \ldots, n\}$, therefore, as one horizontal line in a tree (Fig. 11.1).

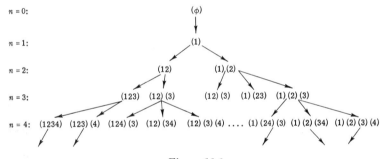

Figure 11.1

In this tree, a line is drawn from each partition $\mathcal{P}$, of a set of n letters into k classes, to each of its $k + 1$ immediate descendants, which are partitions of $n + 1$ letters into k or $k + 1$ classes.

To generate successively all partitions of $\{1, 2, \ldots, n\}$ we want to move from left to right along one horizontal level of this tree. Given a partition $\mathcal{P}$ of $\{1, 2, \ldots, n\}$, to locate its immediate successor $\mathcal{P}'$ we (a) locate the highest active letter m, i.e., the largest integer $1 \leqq m \leqq n$ which is not in a singleton class in $\mathcal{P}$; (b) move m to the next higher class, or create a singleton class for m if m is already in the highest class; (c) put $m + 1, \ldots, n$ into class 1.

For example, here are the five partitions of $\{1, 2, 3\}$, in the order in which this algorithm produces them where, in each case, the highest active letter m is underlined:

$$(1\ 2\ \underline{3})$$
$$(1\underline{2})\ (3)$$
$$(1\underline{3})\ (2)$$
$$(1)\ (2\underline{3})$$
$$(1)\ (2)\ (3)$$

It is convenient to use two arrays, p_i, the population of the ith class in the output partition, and q_j, the class to which element j belongs $(i = 1, n_c; j = 1, n)$.

ALGORITHM NEXEQU

(A) [*First entry*] $p_1 \leftarrow n$; $n_c \leftarrow 1$; $m \leftarrow n$; $q_i \leftarrow 1$ $(i = 1, n)$; $p_l \leftarrow 0$ $(l = 2, n)$; to (E).

(B) [*All later entries*] $k_1 \leftarrow q_m$; If $p_{k_1} = 1$, to (C); $p_{k_1} \leftarrow 0$; $m \leftarrow m - 1$; $n_c \leftarrow n_c - 1$.

(C) $k_2 \leftarrow k_1 + 1$; $q_m \leftarrow k_2$; $p_{k_1} \leftarrow p_{k_1} - 1$; $p_{k_2} \leftarrow p_{k_2} + 1$; If $p_{k_2} \neq 1$, to (D); $n_c \leftarrow n_c + 1$.

(D) If $m = n$, to (E); For $j = m + 1, n : \{q_j \leftarrow 1; p_1 \leftarrow p_1 + 1\}$.

(E) If $n_c = n$, final exit; Exit ∎

Remark   Recall that no significance attaches to the names of the classes within a partition. Yet, on output, the computer is forced to name these classes for reference purposes. Our algorithm does this naming in such a way that the smallest element of class j is the first integer which does not belong to any earlier class $1, 2, \ldots, j - 1$.

FLOW CHART NEXEQU

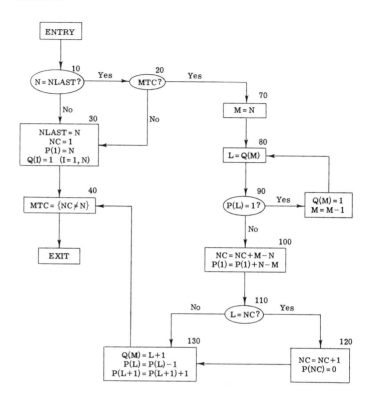

DESCRIPTION OF FLOW CHART

Box 10 New N? If so, new series.

Box 20 Does the user want a new series anyway?

Box 30 Initialize for new series of set-partitions.

Box 40 End of series? (MTC=FALSE).

Box 70 Start descending series.

Boxes 80, 90 Is M a singleton class? If so, move M to class 1 and try next lower M.

Box 100 Adjust NC and P(1) for changes just made.

Box 110 L is the class of the largest M not in a singleton class. Is this the highest class?

Box 120 If so, increase NC; initialize P(NC).

Box 130 Move M to next higher class.

SUBROUTINE SPECIFICATIONS

(1) *Name of subroutine:* NEXEQU.

(2) *Calling statement:* CALL NEXEQU(N,NC,P,Q,MTC).

(3) *Purpose of subroutine:* Generate next equivalence relation on {1, 2, . . . , n}.

(4) *Descriptions of variables in calling statement:*

Name	Type	I/O/W/B	Description
N	INTEGER	I	Number of elements in set to be partitioned.
NC	INTEGER	O	Number of classes in output partition.
P	INTEGER(N)	I/O	P(I) is the number of elements in the Ith class in the output partition (I=1,NC).
Q	INTEGER(N)	I/O	Q(I) is the class to which I belongs (I=1,N).
MTC	LOGICAL	I/O	=.TRUE. if current output is not the last; =.FALSE. otherwise.

(5) *Other routines which are called by this one:* None.

(6) *Approximate number of* FORTRAN *instructions:* 30.

```
        SUBROUTINE NEXEQU(N,NC,P,Q,MTC)
        IMPLICIT INTEGER(A-Z)
        LOGICAL MTC
        DIMENSION P(N),Q(N)
        DATA NLAST/0/
10      IF(N.EQ.NLAST) GO TO 20
30      NLAST=N
        NC=1
        DO 35  I=1,N
35      Q(I)=1
        P(1)=N
40      MTC=(NC.NE.N)
        RETURN
20      IF(.NOT.MTC)  GO TO 30
70      M=N
80      L=Q(M)
90      IF(P(L).NE.1) GO TO 100
95      Q(M)=1
        M=M-1
        GO TO 80
100     NC=NC+M-N
        P(1)=P(1)+N-M
```

```
110    IF(L.NE.NC) GO TO 130
120    NC=NC+1
       P(NC)=0
130    Q(M)=L+1
       P(L)=P(L)-1
       P(L+1)=P(L+1)+1
       GO TO 40
       END
```

SAMPLE OUTPUT

The subprogram NEXEQU was called repeatedly with N=5, until termination. The 52 output vectors $Q(1), Q(2), \ldots, Q(5)$ are shown below.

1	1	1	1	1		1	2	2	1	2
1	1	1	1	2		1	2	2	1	3
1	1	1	2	1		1	2	2	2	1
1	1	1	2	2		1	2	2	2	2
1	1	1	2	3		1	2	2	2	3
1	1	2	1	1		1	2	2	3	1
1	1	2	1	2		1	2	2	3	2
1	1	2	1	3		1	2	2	3	3
1	1	2	2	1		1	2	2	3	4
1	1	2	2	2		1	2	3	1	1
1	1	2	2	3		1	2	3	1	2
1	1	2	3	1		1	2	3	1	3
1	1	2	3	2		1	2	3	1	4
1	1	2	3	3		1	2	3	2	1
1	1	2	3	4		1	2	3	2	2
1	2	1	1	1		1	2	3	2	3
1	2	1	1	2		1	2	3	2	4
1	2	1	1	3		1	2	3	3	1
1	2	1	2	1		1	2	3	3	2
1	2	1	2	2		1	2	3	3	3
1	2	1	2	3		1	2	3	3	4
1	2	1	3	1		1	2	3	4	1
1	2	1	3	2		1	2	3	4	2
1	2	1	3	3		1	2	3	4	3
1	2	1	3	4		1	2	3	4	4
1	2	2	1	1		1	2	3	4	5

12

Random Partition of an n-Set (RANEQU)

The algorithm for a random equivalence relation on $\{1, 2, \ldots, n\}$ follows the basic idea of Chapter 10 and its Postscript, in which we found a recurrence formula and then endowed it with a probabilistic interpretation.

Here, the recurrence is in the quantities $a_0, a_1, \ldots$ where a_n is the number of partitions of a set of n objects. Indeed, let $\mathcal{P}_k$ be a fixed partition of $\{1, 2, \ldots, k\}$. We will extend it to exactly $\binom{n-1}{k}$ partitions of $\{1, 2, \ldots, n\}$. First, choose a subset S of k elements from $\{1, 2, \ldots, n-1\}$. Relabel the k elements of $\mathcal{P}_k$ using the elements of S as labels. Adjoin to the resulting partition all of the $n - k$ remaining elements of $\{1, 2, \ldots, n\}$ regarded as a single class. In this way, we make $\binom{n-1}{k}$ partitions of $\{1, 2, \ldots, n\}$ from each of the a_k partitions of $\{1, 2, \ldots, k\}$ or

$$\sum_{k=0}^{n-1} \binom{n-1}{k} a_k$$

partitions of $\{1, 2, \ldots, n\}$ altogether.

We claim that every partition $\mathcal{P}$ of $\{1, 2, \ldots, n\}$ is constructed just once in this way. For, if $\mathcal{P} = T_1 \cup T_2 \cup \cdots \cup T_h$ where the T_i are the classes of $\mathcal{P}$, suppose T_h is the unique class of $\mathcal{P}$ which contains the element n. Then $\mathcal{P}$ was constructed uniquely from the partition which is formed by relabeling the set $T_1 \cup T_2 \cup \cdots \cup T_{h-1}$ with labels $1, 2, \ldots, k$, where $k = \sum_{i=1}^{h-1} |T_i|$. Hence we have

(1) $$a_n = \sum_{k=0}^{n-1} \binom{n-1}{k} a_k \quad (n \geq 1, a_0 = 1)$$

from which we find $a_1 = 1$, $a_2 = 2$, $a_3 = 5$, $a_4 = 15$, etc.

Usually the use to which (1) is put is to find the generating function

(2) $$f(z) = \sum_{n=0}^{\infty} \frac{a_n}{n!} z^n$$

In fact, (1) implies that

$$f'(z) = e^z f(z)$$

and $f(0) = 1$. The solution of this initial value problem is evidently

(3) $$f(z) = \exp(e^z - 1)$$

which identifies the numbers a_n as

(4) $$a_n = \frac{d^n}{dz^n} (\exp(e^z - 1)) \bigg|_{z=0} \quad (n = 0, 1, 2, \ldots)$$

Our interest, however, lies in the algorithm which results from dividing both sides of (1) by a_n

(5) $$1 = \sum_{k=0}^{n-1} \binom{n-1}{k} \frac{a_k}{a_n}$$

and identifying the terms on the right as probabilities which sum to 1.

The full algorithm is as follows:

ALGORITHM RANEQU

Let $U = \{1, 2, \ldots, n\}$.

(A)   Let $U' \leftarrow U$, $m \leftarrow n$, $\mathcal{P} \leftarrow$ unique partition of empty set.

(B)   Choose an integer k according to the probabilities

(6) $$\text{Prob}(k) = \binom{m-1}{k} \frac{a_k}{a_m} \quad (0 \leq k \leq m - 1)$$

(C)   Let $l = $ largest element of U'; Let S be a random k-subset of $U' - \{l\}$.

(D) Adjoin $U' - S$ to $\mathscr{P}$ as a single class; If $k = 0$, stop; Otherwise, let $m \leftarrow k$, $U' \leftarrow S$ and return to step **(B)** ■

FLOW CHART RANEQU

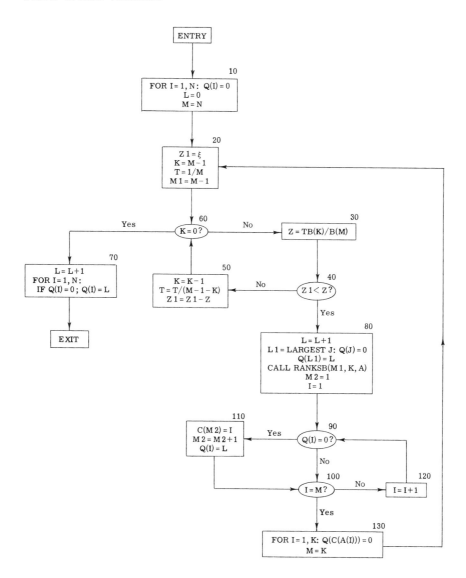

DESCRIPTION OF FLOW CHART

Box 10   Q(I) is the class to which I belongs, or 0 if I is unassigned as yet. L is the number of classes in the current partition; M is the number of unassigned elements.

Boxes 20–50   We select K, $0 \leq K \leq M-1$, according to the probability distribution (6).

Box 70   If K=0, all unassigned elements are assigned to the last class, L. Exit.

Box 80   Otherwise, find L1, the largest unassigned element, and assign it to class L. Find a random K-subset S of the letters 1,2,...,M-1.

Boxes 90–120   Create the array C(J) (J=1,M-1), where C(J) is the Jth currently unassigned letter. Assign all unassigned letters to class L (some of these will become unassigned again in Box 130).

Box 130   Reset the random subset S of the previously unassigned letters back to unassigned status. Set M=K and return to Box 20.

SUBROUTINE SPECIFICATIONS

(1) *Name of subroutine:* RANEQU.
(2) *Calling statement:* CALL RANEQU(N,L,Q,A,B,C).
(3) *Purpose of subroutine:* Generate random equivalence relation on $\{1, 2, \ldots, n\}$.
(4) *Descriptions of variables in calling statement:*

Name	Type	I/O/W/B	Description
N	INTEGER	I	Cardinality of partitioned set.
L	INTEGER	O	Number of classes in output partition.
Q	INTEGER	O	Q(I) is the class to which I belongs (I=1,N).
A	INTEGER(N)	W	Working storage.
B	REAL(N)	B	B(K)=A(K)/K! (see text Eq. (1)) (K=1,N).
C	INTEGER(N)	W	Working storage.

(5) *Other routines which are called by this one:* FUNCTION RAND(I) (random numbers), RANKSB (Chapter 4).
(6) *Approximate number of* FORTRAN *instructions:* 56.

```
SUBROUTINE RANEQU(N,L,Q,A,B,C)
INTEGER Q(N),A(N),C(N)
DIMENSION B(N)
DATA NLAST/1/
B(1)=1
IF(N.LE.NLAST) GO TO 10
```

```
3      M=NLAST
       NLAST=N
       NM1=N-1
       DO 5  L=M,NM1
       SUM=1./FLOAT(L)
       L1=L-1
       DO 6  K=1,L1
6      SUM=(SUM+B(K))/FLOAT(L-K)
5      B(L+1)=(SUM+B(L))/FLOAT(L+1)
10     DO 11  I=1,N
11     Q(I)=0
       L=0
       M=N
20     Z1=RAND(1)
       K=M-1
       T=1.0/FLOAT(M)
       M1=M-1
60     IF(K.EQ.0) GO TO 70
30     Z=T*B(K)/B(M)
40     IF(Z1.LT.Z) GO TO 80
50     K=K-1
       T=T/FLOAT(M-1-K)
       Z1=Z1-Z
       GO TO 60
80     L1=N
81     IF(Q(L1).EQ.0) GO TO 82
       L1=L1-1
       GO TO 81
82     L=L+1
       Q(L1)=L
       CALL RANKSB(M1,K,A)
       M2=1
       I=1
90     IF(Q(I).EQ.0) GO TO 110
100    IF(I.EQ.M) GO TO 130
120    I=I+1
       GO TO 90
110    C(M2)=I
       M2=M2+1
       Q(I)=L
       GO TO 100
130    DO 131  I=1,K
131    Q(C(A(I)))=0
```

```
        M=K
        GO TO 20
70      L=L+1
        DO 71   I=1,N
71      IF(Q(I).EQ.0)   Q(I)=L
        RETURN
        END
```

SAMPLE OUTPUT

The subprogram RANEQU was called 750 times with N=4. The frequencies with which each of the 15 partitions of the set {1, 2, 3, 4} occurred are shown on the next page. The partitions are identified by the output vector Q:Q(I) is the class to which I belongs (I=1,4). Thus, the partition (124) (3) was obtained 49 times, etc. The value $\chi^2 = 12.72$ was calculated from

$$\chi^2 = \sum_{\pi} \frac{(\phi(\pi) - 50)^2}{50}$$

where $\phi(\pi)$ is the observed frequency of the partition π of the set and the sum is over the 15 partitions. In 95% of such experiments, the value of χ^2 would lie between 5.63 and 26.12 if the 15 partitions were in fact equally probable.

```
1  1  1  1     50
2  1  1  1     49
1  2  1  1     38
2  2  1  1     57
3  2  1  1     42
1  1  2  1     49
2  1  2  1     54
3  1  2  1     61
1  2  2  1     57
2  2  2  1     51
3  2  2  1     42
1  3  2  1     54
2  3  2  1     45
3  3  2  1     57
4  3  2  1     44
```

CHI SQ IS 12.72 WITH 14 DEG FREEDOM

13

Renumbering Rows and Columns of an Array (RENUMB)

In this chapter, we study a question which at first sight seems trivial but which in fact is quite substantial. We are given an $m \times n$ matrix A and two permutations

$$\sigma: \{1, \ldots, m\} \to \{1, \ldots, m\}$$
$$\tau: \{1, \ldots, n\} \to \{1, \ldots, n\}$$

We are asked to renumber the rows and columns of A in accordance with the given permutations. More precisely, we are to construct the matrix $\tilde{A}$ whose elements are

$$(1) \qquad (\tilde{A})_{i,j} = (A)_{\sigma^{-1}(i), \tau^{-1}(j)} \quad (i = 1, \ldots, m; j = 1, \ldots, n)$$

This problem is fundamental in the sequel since it will be used in SPANFO (Chapter 14) and MOBIUS (Chapter 22), and in Chapters 16, 18, and 23, which depend on these two; hence it must be handled efficiently.

Yet there seems to be no problem at all, since the one-step "algorithm"

$$(A) \quad \text{For } i = 1, \ldots, m; j = 1, \ldots, n: \tilde{A}(\sigma(i), \tau(j)) = A(i, j) \blacksquare$$

does the whole job. Questions of interest arise, however, when we insist that *no extra array storage* beyond the input data arrays σ, τ, A

be used; in other words, A must be rearranged *in place*. Let us consider a few possible approaches to this problem.

First, we could permute the rows of A according to σ, then permute the columns by τ. This could easily be programmed to use no extra arrays (try it). The disadvantage of this procedure is that each element gets moved twice, an inefficiency.

In the same vein, we could factor the given permutations as products of transpositions, then carry out the successive interchanges of rows or of columns. In this approach each element will be moved several times. For example, let

$$A = \begin{pmatrix} a_{11} & a_{12} & a_{13} \\ a_{21} & a_{22} & a_{23} \\ a_{31} & a_{32} & a_{33} \end{pmatrix}$$

and

$$\sigma = \tau = \{1 \to 3;\ 2 \to 1;\ 3 \to 2\}$$

be the given data. The desired output is the matrix

$$\tilde{A} = \begin{pmatrix} a_{22} & a_{32} & a_{21} \\ a_{32} & a_{33} & a_{31} \\ a_{12} & a_{13} & a_{11} \end{pmatrix}$$

Suppose we observe that

$$\sigma = \tau = t_{12} t_{13}$$

where t_{ij} exchanges letters i and j. Then in this example the number of times each element is moved during the transition from A to $\tilde{A}$ is

$$\begin{pmatrix} 2 & 2 & 3 \\ 2 & 2 & 3 \\ 3 & 3 & 4 \end{pmatrix}$$

We therefore discard this proposal.

A third possibility is this: Store a_{11} in T. Move into a_{11} the element $a_{\sigma^{-1}(1),\,\tau^{-1}(1)}$, then into the latter location move the element which goes there, etc., until the cycle is complete, then move T into the last location in the cycle. Then begin the next cycle, etc. This approach is much closer to what we shall actually do, but it is not deep enough yet, because how, exactly, do we "begin the next cycle?"

What we must do is find some matrix element which was not

moved in the first cycle and then follow around the cycle which it belongs to. How do we recognize a matrix element which was not moved in the first cycle?

The matrix elements will have to be flagged in some way when they are moved, and then we can search for an unflagged entry. One possibility is to use a LOGICAL array for just this purpose, but our stipulation regarding no extra array storage would thereby be violated. If it is known in advance that the matrix entries are positive numbers, then we can flag them in the sign position. Aside from restricting the applicability of the subroutine, this approach also doubles the number of times the entries are moved, because the flags must all be reset before exit.

If the matrix elements are restricted to be integers, of either sign, we can (a) double all entries, (b) use the "1's" bit for a flag, (c) halve all entries before exit. The objections to this are as described in the previous paragraph.

We hope now to have convinced the reader that a question of some depth is posed by the requirements of no extra array space, universal applicability of the method, and movement of each matrix entry at most once. We must seek our answer in the direction of understanding the cycle structure of the induced product permutation

$$\rho: (i, j) \to (\sigma(i), \tau(j)) \quad (i = 1, \ldots, m; j = 1, \ldots, n)$$

Consider the case where σ and τ are both equal to the permutation $1 \to 4 \to 5 \to 1; 2 \to 3 \to 2$ of five letters. The induced permutation ρ of the product set then has the cycle structure shown below.

$$(1, 1) \to (4, 4) \to (5, 5) \to (1, 1)$$
$$(1, 4) \to (4, 5) \to (5, 1) \to (1, 4)$$
$$(1, 5) \to (4, 1) \to (5, 4) \to (1, 5)$$
$$(2, 2) \to (3, 3) \to (2, 2)$$
$$(2, 3) \to (3, 2) \to (2, 3)$$
$$(1, 2) \to (4, 3) \to (5, 2) \to (1, 3) \to (4, 2) \to (5, 3) \to (1, 2)$$
$$(2, 1) \to (3, 4) \to (2, 5) \to (3, 1) \to (2, 4) \to (3, 5) \to (2, 1)$$

Obviously, within one of its cycles ρ is a cyclic permutation, and to reorder elements under a cyclic permutation is easy. Suppose

$$\alpha_1 \to \alpha_2 \to \alpha_3 \to \cdots \to \alpha_r \to \alpha_1$$

is such a cycle. We can then do

(a) $T \leftarrow \alpha_r$
(b) $\alpha_{i+1} \leftarrow \alpha_i \quad (i = r - 1, r - 2, \ldots, 1)$

(c) $\alpha_1 \leftarrow T$

and the rearrangement is accomplished.

We can, in fact, give a complete description of the cycles of the product permutation ρ in terms of the cycles of σ, τ. If

$$C': \quad i_1 \to i_2 \to \cdots \to i_r \to i_1$$

and

$$C'': \quad j_1 \to j_2 \to \cdots \to j_s \to j_1$$

are, respectively, a cycle of σ and a cycle of τ, let $g = $ g.c.d. (r, s) and let $\lambda = $ l.c.m. (r, s). Corresponding to the pair C', C'' of cycles of σ and τ, there are exactly g different cycles of ρ, each of length λ, namely, the cycles

$$
\begin{array}{ll}
1 & (i_1, j_1) \to (i_2, j_2) \to \cdots \\
2 & (i_1, j_2) \to (i_2, j_3) \to \cdots \\
3 & (i_1, j_3) \to (i_2, j_4) \to \cdots \\
\vdots & \qquad \vdots \qquad\qquad \vdots \\
g & (i_1, j_g) \to (i_2, j_{g+1}) \to \cdots
\end{array}
$$

Furthermore, as C' runs over all cycles of σ and C'' runs through all cycles of τ, we obtain every cycle of ρ as above, each one exactly once.

To use this parameterization of the cycles of ρ in terms of those of σ, τ our first thought might be to proceed as follows (our final thought will differ in a small, but very important, detail):

(a)   Run through all elements of one cycle C' of σ, counting them and flagging them, say, by changing the sign of the corresponding entries of the array σ. Let the cycle have r elements.

(b)   Do the same as above for one cycle C'' of τ. Let it have s elements.

(c)   Calculate $g = $ g.c.d. (r, s); $\lambda = $ l.c.m. (r, s).

(d)   For the fixed pair C', C'', move the matrix entries around the set of g cycles of ρ which the pair C', C'' generate, as described above.

(e)   By locating the first unflagged (positive) entry of τ, repeat steps (b)–(d) for the next cycle of τ, keeping C' fixed. Continue in this way until all cycles of τ are done (all entries of the array τ are negative).

(f)   Reset the entries of τ to positive values. Search the array σ for the first unflagged element, and generate the next cycle C' of σ.

Keeping C' fixed, repeat the operations as above.

(g) Proceed until all cycles of σ have been done.

This is, essentially, our method. One difficulty arises if the flagging of elements of σ, τ is done as above. This will become clear if we imagine what happens if the routine is called in the important special case where $\sigma = \tau$, that is, only one linear array is input, and it plays two roles. If we use the sign bits of σ and τ as flags, and if, in fact, σ and τ are the same array, then the logic of the routine will obviously become snarled.

The way out of this problem is to tag, in each cycle of σ, the element $\sigma(i)$ for which i is minimal in that cycle with a minus sign before any actual permuting takes place; a loop achieves this by flagging the elements by means of a method similar to steps (a), (b), and (e) above. However, once the tags are on, they are not changed during the actual permuting of matrix elements. To find out if $\sigma = \tau$, we first tag σ, then test if $\tau(1)$ is negative; if not, we tag τ also.

The core of the subroutine consists of instructions 50 to 55 in which the cycles of (σ, τ) are traced without s, g, and λ having been explicitly computed; we need only r. Before entering a cycle pair (C', C'') we set $k \leftarrow r$, $i_1 \leftarrow i$, $j_1 \leftarrow j_2 \leftarrow j$, where i, j are the tagged elements. Displacements of matrix elements are performed as $i_1 \leftarrow \sigma(i_1)$, $j_1 \leftarrow \tau(j_1)$ until j_1 returns to j_2. At that point, we set $k \leftarrow k - 1$ and test if $i_1 = i$ (return to loop if not) which signifies the completion of a cycle of length λ. We then set $j_1 \leftarrow j_2 \leftarrow \tau(j_1)$ to start a new cycle, provided $k > 0$. Indeed, in each cycle of length λ, k is reduced by λ/s; hence the total number of cycles performed until $k = 0$ is $r/(\lambda/s) = rs/\lambda = g$, and we are finished with the pair (C', C'') of cycles, *without ever having computed g or λ explicitly*.

The number of displacements of matrix elements per cycle pair is, of course, rs; the number of tests is counted as follows. j_1 is tested each time (rs tests); i_1 is tested as k is reduced, (r times). Finally, k is tested g times, so that there is a total of

$$rs + r + g$$

tests. Summed over all pairs (C', C''), this yields

$$mn + m(\text{number of cycles of } \tau) + \Sigma g$$

In average situations, the last sum is small (though it can be as big as mn) while the average number of cycles of τ is $\log n$ (the maximum is n). In any case, the operation count is $O(mn)$ (see Table 13.1).

ALGORITHM TAG

Given a permutation $\sigma(1), \ldots, \sigma(m)$; reverse the sign of each $\sigma(i)$ for which i is the smallest element of its cycle.

(A) $i \leftarrow 1$.
(B) $i_1 \leftarrow \sigma(i)$.
(C)   If $i_1 \leq i$, to (D); $i_2 \leftarrow \sigma(i)$; $\sigma(i_1) \leftarrow -i_2$; $i_1 \leftarrow i_2$; to (C).
(D) $\sigma(i) \leftarrow -\sigma(i)$; If $i = m$, Exit; $i \leftarrow i + 1$, to (B) ∎

ALGORITHM RENUMB

Given a permutation σ of $1, \ldots, m$; a permutation τ of $1, \ldots, n$; a matrix a_{ij} ($i = 1, \ldots, m$; $j = 1, \ldots, n$); move a_{ij} to $a_{\sigma(i)\tau(j)}$.

(A)   Tag σ; If $\tau \neq \sigma$, tag τ; $i \leftarrow 0$.
(B)   [*Find next cycle of σ*] $i \leftarrow i + 1$; If $i > m$, to (G); $i_1 \leftarrow -\sigma(i)$; If $i_1 < 0$, to (B); $l \leftarrow 0$.
(C)   [*Find length of cycle of σ*] $i_1 \leftarrow \sigma(i_1)$; $l \leftarrow l + 1$; If $i_1 > 0$, to (C); $i_1 \leftarrow i$; $j \leftarrow 0$.
(D)   [*Find next cycle of τ*] $j \leftarrow j + 1$; If $j > n$, to (B); If $\tau(j) > 0$, to (D); $j_2 \leftarrow j$; $k \leftarrow l$.
(E)   [*Start new product cycle*] $j_1 \leftarrow j_2$; $t_1 \leftarrow a_{i_1 j_1}$.
(F)   [*Move matrix elements in one product cycle*] $i_1 \leftarrow |\sigma(i_1)|$; $j_1 \leftarrow |\tau(j_1)|$; $t_2 \leftarrow a_{i_1 j_1}$; $a_{i_1 j_1} \leftarrow t_1$; $t_1 \leftarrow t_2$; If $j_1 \neq j_2$, to (F); $k \leftarrow k - 1$; [*End of product cycle?*] If $i_1 \neq i$, to (F); $j_2 \leftarrow |\tau(j_2)|$; [*All product cycles done?*] If $k \neq 0$, to (E); to (D).
(G)   [*Restore arrays*] $\sigma(i) \leftarrow |\sigma(i)|$ ($i = i, \ldots, m$): If $\sigma \neq \tau$, $\tau(j) \leftarrow |\tau(j)|$ ($j = 1, \ldots, n$), Exit ∎

Table 13.1   Structure of SUBROUTINE RENUMB

Instruction number	Purpose
10	Outer DO loop through the cycles of σ
20 and two below	The cycle length LC of a cycle of σ is calculated
30	DO loop through the cycles of τ
40	Start of cycle of length λ
50	Continuation of above cycle
55	Test if more cycles required
60, 70	Remove tags from σ, τ

SUBROUTINE SPECIFICATIONS

(1) *Name of subroutine:* RENUMB.

(2) *Calling statement:* CALL RENUMB(M,N,SIG,TAU,A).

(3) *Purpose of subroutine:* Renumber rows and columns of a matrix.

(4) *Descriptions of variables in calling statement:*

Name	Type	I/O/W/B	Description
M	INTEGER	*I*	Number of rows of matrix.
N	INTEGER	*I*	Number of columns of matrix.
SIG	INTEGER(M)	*I*	SIG(I) is the value at I, of the row permutation (I=1,M).
TAU	INTEGER(N)	*I*	TAU(J) is the value, at J, of the column permutation (J=1,N).
A	INTEGER(M,N)	*I/O*	A(I,J) is the I,J entry of the input matrix, and holds Ā(I,J) after execution (I=1,M;J=1,N).

(5) *Other routines which are called by this one:* None.

(6) *Approximate number of* FORTRAN *instructions:* 52.

(7) *Remarks:* To use on a noninteger matrix, just change type declaration of A.

```
      SUBROUTINE RENUMB(M,N,SIG,TAU,A)
      INTEGER SIG(M),TAU(N),A(M,N),T1,T2
      DO 5  I=1,M
      I1=SIG(I)
6     IF(I1.LE.I) GO TO 5
      I2=SIG(I1)
      SIG(I1)=-I2
      I1=I2
      GO TO 6
5     SIG(I)=-SIG(I)
      IF(TAU(1).LT.0) GO TO 9
      DO 7  J=1,N
      J1=TAU(J)
8     IF(J1.LE.J) GO TO 7
      J2=TAU(J1)
      TAU(J1)=-J2
      J1=J2
      GO TO 8
```

```
7    TAU(J)=-TAU(J)
9    DO 10   I=1,M
     I1=-SIG(I)
     IF(I1.LT.0) GO TO 10
     LC=0
20   I1=SIG(I1)
     LC=LC+1
     IF(I1.GT.0) GO TO 20
     I1=I
     DO 30   J=1,N
     IF(TAU(J).GT.0) GO TO 30
     J2=J
     K=LC
40   J1=J2
     T1=A(I1,J1)
50   I1=IABS(SIG(I1))
     J1=IABS(TAU(J1))
     T2=A(I1,J1)
     A(I1,J1)=T1
     T1=T2
     IF(J1.NE.J2) GO TO 50
     K=K-1
     IF(I1.NE.I) GO TO 50
     J2=IABS(TAU(J2))
55   IF(K.NE.0) GO TO 40
30   CONTINUE
10   CONTINUE
     DO 60   I=1,M
60   SIG(I)=IABS(SIG(I))
     IF(TAU(1).GT.0) RETURN
     DO 70   J=1,N
70   TAU(J)=IABS(TAU(J))
     RETURN
     END
```

SAMPLE OUTPUT

Subroutine RENUMB was called, with M=N=9, SIG as shown in the
first line of the next page, TAU as shown on the second line. The

input 9×9 matrix A appears next, followed by the output rearrangement of A.

```
 2   3   9   6   7   8   5   4   1
 3   4   5   6   7   8   9   1   2

23  24  25  26  27  28  29  21  22
33  34  35  36  37  38  39  31  32
93  94  95  96  97  98  99  91  92
63  64  65  66  67  68  69  61  62
73  74  75  76  77  78  79  71  72
83  84  85  86  87  88  89  81  82
53  54  55  56  57  58  59  51  52
43  44  45  46  47  48  49  41  42
13  14  15  16  17  18  19  11  12

11  12  13  14  15  16  17  18  19
21  22  23  24  25  26  27  28  29
31  32  33  34  35  36  37  38  39
41  42  43  44  45  46  47  48  49
51  52  53  54  55  56  57  58  59
61  62  63  64  65  66  67  68  69
71  72  73  74  75  76  77  78  79
81  82  83  84  85  86  87  88  89
91  92  93  94  95  06  97  98  99
```

14

Spanning Forest of a Graph (SPANFO)

Let G be a graph of N vertices and E edges. One of the most fundamental questions about G concerns its connectivity. G is *connected* if, whenever u and v are distinct vertices of G, there is a path in G which joins u and v. If G is not connected, we can define an equivalence relation on its vertices: u and v are related if there is a path between them. A *connected component* of G is an equivalence class V of vertices of G, under this equivalence relation, together with all of the edges of G which are incident with some vertex of V.

Visually there is usually no problem in determining connectivity. The graph in Fig. 14.1 of fourteen vertices and ten edges has seven connected components, namely, the seven pieces of the drawing.

Computationally, however, we have a substantial question. Imagine that we are given the graph G (Fig. 14.1) in a computer, in the form of an array ENDPT(I,J):

```
ENDPT(1,J) : 2  4  1   7  5  2   6  2  3   4
ENDPT(2,J) : 3  7  9  11  8  5  10  8  8  11
```

Here ENDPT(1,I), ENDPT(2,I) are, respectively, the two ends of the Ith edge of G (I=1,10).

Now we wish to design an algorithm which, from this array and from N, the number of vertices, will produce the following information: (a) K, the number of components of G; (b) X(I), the component to which vertex I belongs (I=1,N); (c) NV(J), the number of vertices in component J (J=1,K); and (d) a rearrangement of the edges in the input ENDPT array so that the first NV(1)−1 edges form a spanning tree for the first component of G, the next NV(2)−1 edges are such a tree for the second component, etc. (The reader may wish to turn to the sample output page of this chapter to see the input and output for the graph of Fig. 14.1.)

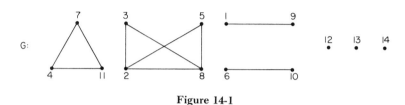

G:

Figure 14-1

There are straightforward algorithms for achieving this purpose, which turn out to cost about N^2 operations beyond scanning the list of edges. We choose here a less straightforward algorithm which does the job in $O(N \log N)$ operations in addition to the edge-scan.

One conceptually simple method of constructing the vertex set and the spanning tree of a component is to choose a vertex, put it in V_1, go through the edges to find any that are incident with a vertex in V_1, and adjoin the other endpoint to V_1, if it is not already in V_1. Edges that produce new vertices are used for the spanning tree; the others are not used. This procedure is continued until a pass through the edges yields no further growth of V_1. If any vertices are left, one is taken to start the next vertex set V_2, etc.

Simple as this method is, it is very inefficient as it requires many passes through the list of edges.

The method below goes through only one search of the edges, and assigns vertices to components the best it can. Rooted trees are started at each vertex, and are joined together into larger trees as edges connecting them are uncovered. Initially, each vertex I is a one-vertex tree, numbered I and rooted at I. When an edge has endpoints that belong to the same tree, it is moved to the end of the list and not processed further. When it connects two trees, these are joined together, and the new tree has the name and the root of the larger one of the two. When the edge-list is exhausted (or sooner, if we find a spanning tree), a spanning forest has been constructed.

The bookkeeping requires several items. First, an array ENDPT holds the endpoint pairs of the edges; ENDPT(1,J) and ENDPT(2,J) are the endpoints of edge J; J=1,...,E. An array X

holds in X(I) the name of the component to which vertex I belongs
(I=1,...,N). The name of each tree is that of its root; therefore,
when I is a root, X(I) may (and will) hold other information. We
will give X(I) some negative value to distinguish it from a component number.

Then there is an array NV; its entry NV(T) holds the number of vertices in tree number T; initially NV(T)=1 for T=1,...,N. As trees
merge, these values are adjusted. Finally, there is a purely auxiliary
array Y, which is used for two purposes. The first use is as a set of so-
called *links:* When the trees are being merged, Y(I) is the name of a
vertex in the same tree as I. The assignment is such that, starting
with a root and going down Y (i.e., going from I to Y(I), then to
Y(Y(I)), etc.), all vertices of a tree are encountered exactly once; the
last-visited member of a tree has Y(I)=0. When two trees are
merged into one, the Y-lists are connected by making the Y of the last
element of the larger tree point to the root of the smaller one. To
simplify this process, the name L of the "last" element of tree T is
stored in X(T) as −L. The second use of Y is in the sorting of the
edges at the end: Y(I) is the position in the edge-list to which edge
I must be moved for output (I=1,E1).

It is interesting to estimate the amount of work involved in this
method. First, the pass through the edges and some simple bookkeeping on them requires $O(E)$ operations, that is, roughly E times a
small constant. Similarly, there are $O(N)$ operations for some simple
bookkeeping and initializing of arrays. Most interesting is, however,
an estimate of the work involved in merging trees, which we show is
$O(N \ln N)$. To show this, we count the total number of name changes
needed to produce a tree of n vertices, for which we assert that
$\frac{1}{2}n \log_2 n$ is an (attainable) upper bound. Indeed, by induction on the
number of vertices of the tree, the statement is true for $n = 1$. Furthermore, let an n-vertex tree be constructed by merging an x-vertex
tree and an $(n-x)$-vertex tree; $x \leqslant \frac{1}{2}n$. These two were obtained (by
induction) at the cost of at most $\frac{1}{2}x \log_2 x$, resp. $\frac{1}{2}(n-x) \log_2(n-x)$,
renamings; the merging requires another x renamings. Now con-
sider, therefore,

$$f(x) = x + \tfrac{1}{2}x \log_2 x + \tfrac{1}{2}(n-x) \log_2(n-x), \quad 0 \leqslant x \leqslant \tfrac{1}{2}n$$

It is easy to verify that $f'(x)$ is negative when $x < \dfrac{n}{5}$ and positive

when $x > \dfrac{n}{5}$. Furthermore,

$$f(0) = f\left(\frac{n}{2}\right) = \frac{n}{2} \log_2 n$$

so

$$f(x) \leq \frac{n}{2} \log_2 n \quad \text{for} \quad 0 \leq x \leq \frac{n}{2} \quad \blacksquare$$

This seems to be the only known spanning forest algorithm with $O(n \log n) + O(E)$ operations, uniformly.

ALGORITHM SPANFO

(A) [*Initialize arrays to correspond to totally disconnected graph*] For I=1,N:

$$X(I) \leftarrow I, \quad NV(I) \leftarrow 1, \quad Y(I) \leftarrow 0.$$

Set J←1 (J counts edges); E1←E (E1 is the last edge to be processed).

(B) [*Process next edge in list*] $V\frac{1}{2} \leftarrow$ENDPT$(\frac{1}{2},J)$; T1=X(V1) and T2=X(V2) are the trees to which V1,V2 belong;
If T1=T2, check if J=E1; If so, set E1←E1-1; To (D);
 Otherwise, interchange edges
 J,E1; E1←E1-1; To (B);
If T1≠T2, check if NV(T1)≤NV(T2); If not, interchange T1,T2.

(C) [*Merge trees* T1,T2] Link the root of T1 (which is named T1) to the last element of T2; The new root is that of T2; The new last element is that of T1; Change component numbers in T1 by changing X(I) to T2 at I=T1,Y(T1),Y(Y(T1)),...; Increment NV(T2) by NV(T1); Set NV(T1)←0; J←J+1; If J≤E1 and J<N, to (B).

(D) [*Edge sweep complete renumber components consecutively; use* Y *for cross-reference*]
Set K←0; For I=1,N do:
 If NV(I)=0, do nothing;
 Else, set K←K+1, NV(K)←NV(I), Y(I)←K;
[*Assign new component numbers to the vertices*]
For I=1,N do:
 C←X(I);
 If C<0, set C←I; X(I)←Y(C).

(E) If K=1, exit; Otherwise find the permutation Y of edges 1,E1 which arranges them by components: Set NV(L) ← number of edges in components L'<L (L=1,K); Then Y(I) ← position of edge I in output list (I=1,E1); Call RENUMB to carry out the permutation Y on the first E1 columns of ENDPT; Restore NV(L) (L=1,K) to number of vertices in component L; Exit ∎

SUBROUTINE SPECIFICATIONS

(1) *Name of subroutine:* SPANFO.

(2) *Calling statement:* CALL SPANFO(N,E,ENDPT,K,X,NV,Y).

(3) *Purpose of subroutine:* Determine connectivity of a graph; find spanning forest.

(4) *Descriptions of variables in calling statement:*

Name	Type	I/O/W/B	Description
N	INTEGER	I	Number of vertices in input graph G.
E	INTEGER	I	Number of edges in G.
ENDPT‡	INTEGER(2,E)	I/O	ENDPT(1,I), ENDPT(2,I) are the two vertices in edge I (I=1,E).
K	INTEGER	O	Number of connected components in G.
X	INTEGER(N)	O	X(I) is the component to which vertex I belongs (I=1,N).
NV	INTEGER(N)	O	NV(I) is the number of vertices in the Ith component (I=1,K) (also used for working storage).
Y	INTEGER(N)	W	Working storage.

‡ See text for arrangement of output array ENDPT.

(5) *Other routines which are called by this one:* RENUMB.

(6) *Approximate number of* FORTRAN *instructions:* 70.

```
      SUBROUTINE SPANFO(N,E,ENDPT,K,X,NV,Y)
      IMPLICIT INTEGER(A-Z)
      DIMENSION ENDPT(2,E),X(N),NV(N),Y(N),S(2)
      DATA S(1),S(2),M/1,2,2/
      DO 10  I=1,N
      X(I)=-I
      NV(I)=1
10    Y(I)=0
      J=1
      E1=E
20    V1=ENDPT(1,J)
      V2=ENDPT(2,J)
25    T1=X(V1)
      IF(T1.LT.0)  T1=V1
      T2=X(V2)
      IF(T2.LT.0)  T2=V2
      IF(T1.NE.T2) GO TO 40
```

```
        IF(J.LT.E1)   GO TO 30
        E1=E1-1
        GO TO 60
30      ENDPT(1,J)=ENDPT(1,E1)
        ENDPT(2,J)=ENDPT(2,E1)
        ENDPT(1,E1)=V1
        ENDPT(2,E1)=V2
        E1=E1-1
        GO TO 20
40      IF(NV(T1).LE.NV(T2))   GO TO 50
        T=T1
        T1=T2
        T2=T
50      Y(-X(T2))=T1
        X(T2)=X(T1)
        I=T1
55      X(I)=T2
        I=Y(I)
        IF(I.NE.0) GO TO 55
        NV(T2)=NV(T2)+NV(T1)
        NV(T1)=0
        J=J+1
        IF(J.LE.E1.AND.J.LT.N)   GO TO 20
60      K=0
        DO 70   I=1,N
        IF(NV(I).EQ.0)   GO TO 70
        K=K+1
        NV(K)=NV(I)
        Y(I)=K
70      CONTINUE
        DO 80   I=1,N
        T=X(I)
        IF(T.LT.0)   T=I
80      X(I)=Y(T)
        IF(K.EQ.1)   RETURN
90      I2=NV(1)
        NV(1)=1
        DO 100   L=2,K
        I1=NV(L)
        NV(L)=NV(L-1)+I2-1
100     I2=I1
        DO 110   I=1,E1
```

```
        Z=X(ENDPT(1,I))
        Y(I)=NV(Z)
110     NV(Z)=NV(Z)+1
        CALL RENUMB(M,E1,S,Y,ENDPT)
        I1=1
        DO 120  L=1,K
        I2=NV(L)
        NV(L)=I2-I1+1
120     I1=I2
        RETURN
        END
```

SAMPLE OUTPUT

SPANFO was called for the graph of Fig. 14.1. The input and output array ENDPT is shown on the next page together with the output arrays X, NV, and the number of connected components K=7.

The first two (=NV(1)-1) edges in the output ENDPT array are a spanning tree for the first component (Fig. 14.2). The next three

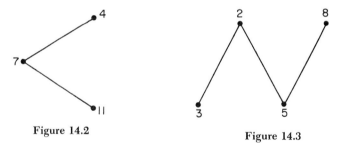

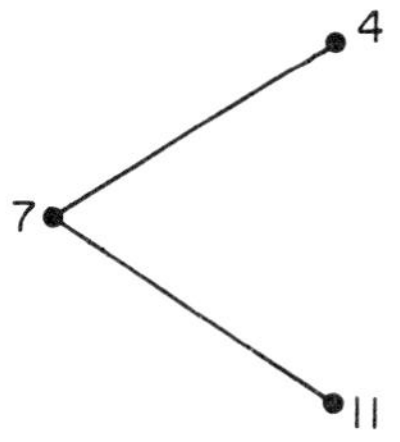

Figure 14.2

Figure 14.3

(=NV(2)-1) edges are a spanning tree for the second component (Fig. 14.3). The next one (=NV(3)-1) spans the third component

Figure 14.4

Figure 14.5

(Fig. 14.4). Finally, the last one (=NV(4)-1) spans the fourth component (Fig. 14.5).

```
INPUT

ENDPT(1,J) :   2   4   1    7   5   2    6   2   3    4
ENDPT(2,J) :   3   7   9   11   8   5   10   8   8   11

OUTPUT

ENDPT(1,J) :   4    7   2   5   2   1    6   3    4   2
ENDPT(2,J) :   7   11   3   8   5   9   10   8   11   8
 X:   3   2   2   1   2   4   1   2   3   4   1   5   6   7
NV:   3   4   2   2   1   1   1

K=7
```

15

Newton Forms of a Polynomial (POLY)

A polynomial $f(x)$ of degree $n - 1$ is said to be in Newton form with respect to $x_1, \ldots, x_{n-1}$ if it is written as

(1) $\quad f(x) = a_1 + a_2(x - x_1) + a_3(x - x_1)(x - x_2)$
$$+ \cdots + a_n(x - x_1) \cdots (x - x_{n-1}).$$

In this chapter, we consider (primarily for use in Chapter 16) algorithms for transforming the coefficients of f from one Newton form to another and related questions.

First, values of f can easily be calculated by rewriting (1) as

(2) $\quad f(x) = a_1 + (x - x_1)(a_2 + (x - x_2)(a_3 + (x - x_3)$
$$\times (\cdots + (a_{n-1} + (x - x_{n-1})a_n) \cdots)$$

More explicitly, $V = f(z)$ is the result of

ALGORITHM VALUE

(A) $\quad V \leftarrow a_n$.
(B) $\quad V \leftarrow (z - x_k)V + a_k \ (k = n - 1, n - 2, \ldots, 1)$ ∎

The following special cases are of interest here:

(i) $\quad x_1 = \cdots = x_{n-1} = 0$. Then (1) is the usual form of a polynomial as a series of powers of x.

(ii) $x_1 = \cdots = x_{n-1} = c$. Then (1) is the Taylor expansion of $f(x)$ at c.

(iii) $x_i = i - 1$ $(i = 1, \ldots, n-1)$. Here $f(x)$ is expanded as

(3) $$f(x) = a_1(x)_0 + a_2(x)_1 + \cdots + a_n(x)_{n-1}$$

as a series in the factorial polynomials

(4) $$(x)_m = x(x-1) \cdots (x-m+1); \quad (x)_0 = 1$$

Transitions between the different forms can be obtained by a well-known theorem of interpolation theory (see, for example, Conte and de Boor [CB1, p. 199]) which asserts that the coefficients $b_1, \ldots, b_n$ of the Newton form of f with respect to $z, x_1, \ldots, x_{n-2}$ are found from the coefficients $a_1, \ldots, a_n$ of the Newton form of f with respect to $x_1, \ldots, x_{n-1}$ by means of

ALGORITHM NEWTON

(A) $b_n \leftarrow a_n$.
(B) $b_i \leftarrow a_i + (z - x_i)b_{i+1}$ $(i = n-1, \ldots, 1)$ ∎

To prove this, rewrite (A) and (B) as

$$a_n = b_n$$
$$a_i = b_i - (z - x_i)b_{i+1} \quad (i = n-1, \ldots, 1)$$

and substitute in (1). There are two terms which involve b_i, namely,

$$b_i(x - x_1) \cdots (x - x_{i-1}) - (z - x_{i-1})b_i(x - x_1) \cdots (x - x_{i-2})$$
$$= b_i(x - x_1) \cdots (x - x_{i-2})(x - x_{i-1} - z + x_{i-1})$$
$$= b_i(x - z)(x - x_1) \cdots (x - x_{i-2})$$

which is exactly the term with b_i in the Newton form with respect to $z, x_1, \ldots, x_{n-2}$, as claimed.

Consider the result of repeatedly applying Algorithm Newton with $z = c$, to the ordinary polynomial form of f (i.e., $x_1 = x_2 = \cdots = x_{n-1} = 0$)

$$f = a_1 + a_2 x + \cdots + a_n x^{n-1}$$

We would first obtain the form

$$f = b_1 + (x - c)\{b_2' + b_3'x + \cdots + b_n'x^{n-2}\}$$

then

$$f = b_1 + b_2(x - c) + (x - c)^2\{b_3'' + b_4''x + \cdots + b_n''x^{n-3}\}$$

and so forth. Hence, each application of Algorithm Newton would produce one additional coefficient of the Taylor expansion of f at c. This can be summarized as a procedure for finding the Taylor coefficients of f.

ALGORITHM TAYLOR

[Input] $(a_1, \ldots, a_n)$, the coefficients of f as a series of powers of x.

(A) For $m = 1, \ldots, n - 1$ do:
For $i = n - 1, \ldots, m$ do:

$$a_i \leftarrow a_i + ca_{i+1}$$

(B) [Exit] $a_1, \ldots, a_n$ are the coefficients of $f(x)$ as a series of powers of $(x - c)$ ∎

Observe that if $a_1, \ldots, a_n$ are the coefficients of f in an expansion in powers of $x - d$, then the output will be the coefficients of an expansion in powers of $x - d - c$. The case $c = -d$ is of particular importance.

As a second application of Algorithm Newton, we again begin with f in ordinary polynomial form

$$f(x) = a_1 + a_2 x + \cdots + a_n x^{n-1}$$

and we apply Algorithm Newton with $z = 1$ to the truncated coefficient sequence $a_2, a_3, \ldots, a_n$. There results

$$f(x) = a_1 + x(a_2' + (x - 1)(a_3' + a_4'x + \cdots + a_n'x^{n-3}))$$

Next we apply Algorithm Newton again, this time with $z = 2$, and only to the shorter sequence $a_3', a_4', \ldots, a_n'$. This gives an expansion of $a_3' + a_4'x + \cdots + a_n'x^{n-3}$ in the form $a_3'' + (x - 2)(a_4'' + a_5''x + a_n''x^{n-4})$, and our original function f has been so far transformed into

$$f(x) = b_1 + x(b_2 + (x - 1)(b_3 + (x - 2)(b_4 + b_5x + \cdots + b_nx^{n-4}))$$

As we repeat the process, we successively generate the coefficients of the factorial expansion (3) of f. Each time, we increase z by 1 and one less coefficient is subjected to Algorithm Newton. This is formalized as

ALGORITHM STIRLING

[*Input*] $a_1, \ldots, a_n$, coefficients of f as a power series.

(A)   For $m = n - 1, \ldots, 2$ do:

$$z \leftarrow n - m$$

For $i = m, \ldots, 2$ do:

$$a_i \leftarrow a_i + za_{i+1}$$

(B)   [*Exit*] $a_1, \ldots, a_n$ are the coefficients of $f(x)$ in (3) ■

The same result might have been obtained by applying Algorithm Newton more straightforwardly to all of $a_1, \ldots, a_n$, starting with $x_1 = \cdots = x_{n-1} = 0$, $z = n - 1$; then $x_1 = n - 1$, $x_2 = \cdots = x_{n-1} = 0$, $z = n - 2$; then $x_1 = n - 2$, $x_2 = n - 1$, $x_3 = \cdots = x_{n-1} = 0$, $z = n - 3$, etc. On balance, Algorithm Stirling above seems more efficient.

If Algorithm Stirling is applied to $f(x) = x^{n-1}$, the output values of $a_1, \ldots, a_n$ express x^{n-1} as a linear combination of $(x)_0, \ldots, (x)_{n-1}$. These are the *Stirling numbers of the second kind*.

A third application of Algorithm Newton will convert factorial series to ordinary power series. If $f(x)$ in the form (3) is given, then

$$f(x) = a_1 + x(a_2 + (x - 1)(a_3 + \cdots + (x - n + 3))(a_{n-1} + (x - n + 2)a_n) \cdots).$$

Then we would first work out the innermost brackets and find

$$a_{n-1} + (x - n + 2)a_n = (a_{n-1} - (n - 2)a_n) + xa_n$$

If we rename $a_{n-1} \leftarrow a_{n-1} - (n - 2)a_n$, then we have $a_{n-1} + xa_n$. This expression is now used in calculating the next bracket, and so forth. The name changing is most unambiguously expressed by the formal

ALGORITHM REVERSE STIRLING

[*Input*] $a_1, \ldots, a_n$, coefficients of f in factorial form (3).

(A)   For $m = n - 1, \ldots, 2$ do:

$$z \leftarrow m - 1$$

For $i = n - 1, \ldots, m$ do:

$$a_i \leftarrow a_i - za_{i+1}$$

(B) [*Exit*] $a_1, \ldots, a_n$ are the coefficients of f as a power series ■

If Algorithm Reverse Sterling is applied to $f(x) = (x)_{n-1}$ the output values $a_1, \ldots, a_n$ give $(x)_{n-1}$ as a linear combination of $x^0, \ldots, x^{n-1}$. These are the *Stirling coefficients of the first kind* (with alternating signs).

It may be an interesting exercise to turn the above algorithms into programs. We have chosen, however, not to program Algorithm Newton, and to combine Taylor, Stirling, and Reverse Stirling into a single Algorithm POLY. This program will have the following parameters and capabilities:

A(1), ..., A(N) (Coefficients of the input polynomial); N (N–1 is the degree); B(1), ..., B(N) (Coefficients of the output polynomial).

XO: Takes the place of c in Taylor.

VAL: Holds the value of $f(c)$ upon return from a call.

OPTION: Directs the routine to its various possibilities.

OPTION=0: Returns the value of the usual polynomial at XO in VAL.

OPTION>0: The numerical value of OPTION is the number of terms of the Taylor expansion at XO which the program returns in B(1), ..., B(OPTION), and leaves in the remaining B the coefficients of the last quotient.

OPTION=−1: Return in VAL the value of $f(x)$ with A(1), ..., A(N) considered as the coefficients in the factorial form (3).

OPTION=−2: Returns in B the coefficients of $f(x)$ in the form (3) assuming A(1), ..., A(N) are the coefficients as a power sum; i.e., Algorithm Stirling is executed.

OPTION=−3: Algorithm Reverse Stirling is executed.

The FORTRAN program is a straightforward joining of these separate programs as no significant economies seem possible despite the similarities in the algorithms.

The flow chart explains the logic which controls the choice of algorithms (Taylor, Stirling, Reverse Stirling) to be used. It should be self-explanatory.

FLOW CHART POLY

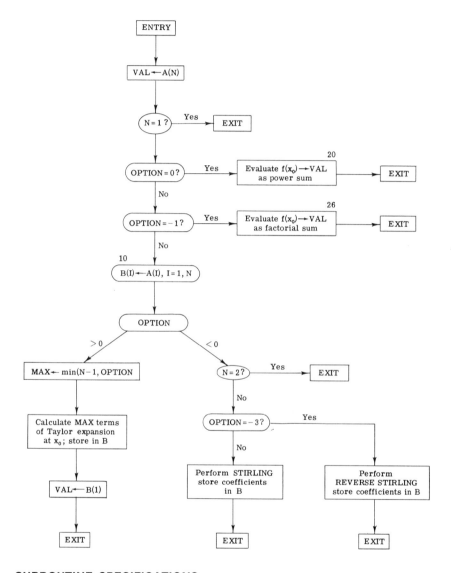

SUBROUTINE SPECIFICATIONS

(1) *Name of subroutine:* POLY.

(2) *Calling statement:* CALL POLY(N,A,XO,OPTION,VAL,B).

(3) *Purpose of subroutine:* Operations on polynomials in power and factorial form.

(4) *Descriptions of variables in calling statement:*

Name	Type	I/O/W/B	Description
N	INTEGER	I	N−1 is the degree of the input polynomial.
A	INTEGER(N)	I	A(I) is the [I-1]th coefficient of the input polynomial (I=1,N).
XO	INTEGER	I	This is the parameter c in Taylor's formula.
OPTION	INTEGER	I	See text.
VAL	INTEGER	O	Holds the value $f(x_0)$ after execution.
B	INTEGER(N)	O	Coefficients of output polynomial.

(5) *Other routines which are called by this one:* None.
(6) *Approximate number of* FORTRAN *instructions:* 49.
(7) *Remarks:* Correct results will be be obtained if called with B=A.

```
      SUBROUTINE POLY(N,A,XO,OPTION,VAL,B)
      IMPLICIT INTEGER (A-Z)
      DIMENSION A(N),B(N)
      VAL=A(N)
      IF(N.EQ.1) RETURN
      N1=N-1
      IF(OPTION.EQ.0) GO TO 20
      IF(OPTION.EQ.-1) GO TO 26
      DO 10  I=1,N
   10 B(I)=A(I)
      IF(OPTION) 50,30,30
   20 DO 25  I=1,N1
   25 VAL=VAL*XO+A(N-I)
      RETURN
   26 DO 27  I=1,N1
   27 VAL=VAL*(XO-N1+I)+A(N-I)
      RETURN
   30 MAX=MINO(N1,OPTION)
      DO 35  J=1,MAX
      M=N1
      V=VAL
   37 V=B(M)+V*XO
      B(M)=V
      M=M-1
      IF(M.GE.J) GO TO 37
   35 CONTINUE
      VAL=B(1)
```

```
      RETURN
50    IF(N.EQ.2) RETURN
      N2=N-2
      IF(OPTION.EQ.-3) GO TO 70
      DO 55  J=1,N2
      V=VAL
      M=N1
60    V=B(M)+J*V
      B(M)=V
      M=M-1
      IF(M.GT.J) GO TO 60
55    CONTINUE
      RETURN
70    DO 75  J=1,N2
      Z=N1-J
      M=Z+1
80    B(M)=B(M)-Z*B(M+1)
      M=M+1
      IF(M.LE.N1) GO TO 80
75    CONTINUE
      RETURN
      END
```

SAMPLE OUTPUT

POLY was called, with $N=6$, $A(1)= \cdots =A(5)=0$, $A(6)=1$ (i.e., $f(x) = x^5$ or $f(x) = (x)_5$ depending on OPTION).

First call: X0=1, OPTION=6
    Output: binomial coefficients $\binom{5}{k}$, $k = 0, \ldots , 5$.
Second call: X0=-1, OPTION=6
    Output: $(-1)^{k+1}\binom{5}{k}$, $k = 0, \ldots , 5$.
Third call: OPTION=-2
    Output: Stirling coefficients of the second kind, with alternating signs.
Fourth call: OPTION=-3
    Output: Stirling coefficients of the first kind.

1	5	10	10	5	1
-1	5	-10	10	-5	1
0	24	-50	35	-10	1
0	1	15	25	10	1

16

Chromatic Polynomial of a Graph (CHROMP)

Let G be a graph of n vertices. By a *proper coloring* of G we mean an assignment of colors to the vertices of G in such a way that the endpoints of no edge of G have the same color. In Fig. 16.1, we show a graph G of 4 vertices and a proper coloring of G in three colors R, Y, B.

For a fixed positive integer λ, the number of proper colorings of G in λ *or fewer* colors is denoted by $P(\lambda)$. In counting $P(\lambda)$, the vertices of G are regarded as labeled with the labels $1, 2, \ldots, n$, and two proper colorings of G are different if any one of the ordered pairs $(V, color\ of\ V)$ $(V = 1, 2, \ldots, n)$ are different in the two colorings. If G, for example, is a triangle, then $P(0) = 0$, $P(1) = 0$, $P(2) = 0$, $P(3) = 6$, $P(4) = 24, \ldots, P(\lambda) = \lambda(\lambda - 1)(\lambda - 2)$ $(\lambda \geqq 0)$.

The values $P(\lambda)$ $(\lambda = 0, 1, 2, \ldots)$ turn out to be the values of a polynomial P at the nonnegative integers λ. This polynomial is called

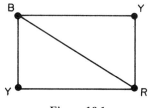

Figure 16.1

the *chromatic polynomial* of the graph G. Thus, the chromatic polynomial of the triangle is $\lambda(\lambda - 1)(\lambda - 2)$. We develop, in this chapter, a new algorithm for the computation of the coefficients of the powers of λ in the chromatic polynomial of a graph.

For a given graph G, let u and v be any two vertices which are joined by an edge, E_{uv}. Let $G - E_{uv}$ denote the new graph which is obtained from G by deleting the edge E_{uv}. Let G_{uv} denote the new graph which is obtained from G by *identifying* the two vertices u, v. This means that G_{uv} has, instead of the two vertices u and v, a single vertex uv such that uv is joined by an edge to every vertex w which was joined, in G, to *either u or v*. All other vertices and edges of G_{uv} are as they were in G.

Consider the collections of all $P(\lambda; G)$ proper colorings of G, the $P(\lambda; G - E_{uv})$ proper colorings of $G - E_{uv}$, and the $P(\lambda; G_{uv})$ proper colorings of G_{uv}. Clearly, there are more colorings of $G - E_{uv}$ than of G because there is one less edge-constraint on the colorings. Indeed, the excess of $P(\lambda; G - E_{uv})$ over $P(\lambda; G)$ is exactly the number of colorings of G which are proper except that the two ends u, v of E_{uv} are given the same color. But such colorings are identical with proper colorings of G_{uv}: from any such coloring C of G_{uv}, construct a coloring C' of G in which u and v are both given the color of uv in C and all other vertices are given the colors which they had in C. It follows that

(1) $$P(\lambda; G) = P(\lambda; G - E_{uv}) - P(\lambda; G_{uv})$$

Observe that in this fundamental and well-known relation G has n vertices and E edges, $G - E_{uv}$ has n vertices and $E - 1$ edges, and G_{uv} has $n - 1$ vertices and $< E$ edges. Hence, (1) is actually a *reduction* formula. For theoretical purposes, (1) is useful because from it we can prove theorems by induction. For practical purposes, (1) can be used iteratively to compute $P(\lambda; G)$.

As an example, let us prove that $P(\lambda; G)$ is a polynomial in λ of degree n. If G has 0 edges and n vertices, then $P(\lambda; G) = \lambda^n$, so the theorem holds. If true for graphs of $< E$ edges and any number of vertices, then by (1) it remains true for graphs of E edges and any number of vertices, completing the proof. It follows that if G has n vertices, we may write $P(\lambda; G)$ in the form

(2) $$P(\lambda; G) = \lambda^n - a_{n-1}\lambda^{n-1} + a_{n-2}\lambda^{n-2} - \cdots + (-1)^{n-1}a_1\lambda$$

A similar induction will prove that $a_j \geq 0$ $(j = 1, \ldots, n - 1)$ in (2), so that the coefficients alternate in sign.

We return now to our algorithm for computation of $a_1, \ldots, a_{n-1}$, by considering a certain *binary tree* which can be constructed from our given graph G. In case G is the graph of Fig. 16.1, the tree in question looks like Fig. 16.2.

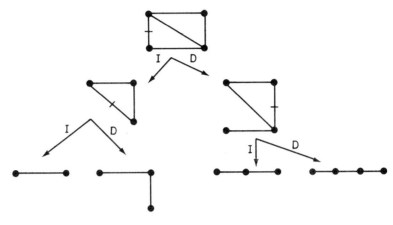

Figure 16.2

At the top of the tree is the original graph G with one of its edges marked. It has two descendants, IG and DG. IG is obtained from G by identifying the two endpoints of the marked edge. DG is obtained from G by deleting the marked edge. Next, in IG and DG, we mark an edge and repeat the process. According to Eq. (1),

$$(3) \quad P(\lambda; G) = P(\lambda; DG) - P(\lambda; IG)$$
$$= P(\lambda; DDG) - P(\lambda; IDG) - P(\lambda; DIG) + P(\lambda; IIG)$$

Why, in Fig. 16.2, did we choose to halt when we did? Because the graphs in the bottom line are all trees (connected, with no circuits). In the present context, the advantage of a tree is that *all trees on n vertices have the same chromatic polynomial*, namely

$$(4) \qquad\qquad t_n(\lambda) = \lambda(\lambda - 1)^{n-1} \quad (n \geq 1)$$

We can prove this by induction on n: If T is a tree on n vertices, choose a terminal vertex (vertex with just one incident edge) u of T and let v be the unique other vertex of T which is connected to u. Then $T - E_{uv}$ is a tree of $n - 1$ vertices and an isolated point, which, inductively, has the chromatic polynomial

$$P(\lambda; T - E_{uv}) = \lambda \cdot (\lambda - 1)^{n-2} \cdot \lambda = \lambda^2(\lambda - 1)^{n-2}$$

On the other hand, if we identify u and v in T, we obtain a tree of

$n - 1$ vertices so that, inductively,

$$P(\lambda; T_{uv}) = \lambda(\lambda - 1)^{n-2}$$

Then (1) yields

$$P(\lambda; T) = \lambda^2(\lambda - 1)^{n-2} - \lambda(\lambda - 1)^{n-2} = \lambda(\lambda - 1)^{n-1}$$

as claimed.

Hence, if b_i is the number of trees on i vertices which are produced by the delete-and-identify algorithm above, then the characteristic polynomial of G is exactly

(5)
$$P(\lambda; G) = \sum_{j=1}^{n} (-1)^{n-j} b_j \lambda(\lambda - 1)^{j-1}$$

As a by-product of the algorithm, notice that we have just proved the following well-known

Theorem If the chromatic polynomial of a graph is written in the form (5), then the coefficients b_j are nonnegative ($j = 1, n$).

Equation (5) is called the *Tutte polynomial* form of $P(\lambda; G)$. For example, Eq. (3) now implies that for the graph G of Fig. 16.1,

$$\begin{aligned}
P(\lambda; G) &= t_4(\lambda) - t_3(\lambda) - t_3(\lambda) + t_2(\lambda) \\
&= \lambda(\lambda - 1)^3 - 2\lambda(\lambda - 1)^2 + \lambda(\lambda - 1) \\
&= \lambda(\lambda - 1)(\lambda - 2)^2
\end{aligned}$$

Next, how can we be sure that every downward path terminates at a tree? By taking care that, at each stage, the edge which we mark has the property that its removal will not disconnect the graph. One convenient way of doing this is, after having previously found a spanning tree for the graph, to mark only edges which lie outside that spanning tree. Evidently, the removal of any such edge will not disconnect G, and, having removed all such edges, we will be left with a tree.

How can we be sure to carry out every possible combination of I's and D's? A well-known algorithm for doing this is to throw all the work to be done later onto a "stack."

(A) $G' \leftarrow G$; stack $\leftarrow$ empty stack.
(B) If G' is a tree, to (C); Stack $\leftarrow DG'$; $G' \leftarrow IG'$; To (B).
(C) Tabulate G'; If stack is empty, exit; Otherwise, $G' \leftarrow$ top graph on stack, and return to (B) ■

The method utilizes a stack of graphs, and, as we work our way down Fig. 16.2, we travel to the left at each fork while at the same time throwing the right hand graph DG' on top of the stack. When we reach the end of a path (G' is a tree) we take next the top graph on the stack at that time.

Several technical problems need to be discussed before our description is complete.

Question Which edge gets marked for deletion at each step?

Answer At the outset, we construct a spanning tree for G. We list the edges of G in order so that the first $n - 1$ edges in the list are those of the spanning tree. The remaining $E - n + 1$ edges are then listed, and any one of them can be deleted from G without disconnecting it. We therefore mark the last edge in the list each time.

Question How do we recognize the bottom of a path, i.e., when G' is a tree?

Answer When $E = n - 1$.

Question Doesn't a spanning tree get destroyed by the act of identifying two vertices?

Answer Yes, except in the special case where the path in the spanning tree which connects the two vertices which are being identified is a figure V, in which case the two edges are simply identified, and the spanning tree is intact.

Question Is it, then, necessary to find a new spanning tree in the identified graph IG', except in the special case above?

Answer No! Even though identification may destroy the spanning tree, it does so in a way which can be undone, so that at each identification a spanning tree of the new graph can very quickly be found from the ruins of the old one.

Question How is this done?

Answer When IG' is constructed, and vertices I_1 and I_2 are identified, the path in a spanning tree of G' which connects I_1 and I_2 becomes a cycle (unless that path consists of a figure V). The deletion from the "identified" tree of one edge from the cycle will make it a spanning tree for IG'. The problem is to find an edge which is in this cycle. To find such an edge, we give the spanning tree of G' a *root* R, and list the vertex pair in each edge in such a way that the second one is farthest from the root. The edges are listed so each edge is preceded by those that connect it to the root. Let I_2 follow I_1 in the pairs of vertices that constitute the edge-list. Deletion of the incoming edge to I_2 will then cut the cycle.

In order to carry out the above procedure, the edges of the initial spanning tree T of G have to be oriented. This is done by building up T from smaller rooted trees whose edges are oriented. Initially, we have N one-vertex rooted trees, one at each vertex. Then the edges are joined. Let edge J have endpoints I_1 and I_2 which are vertices of trees T_1 and T_2. Then the new tree has I_1 at its root. To orient the edges of the new tree, all edges on the path from I_1 to the root of T_1 have to be reoriented and, similarly, those from I_2 to the root of T_2.

The stack will be a $2 \times (E \cdot N)$ array consisting of (at most) N trees whose edges are listed in $2 \times (E - 1)$ or fewer locations. The last location for each graph on the stack is used to store $N1$ and $E1$, the vertex and edge counts.

In the identification process the array ENDPT is searched for the occurrence of I_1 and I_2, and I_2 is replaced by I_1. At the same time, a notation is made for each vertex I_0 to which I_1 and I_2 are joined. The edge of T' which runs into I_2 is moved to the list of edges which do not belong to the spanning tree of G'. Next, this list is scanned, I_2 is replaced by I_1, and duplications are removed; this pruned list belongs to IG'.

We now summarize the entire procedure as an algorithm for the calculation of B(I) (same as b_i in Eq. (5)) by counting trees:

(A) B(I)←0 (I=1,N), $G' \leftarrow G$; Construct a spanning tree T' for G'; Orient the edges of T' to point away from the root.

(B) Is G' a tree? If not, to (C); Otherwise register one tree: B(M)←B(M)+1, where M is the number of vertices of G'; To (E).

(C) Is DG' a tree? If so, register one tree: B(M)←B(M)+1, where M is the number of vertices of DG'; If not, $DG' \rightarrow$ STACK; Increase stack counter by one unit.

(D) Carry out identification on G'; Construct a spanning tree for G'; To (B).

(E) STACK empty? If so, go to exit routine; Otherwise $G' \leftarrow$ STACK; Let N' (resp. E') count the vertices (resp. edges) of G'; If

E'>N', reduce E' for G' on stack by one unit (i.e., replace G' on the stack by DG'); If E'=N', register one N'-tree: B(N')←B(N')+1; Then reduce stack counter by one; To (**D**) ■

For many purposes it is desirable also to have the coefficients a_j of the form (2). These are computed by the program through a call to the subroutine POLY of Chapter 15. Indeed, let $\lambda' = \lambda - 1$; then

$$P(\lambda)/\lambda = \sum_{j=1}^{n} \lambda'^{j-1}(-1)^{n-j}b_j$$

is a polynomial which, if arranged in powers of $\lambda' + 1$ $(=\lambda)$, gives the form (2) (after multiplying both sides again by λ). This is just what POLY does, if OPT=N. Similarly, a call to POLY, with OPT=−2 causes $P(\lambda)/\lambda$ to be written as a sum of factorial polynomials $(\lambda')_{j-1}$; this expression has the same coefficients as the expression of $P(\lambda)$ in terms of

$$\lambda, \lambda(\lambda - 1), \lambda(\lambda - 1)(\lambda - 2), \ldots, \lambda(\lambda - 1)(\lambda - 2) \cdots (\lambda - n + 1)$$

The coefficient of $\lambda(\lambda - 1) \cdots (\lambda - i + 1)$ is $1/i!$ times the number of colorings of G in *exactly* i colors.

DESCRIPTION OF FLOW CHART

Box 10   Call SPANF0; initialize A and B. In the first phase, pass through the edges of the spanning tree. A(I) will contain the edge J whose 2nd endpoint is I. B(J) will contain ±1 to indicate whether the endpoints as listed in edge-list are correct or should be reversed.

Boxes 20–40   Each edge of the spanning tree is in turn used to connect two trees.

Boxes 50–80   Beginning with vertex I0 in Box 50, edge references move in and out of A as edges are reversed (B(J0)← −B(J0)) while a path is traversed down to the root of a tree (J0=0, Box 70). The new root is at I0 in Box 50.

Box 90   As both vertices of an edge were made roots, the edge assignment for the second one is changed.

Box 100   The last root constructed is the actual root R of the spanning tree.

Boxes 110–150   Endpoints of edges are interchanged as needed. The edge-list of the spanning tree is copied into STACK.

Boxes 150–170   A loop copies the edges of the spanning tree from STACK back into ENDPT in an order such that each edge is preceded by the ones that connect it to the root. The edge references are still in A; as edges are copied back into ENDPT the value of A is set to zero. Each edge is traced down in loop

150 (the labels along the way stored in C) until an edge is encountered which has already been transferred. Then the edges are copied (Box 155). J0 acts as counter of copied edges. (Incidentally, B is zeroed out.)

FLOW CHART CHROMP

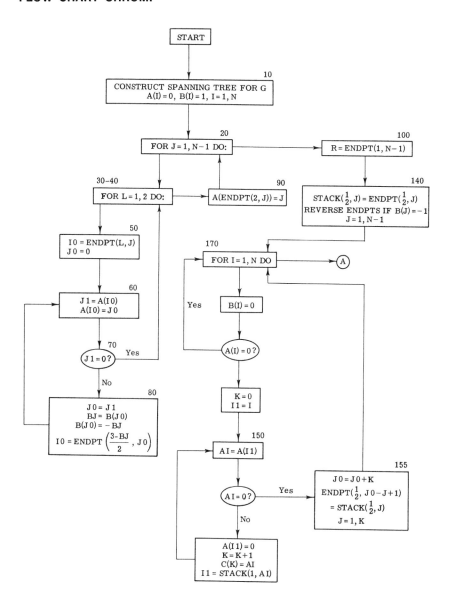

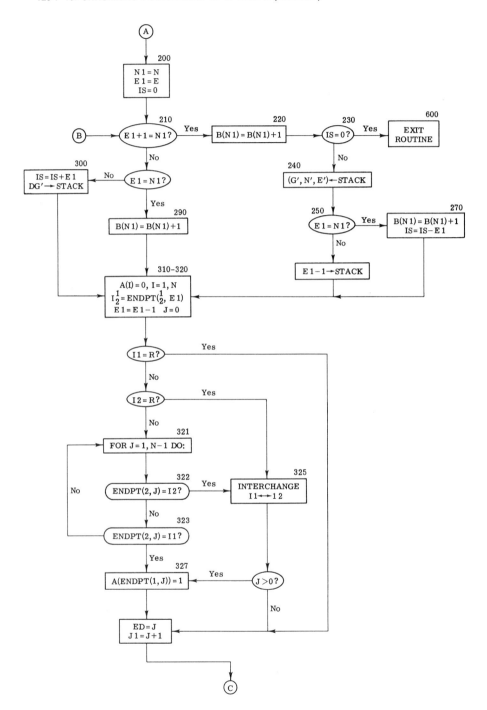

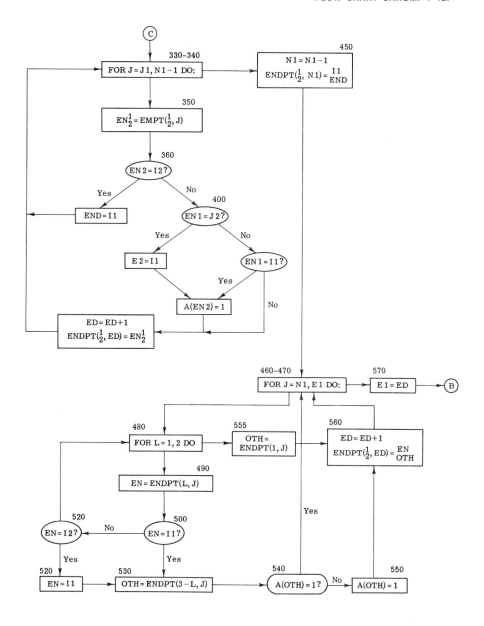

Box 200   Initialization of variables N1,E1 to contain vertex and edge counts of running graph G'. IS keeps count of stack content.

Boxes 210–220 G' a tree? If so, register. Otherwise to Box 280.

Boxes 230–240   Get next graph G'; if none, go to exit routine.

Boxes 250–270   Is DG' a tree? If so, register (Box 270) and delete G' from stack. If not, change G' on stack to DG'.

Boxes 280–300   Is DG' a tree? If so, register. If not, place on stack.

Boxes 310–327   Beginning of contraction on edge E1 endpoints I1,I2; interchange if I2=R. A is zeroed out.

Boxes 330–340   The endpoints EN1 and EN2 of edge J are compared with I1 and I2. In only one edge J is EN2=I2 (its other endpoint is END); there is one edge J for which EN2=I1 (none if I1=R). Except for the former edge, in all other edges with one vertex = I2 the I2 is replaced by I1; furthermore, a record is kept in A of the occurrence of the other endpoints of these edges (Box 430). These edges are copied back into ENDPT; the edge counter is ED. No vertex I will occur twice (except perhaps END) in the list of A's, since we are dealing with a tree.

Box 450   Edge (I1,END) is copied back into ENDPT; N1 is reduced by 1, since this edge is not in the spanning tree (of IG).

Boxes 460–480   The remaining edges are processed.

Boxes 490–560   I2 is replaced by I1; the second vertex OTH of each edge with endpoints I1 or I2 is checked against A and the edge deleted if A=1 (Box 540). If not, A is set = 1 and the edge is copied (Box 560). Edges with no endpoint I1 or I2 pass through Box 555.

Box 570   E1 is redefined (N1 was done in Box 450).

Box 600   The B's are copied into A and POLY is invoked. A now contains the coefficients of $P(\lambda)$ as in (2). Exit.

Remark   The graphs stored in STACK have the property that both their vertex and their edge counts are strictly decreasing. Also, no graph has fewer than three vertices, as there are never any trees on the stack. Also, none has E edges, as all the graphs are DG's.

An upper estimate for the number of pairs in STACK (including the N1 and E1) is therefore

$$E + (E - 1) + \cdots + (E - N + 3)$$
$$= (N - 2)(E - (N - 3)/2) \leqslant N(E - N + \tfrac{1}{2})$$

SUBROUTINE SPECIFICATIONS

(1) *Name of subroutine:* CHROMP.
(2) *Calling statement:* CALL CHROMP(N,E,ENDPT,A,B,C,STACK, NSTK).
(3) *Purpose of subroutine:* Calculate coefficients of chromatic polynomial of a connected graph.
(4) *Descriptions of variables in calling statement:*

Name	Type	I/O/W/B	Description
N	INTEGER	I	Number of vertices of G.
E	INTEGER	I	Number of edges of G.
ENDPT	INTEGER(2,E)	‡	ENDPT(1,I), ENDPT(2,I) are the two ends of edge I of G(I=1,E). This array is destroyed by operation CHROMP.
A	INTEGER(N)	O	Coefficient of $(-1)^I \lambda^I$ in $P(\lambda)$ is A(I) (I=1,N).
B	INTEGER(N)	O	Coefficient of $P(\lambda)$ in Eq. (5).
C	INTEGER(N)	O	$P(\lambda) = \sum\limits_{I=1}^{N} C(I)(\lambda)_I.$
STACK	INTEGER(2,NSTK)	W	Working storage.
NSTK	INTEGER	I	Maximum size of stack; see text.

‡ This array is input data and is destroyed by operation of the routine.

(5) *Other routines which are called by this one:* SPANFO, RENUMB, POLY.
(6) *Approximate number of* FORTRAN *instructions:* 143.
(7) *Remarks:* Input list ENDPT destroyed.

```
      SUBROUTINE CHROMP(N,E,ENDPT,A,B,C,STACK,NSTK)
      IMPLICIT INTEGER (A-Z)
      DIMENSION ENDPT(2,E),STACK(2,NSTK),A(N),B(N),C(N)
10    CALL SPANFO(N,E,ENDPT,K,A,B,C)
      IF (K.GT.1) STOP
12    DO 13  I=1,N
      A(I)=0
13    B(I)=1
20    N1=N-1
      DO 90  J=1,N1
30    DO 40  L=1,2
50    IO=ENDPT(L,J)
      JO=0
```

```
60    J1=A(I0)
      A(I0)=J0
70    IF(J1.EQ.0) GO TO 40
80    J0=J1
      BJ=B(J0)
      B(J0)=-BJ
      I0=ENDPT((3-BJ)/2,J0)
      GO TO 60
40    CONTINUE
90    A(ENDPT(2,J))=J
      R=ENDPT(1,N1)
      DO 140  J=1,N1
      DO 140  L=1,2
140   STACK(L,J)=ENDPT((3+B(J)*(2*L-3))/2,J)
      DO 170   I=1,N
      B(I)=0
      IF(A(I).EQ.0) GO TO 170
      K=0
      I1=I
150   AI=A(I1)
      IF(AI.EQ.0) GO TO 155
      A(I1)=0
      K=K+1
      C(K)=AI
      I1=STACK(1,AI)
      GO TO 150
155   I1=I
      J0=J0+K
      DO 160  J=1,K
      DO 160  L=1,2
160   ENDPT(L,J0-J+1)=STACK(L,C(J))
170   CONTINUE
200   N1=N
      E1=E
      IS=0
210   IF(E1+1.NE.N1) GO TO 280
220   B(N1)=B(N1)+1
230   IF(IS.EQ.0) GO TO 600
240   N1=STACK(1,IS)
      E1=STACK(2,IS)
      J0=IS-E1
      DO 241  J=1,E1
```

```
        DO 242  L=1,2
242     ENDPT(L,J)=STACK(L,JO)
241     JO=JO+1
250     IF(E1.NE.N1) GO TO 260
270     B(N1)=B(N1)+1
        IS=IS-E1-1
        GO TO 310
280     IF(E1.NE.N1) GO TO 300
290     B(N1)=B(N1)+1
        GO TO 310
300     DO 301  J=1,E1
        IS=IS+1
        DO 301  L=1,2
301     STACK(L,IS)=ENDPT(L.J)
        STACK(1,IS)=N1
        STACK(2,IS)=E1-1
        GO TO 310
260     IS=IS-1
        STACK(1,IS)=N1
        STACK(2,IS)=E1-1
310     DO 311  I=1,N
311     A(I)=0
320     I1=ENDPT(1,E1)
        I2=ENDPT(2,E1)
        E1=E1-1
        TR=N1-1
        J=0
        IF(I1.EQ.R) GO TO 327
        IF(I2.EQ.R) GO TO 325
        DO 321  J=1,TR
        EN2=ENDPT(2,J)
322     IF(EN2.EQ.I2) GO TO 325
323     IF(EN2.EQ.I1) GO TO 326
321     CONTINUE
325     IO=I1
        I1=I2
        I2=IO
326     IF(J.GT.0) A(ENDPT(1,J))=1
327     ED=J
        J1=J+1
330     DO 340  J=J1,TR
350     EN1=ENDPT(1,J)
```

```
      EN2=ENDPT(2,J)
360   IF(EN2.NE.I2) GO TO 400
370   END=EN1
      GO TO 340
400   IF(EN1.NE.I2) GO TO 420
      EN1=I1
      GO TO 430
420   IF(EN1.NE.I1) GO TO 440
430   A(EN2)=1
440   ED=ED+1
      ENDPT(1,ED)=EN1
      ENDPT(2,ED)=EN2
340   CONTINUE
450   N1=TR
      ENDPT(1,N1)=I1
      ENDPT(2,N1)=END
460   DO 470  J=N1,E1
480   DO 485  L=1,2
490   EN=ENDPT(L,J)
500   IF(EN.EQ.I1) GO TO 530
510   IF(EN.EQ.I2) GO TO 520
485   CONTINUE
555   OTH=ENDPT(1,J)
      GO TO 560
520   EN=I1
530   OTH=ENDPT(3-L,J)
540   IF(A(OTH).EQ.1) GO TO 470
550   A(OTH)=1
560   ED=ED+1
      ENDPT(1,ED)=EN
      ENDPT(2,ED)=OTH
470   CONTINUE
570   E1=ED
      GO TO 210
600   DO 601  I=1,N
601   A(I)=(1-2*MOD(N-I,2))*B(I)
      CALL POLY(N,A,0,-2,V,C)
      CALL POLY(N,A,-1,N,V,A)
      DO 602  I=1,N
602   A(I)=IABS(A(I))
      RETURN
      END
```

SAMPLE OUTPUT

The chromatic polynomial of the graph shown in Fig. 16.3 was computed by CHROMP.

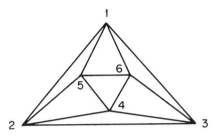

Figure 16.3

The input arrays are shown below, along with the polynomial coefficients $A(1), A(2), A(3), A(4), A(5)$, the "tree coefficients," $B(1), B(2), B(3), B(4), B(5)$, and the Stirling coefficients $C(1), C(2), C(3), C(4), C(5)$.

```
ENDPT(1,I):   1   1   1   1   2   2   2   3   3   4   4   5
ENDPT(2,I):   2   3   4   5   3   4   6   5   6   5   6   6
```

$A(I):$	64	154	137	58	12	1
$B(I):$	0	11	25	20	7	1
$C(I):$	0	0	1	3	3	1

The chromatic polynomial of this graph is therefore

$$
\begin{aligned}
P(\lambda) &= \lambda^6 - 12\lambda^5 + 58\lambda^4 - 137\lambda^3 + 154\lambda^2 - 64\lambda \\
&= \lambda(\lambda - 1)^5 - 7\lambda(\lambda - 1)^4 + 20\lambda(\lambda - 1)^3 \\
&\quad - 25\lambda(\lambda - 1)^2 + 11\lambda(\lambda - 1) \\
&= (\lambda)_3 + 3(\lambda)_4 + 3(\lambda)_5 + (\lambda)_6
\end{aligned}
$$

17

Composition of Power Series (POWSER)

Suppose that we are given two power series

$$(1) \qquad g(z) = b_1 z + b_2 z^2 + b_3 z^3 + \cdots$$
$$(2) \qquad h(z) = c_1 z + c_2 z^2 + c_3 z^3 + \cdots$$

and that we want to calculate the coefficients of the composite

$$(3) \qquad f(z) = g(h(z)) = a_1 z + a_2 z^2 + \cdots$$

Such problems arise frequently in combinatorics, for instance, if

$$(4) \qquad g(z) = h(z) = e^z - 1$$

the numbers $n! a_n$ ($n = 1, 2, \ldots$) represent the number of partitions of an n-set (see Chapter 11).

As so often is the case, the most explicit method is the least desirable computationally. There is a closed formula, due to Faà di Bruno, which expresses the coefficients of $g(h(z))$ in terms of those of $g(z)$ and of $h(z)$. It states that

$$(5) \qquad a_j = \sum b_\mu \mu! \tau_\mu^{(j)} \quad (j \geqq 1)$$

in which

$$(6) \qquad \tau_k^{(j)} = \sum \frac{c_1^{m_1} c_2^{m_2} \cdots}{m_1! m_2! \cdots} \quad (j \geqq 1; 1 \leqq k \leqq j)$$

where the sum runs over the partitions Π of j into exactly k parts, and m_i is the multiplicity of i in Π. The amount of computational labor involved here is astronomical compared to that in either of the next two approaches, and so we shall not discuss (5) further.

Next, a rather neat algorithm can be constructed by the use of two linear arrays, say $\rho_1, \ldots, \rho_n; a_1, \ldots, a_n$:

(**B1**) $\rho_i \leftarrow c_i$ $(i = 1, n)$; $a_i \leftarrow 0$ $(i = 1, n)$; $q \leftarrow 1$.

(**B2**) $a_i \leftarrow b_q\rho_i + a_i$ $(i = 1, n)$; If $q = n$, exit.

(**B3**) $q \leftarrow q + 1$; $\rho_i \leftarrow \sum_l \rho_l c_{i-l}$ $(i = 1, n)$; To (**B2**) ∎

Thus, we find the coefficients c_i of a single power of $h(z)$, the qth power, accumulate the contribution $b_q h(z)^q$ to the coefficients of $f(z)$, then go to the next power of $h(z)$, etc.

The algorithm is quite nice, but we shall not use it here. Its disadvantages relative to our final choice of a method are, first, that if we want to raise $h(z)$ to the 100th power, all lower powers would have to be calculated and, second, that the powers of h are calculated each from its predecessor so that buildup of round-off error can take place. The next method calculates each power of $h(z)$ independently of the others, and only the powers that are needed (i.e., such that $b_i \neq 0$) are computed.

Suppose that the first nonvanishing coefficient of $h(z)$ is c_q $(q \geqq 1)$, so that

$$h(z) = c_q z^q + c_{q+1}z^{q+1} + \cdots \quad (c_q \neq 0)$$

and consider the special case where $g(t) = t^m$, i.e.,

$$f(z) = h(z)^m$$

where, for the moment, m need not even be an integer. By logarithmic differentiation, we find

(7) $$f'(z)h(z) = mf(z)h'(z)$$

and if we equate coefficients of like powers of z on both sides of (7), we find the recurrence formula

(8) $a_j = \{(j - mq)c_q\}^{-1} \sum_{\mu=mq}^{j-1} a_\mu c_{q+j-\mu}\{m(j+q-\mu) - \mu\}$ $(j > mq)$

with the starting value

(9) $$a_{mq} = c_q^m$$

We can now return to the general case where

(10) $$f(z) = g(h(z)) = \sum_{m=1}^{\infty} b_m h(z)^m$$

We calculate $a_1, \ldots, a_n$ by summing the results of the special case (8) and (9), multiplied by b_m, from $m = 1, \ldots, \lfloor n/q \rfloor$.

If $b_m = 0$ for some m, we immediately increase m, thereby avoiding all calculations for that m. Thus, if $g(t) = t^{20}$, for example, we will do no computation until m reaches 20, so we can raise a power series to a high power without computing any lower powers in the process.

ALGORITHM POWSER

(A) $a_l \leftarrow b_1 c_l$ $(l = 1, n)$; $q \leftarrow min\{i \mid c_i \neq 0\}$; $n_1 \leftarrow \lfloor n/q \rfloor$; $m \leftarrow 2$.
(B)   If $b_m = 0$, to (D); $f_{mq} \leftarrow c_q{}^m$; $j \leftarrow mq$.
(C) $a_j \leftarrow a_j + b_m f_j$; If $j = n$, to (D); $j \leftarrow j + 1$; $f_j \leftarrow$ {right hand side of (8)}; To (C).
(D)   If $m = n$, exit; $m \leftarrow m + 1$; To (B) ■

A closely related problem is the "reversion" problem for power series: Suppose $f(z)$, $g(z)$ are given, with $f(0) = g(0) = 0$, $g'(0) \neq 0$. Find $h(z)$ such that $f(z) = g(h(z))$. This can be solved numerically by an iterated use of POWSER. Inductively, suppose we have a partial series

(11) $$h_{m-1}(z) = c_1 z + c_2 z^2 + \cdots + c_{m-1} z^{m-1}$$

which has the property that

(12) $$g(h_{m-1}(z)) = f(z) + \alpha z^m + O(z^{m+1})$$

Then we have

$$\begin{aligned}
(13) \quad g(h_{m-1}(z) + c_m z^m) &= g(h_{m-1}(z)) + c_m z^m g'(h_{m-1}(z)) + O(z^{2m}) \\
&= f(z) + \alpha z^m + O(z^{m+1}) \\
&\quad + c_m z^m (b_1 + O(z)) + O(z^{2m}) \\
&= f(z) + (c_m b_1 + \alpha) z^m + O(z^{m+1})
\end{aligned}$$

Hence, we should take $c_m b_1 + \alpha = 0$, which defines the following iterative process:

(14) $c_m = b_1{}^{-1}\{a_m - $ coefficient of z^m in $g(h_{m-1}(z))\}$

$$(m = 1, 2, \ldots; h_0 \equiv 0)$$

Our computer program solves this reversion problem also, as one of its options (OPTION=4). It does so by treating Algorithm POWSER as a subroutine in order to calculate the composition $g(h_{m-1}(z))$ which appears on the right of (14).

Two special cases of the composition operation merit special attention. In the case where

$$(15) \qquad f(z) = \exp\{h(z)\} - 1$$

our algorithm is, of course, able to handle the problem if we take $g(t) = e^t - 1$, in the way already discussed. The calculation of n coefficients of $f(z)$ would require $O(n^3)$ operations. We can, however, calculate these n coefficients of f in $O(n^2)$ operations. Indeed, by direct logarithmic differentiation of (15) we find a recurrence formula

$$(16) \qquad \begin{cases} a_j = \dfrac{1}{j} \sum_{\mu=1}^{j-1} a_\mu c_{j-\mu}(j-\mu) + c_j \quad (j \geq 2) \\[2mm] a_1 = c_1 \end{cases}$$

for the required $a_1, \ldots, a_n$. Our program POWSER provides for this case under OPTION=2.

Next, if α is a real number, then the coefficients of

$$(17) \qquad f(z) = (1 + h(z))^\alpha - 1$$

can also be treated by our general algorithm in $O(n^3)$ operations, but once more, direct logarithmic differentiation of (17) yields the recurrence

$$(18) \quad a_1 = \alpha c_1; \qquad a_j = \alpha c_j + \frac{1}{j} \sum_{\mu=1}^{j-1} a_\mu c_{j-\mu}\{\alpha(j-\mu) - \mu\} \quad (j \geq 2)$$

from which $a_1, \ldots, a_n$ can be found in $O(n^2)$ operations. This is done by POWSER if OPTION=1 (see Table 17.1).

Table 17.1 Description of Options in Powser Subroutine

Purpose[a]	OPTION=	Input	Output	Operation time
$f = (1+h)^\alpha - 1$	1	$n; \alpha; c_1, \ldots, c_n;$	$a_1, \ldots, a_n$	$O(n^2)$
$f = e^h - 1$	2	$n; c_1, \ldots, c_n;$	$a_1, \ldots, a_n$	$O(n^2)$
$f = g(h)$	3	$n; b_1, \ldots, b_n;$ $c_1, \ldots, c_n;$	$a_1, \ldots, a_n$	$O(n^3)$
$f = g(?)$	4	$n; b_1, \ldots, b_n; b_1 \neq 0$ $a_1, \ldots, a_n;$	$c_1, \ldots, c_n$	$O(n^4)$

[a] $f(z) = a_1 z + a_2 z^2 + \cdots, \quad g(z) = b_1 z + b_2 z^2 + \cdots, \quad h(z) = c_1 z + c_2 z^2 + \cdots.$

FLOW CHART POWSER

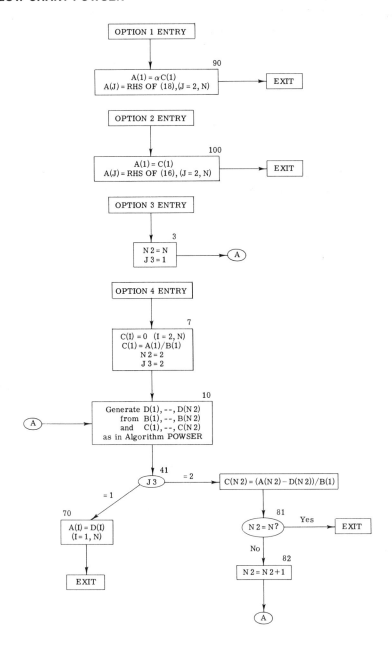

DESCRIPTION OF FLOW CHART

Box 90   Option 1 calculations done. Exit.

Box 100   Option 2 calculations done. Exit.

Box 3   We will now call Box 10 as a subroutine. Variable exit J3 is set to 1, N2=N.

Box 7   In Option 4 we will also call Box 10 as a subroutine. Variable exit J3 set to 2, N2=2, C(I) are initialized.

Box 10   Here we compose the series $g(h(z))$, to get $f(z)$, where the coefficients of g are B(1),...,B(N2), of h are C(1),...,C(N2), and of f are D(1),...,D(N2).

Box 70   After calculation of D(1),...,D(N) above, we transfer them to output locations A(1),...,A(N), and exit.

Box 80   Here we find next coefficient C(N2) of unknown $h(z)$ as in Eq. (14). If N2<N, increase it to find next coefficient and return to Box 10.

SUBROUTINE SPECIFICATIONS

(1) *Name of subroutine:*   POWSER.
(2) *Calling statement:*   CALL POWSER(A,B,C,N,ALPHA,OPTION, D,F).
(3) *Purpose of subroutine:*   Compose power series.
(4) *Descriptions of variables in calling statement:*

Name	Type	I/O/W/B	Description
A	REAL(N)	I/O	$f(z) = A(1)z + A(2)z^2 + \cdots + A(N)z^N$.
B	REAL(N)	I	$g(z) = B(1)z + \cdots + B(N)z^N$.
C	REAL(N)	I/O	$h(z) = C(1)z + \cdots + C(N)z^N$.
N	INTEGER	I	Number of coefficients to be calculated.
ALPHA	REAL	I	Exponent of $1 + h(z)$ if OPTION=1.
OPTION	INTEGER	I	See Table 17.1.
D	REAL(N)	W	Working storage.
F	REAL(N)	W	Working storage.

(5) *Other routines which are called by this one:*   None.
(6) *Approximate number of* FORTRAN *instructions:*   58.
(7) *Remarks:*   If OPTION=4 then B(1)≠0.

```
SUBROUTINE POWSER(A,B,C,N,ALPHA,OPTION,D,F)
INTEGER Q,OPTION
DIMENSION A(N),B(N),C(N),D(N),F(N)
```

```
        GO TO (90,100,3,7),OPTION
3       N2=N
        J3=1
        GO TO 10
7       DO 8   I=2,N
8       C(I)=0
        C(1)=A(1)/B(1)
        N2=2
        J3=2
10      DO 11   L=1,N2
11      D(L)=B(1)*C(L)
20      DO 21   Q=1,N2
        IF(C(Q).NE.0) GO TO 30
21      CONTINUE
30      N1=N2/Q
40      DO 41   M=2,N1
        IF(B(M).EQ.0) GO TO 41
        M1=M*Q
        F(M1)=C(Q)**M
        J=M1
50      D(J)=D(J)+B(M)*F(J)
        IF(J.EQ.N2) GO TO 41
        J=J+1
        S=0
        J1=J-1
60      DO 61   MU=M1,J1
61      S=S+FLOAT(M*(J+Q-MU)-MU)*F(MU)*C(J+Q-MU)
        F(J)=S/(C(Q)*FLOAT(J-M1))
        GO TO 50
41      CONTINUE
        GO TO (70,80),J3
70      DO 71   I=1,N
71      A(I)=D(I)
        RETURN
80      C(N2)=(A(N2)-D(N2))/B(1)
81      IF(N2.EQ.N)    RETURN
82      N2=N2+1
        GO TO 10
90      A(1)=ALPHA*C(1)
        DO 91   J=2,N
        J1=J-1
```

```
      S=0
      DO 95   MU=1,J1
95    S=S+A(MU)*C(J-MU)*(ALPHA*FLOAT(J-MU)-MU)
91    A(J)=ALPHA*C(J)+S/FLOAT(S)
      RETURN
100   A(1)=C(1)
      DO 105   J=2,N
      J1=J-1
      S=0
      DO 110   MU=1,J1
110   S=S+A(MU)*C(J-MU)*FLOAT(J-MU)
105   A(J)=C(J)+S/FLOAT(J)
      RETURN
      END
```

FIRST SAMPLE OUTPUT, OPTION 1

With OPTION=1, $h(z) = z$, the program computes binomial coefficients. Output with $\alpha = 7$, $n = 10$ is shown below.

```
7.0000000   21.0000000   35.0000000   35.0000000   21.0000000
7.0000000    1.0000000    0.0000000    0.0000000    0.0000000
```

SECOND SAMPLE OUTPUT, OPTION 1

If b_j is the number of binary trees on j vertices, then the generating function

$$\sum_{j=0}^{\infty} b_j z^i = \frac{1}{2z} (1 - \sqrt{1 - 4z})$$

is well known. We took OPTION=1, $h(z) = -4z$, $\alpha = 0.5$, $N = 11$, and thereby obtained $a_n = -2b_{n-1}$ $(n = 1, \ldots, 11)$ which are shown below.

```
   -2.0000000       -2.0000000       -4.0000000
  -10.0000000      -28.0000000      -84.0000000
 -264.0000000     -857.9999999    -2859.9999999
-9723.9999999   -33591.9999994
```

SAMPLE OUTPUT, OPTION 3

Let $\Phi(n)$ denote the number of ways of writing

$$n = 5x + 10y + 17z \quad (x, y, z \geq 0)$$

Then evidently

$$\frac{1}{(1 - t^5)(1 - t^{10})(1 - t^{17})} = \sum_{n=0}^{\infty} \Phi(n) t^n$$

$$= \exp\left\{\log \frac{1}{1 - t^5} + \log \frac{1}{1 - t^{10}} + \log \frac{1}{1 - t^{17}}\right\}$$

$$= \exp\left\{\sum_{r=1}^{\infty} \frac{\bar{c}_r t^r}{r}\right\}$$

where $\bar{c}_r$ is the sum of those elements of the subset of $\{5, 10, 17\}$ which divide r. We can calculate $\Phi(n)$ from POWSER with input OPTION=3 and

$$b_i = \frac{1}{i!} \quad (i = 1, \ldots, n)$$

$$c_i = \frac{1}{i} \sum_{d|i} \{\delta_{d,5} + \delta_{d,10} + \delta_{d,17}\} d \quad (i = 1, n)$$

The output of such a calculation, with N=50, follows. The numbers printed are $\Phi(n)$ $(n = 1, 50)$.

```
0.00   0.00   0.00   0.00   1.00   0.00   0.00   0.00
1.00   1.00   0.00   0.00   0.00   1.00   1.00   0.00
1.00   1.00   1.00   1.00   0.00   1.00   1.00   1.00
1.00   1.00   2.00   1.00   1.00   1.00   1.00   2.00
1.00   2.00   2.00   2.00   2.00   1.00   2.00   2.00
2.00   2.00   2.00   3.00   3.00   2.00   2.00   2.00
3.00   3.00
```

SAMPLE OUTPUT, OPTION 4

With OPTION=4, $b_i = 1/i$ $(i = 1, n)$, $n = 10$, and $f(z) = z$, the program will find the coefficients $a_1, \ldots, a_{10}$ of the inverse function of $\log 1/(1 - z)$, namely, of $1 - e^{-z}$. The output follows.

```
 1.0000000   -0.5000000    0.1666667   -0.0416667    0.0083333
-0.0013889    0.0001984   -0.0000248    0.0000028   -0.0000003
```

18

Network Flows (NETFLO)

In this chapter we will consider a remarkable family of combinatorial algorithms first dealt with by Ford and Fulkerson. These are the "network flow" problems, and included as special cases are (a) finding a maximum matching of a bipartite graph, (b) discovering if a family of sets possesses a system of distinct representatives, (c) computing the Dilworth number of a partially ordered set, (d) finding the edge-connectivity or vertex-connectivity of a graph, and (e) determining if a given pair of vectors are or are not the row and column sum vectors of a matrix of zeros and ones, and if so, finding such a matrix, etc.

All of the above problems and many more can be solved with an amount of labor which is a low power of the order of complexity of the problem, i.e., the algorithm is in each case a very efficient method for handling the problem.

The general framework in which we will deal with all of these problems simultaneously is a small variation of the method of network flows. We define a *capacity matrix* to be an $n \times n$ matrix C of nonnegative integer entries, which has zeros on the main diagonal. Let x, z be two distinct elements of $\{1, 2, \ldots, n\}$ called, respectively, the source and the sink. On the set of all capacity matrices we define an equivalence relation, viz., $C \sim C'$ if $C - C'$ is a skew symmetric matrix whose row sums are all zero except in rows x and z (evidently, these two row sums r_x and r_z are negatives of each other).

The Network Flow Problem: Given a capacity matrix C_0, a source

x and a sink z. Find a capacity matrix C^*, equivalent to C_0, such that $r_x(C^*)$ is minimum.

Let $S \subset \{1, 2, \ldots, n\}$, $z \notin S$, $x \in S$. By a *cut* K we mean $S \times \bar{S}$, and by the capacity of K we mean

$$\operatorname{cap}(K) = \sum_{(\mu,\nu)\in K} (C_0)_{\mu,\nu}$$

The max-flow–min-cut theorem of Ford and Fulkerson asserts that

(1) $$\max_{C \sim C_0} r_x (C_0 - C) = \min_K \operatorname{cap}(K)$$

The reader will have noted that graphs, edges, flows, etc. have not been mentioned. We pause to indicate the correspondence between our presentation (which is motivated by greater clarity and ease of application of the resulting algorithms) and the more traditional one. To do this, consider a graph G on vertices $\{1, 2, \ldots, n\} = V$, join p and q by an edge if $C_{p,q} > 0$ or $C_{q,p} > 0$. $C_{p,q}$ denotes the capacity of flow through the edge from p to q. A flow φ is a function on $V \times V$ such that $\varphi(i, j) = -\varphi(j, i)$ (it is considered to go from i to j if $\varphi(i, j) > 0$) which satisfies Kirchhoff's law

$$\sum_i \varphi(i, j) = 0 \qquad (j \neq x, z)$$

Say that φ is admissible with respect to C if $\varphi(i, j)$ does not exceed the capacities of the edge (i, j), i.e., if

$$-C_{j,i} \leq \varphi(i, j) \leq C_{i,j} \qquad (\forall i, j)$$

If φ is an admissible flow with respect to C then $C - \varphi = C'$ is an equivalent capacity matrix, and $-\varphi$ is admissible with respect to C'. Conversely, if C and C' are equivalent capacity matrices, then $C - C'$ is an admissible flow with respect to C. A traditional network flow problem is one in which for each edge (i, j) either $C_{i,j}$ or $C_{j,i}$ is 0, and the edge itself is considered to be directed.

We will now describe in broad outline the algorithm for this problem using the traditional language, though the consequences of our formal definition of the problem will be clearly visible in the capacity reallocation which replaces the usual flow augmentation.

At first glance, implementation of the max-flow–min-cut theorem would seem to imply a search for a cut of minimum capacity, or around 2^n operations. Actually the algorithm we give in this chapter, a slight modification of a method of E. A. Dinic, is much faster than that. In general, the Dinic algorithm requires only $O(n^2E)$ operations for a network of n vertices and E edges. S. Even and R. E. Tarjan have shown that if the edge capacities are all 1 (as in many important applications) the work done is $O(n^{2/3}E)$ and if vertex capacities are 1 also, by the usual method of splitting vertices, the work required is $O(n^{1/2}E)$.

The main idea of the algorithm is, as it was in Ford and Fulkerson's original procedure, to carry out a search for a path P from source to sink such that each edge, (p, q) of P can carry a flow, i.e., $C_{p,q} > 0$. The search is done, also as in the original procedure, by a scanning and labeling process.

To scan a vertex p is to examine each of its neighbors in the network, to label those which have not yet been labeled to which p is joined by a useable edge (one which can carry a flow), and in any case, to keep a record of all useable edges whose initial point is p. The label of a vertex is always $l + 1$ where l is the label of the vertex being scanned at the time. When p has been scanned, we scan the next labeled-but-so-far-unscanned vertex, etc. If by this process the sink does not acquire a label, the flow is at its maximum value, the set of unlabeled vertices defines a cut of minimum capacity, and we exit. Once the sink is labeled, we continue labeling until the next label value is required. Then we have before us the set of all useable edges which constitute a new graph G_U, and in G_U we search for a path from source to sink.

To do this we begin with an edge of G_U adjacent to the source. Generically, if we have a partial path, we extend it by one more edge of G_U, if possible. Otherwise, we delete the last edge of the path from G_U and from the path, and backtrack to the end of the shortened path. If eventually we reach the sink, we increase the flow on every edge of the path by δ units, where δ is the smallest current capacity of any edge in the path. We then decrease the current capacity of every edge in the path by δ units, and *increase* by δ the current capacity of every edge (j, i) where (i, j) is in the path. Any edge which acquires 0 capacity is deleted from G_U. Note that an edge is useable if and only if its current capacity is positive.

Next, without any rescanning or relabeling, we attempt, as before, to find another flow-augmenting path in the new G_U, beginning the new search from the initial vertex of the edge nearest the source which acquired zero capacity from the previous augmentation. This process continues until no further paths exist in G_U. We then return to the scanning and labeling process.

We describe briefly the use of this algorithm in the solution of the five problems mentioned above.

(a) Maximum Matching

Given a bipartite graph $G(S, T)$. Adjoin a source and a sink. Connect the source to each $s \in S$, and connect each $t \in T$ to the sink, using edges of capacity 1. Assign to each edge (s, t) capacity $|S|$ (all other edges have capacity 0). All edges are directed as source→S→T→sink. The maximum value of a flow is then equal to the maximum number of edges in a matching. Any minimal cut defines a minimum edge-covering set of vertices.

(b) Systems of Distinct Representatives (SDR)

Given sets $S_1, \ldots, S_n$ composed of elements $x_1, \ldots, x_m$. Construct a bipartite graph by joining (S_i, x_j) if the element belongs to the set. A maximum matching consists of n edges if and only if there is an SDR. A maximal flow describes the SDR.

(c) Dilworth Number

Given a partially ordered set P: $\{1, 2, \ldots, n\}$. Let $S = \{x_1, \ldots, x_n\}$, $T = \{y_1, \ldots, y_n\}$ and draw edge (x_i, y_j) if $i \alpha j$ in P. If there are d edges in a maximum matching of this bipartite graph, then the Dilworth number of P is $n - d$, i.e., P can be covered by $n - d$ linearly ordered sets but not by fewer. A minimum cut defines an independent set in P of $n - d$ elements.

(d) Edge-Connectivity of a Graph (after Even and Tarjan)

To find the edge-connectivity of an undirected graph G, fix j, $2 \leq j \leq n$. Take vertex 1 as source, j as sink, in the graph G. Give all edges unit capacity in both directions. If $\Phi(j)$ is the value of a maximum flow in this network, then the edge-connectivity is

$$\kappa(G) = \min_{2 \leq j \leq n} \Phi(j)$$

(e) 0–1 Matrices

Given vectors $(r_1, \ldots, r_m)$ and $(s_1, \ldots, s_n)$, a network is constructed from a source, vertices $x_1, \ldots, x_m, y_1, \ldots, y_n$, and a sink. There are edges (source, x_i) of capacity $r_i (i = 1, m)$; edges (x_i, y_j) of capacity 1 $(i = 1, m; j = 1, n)$; and edges (y_i, sink) of capacities $s_i (i = 1, n)$. A 0–1 matrix A having the given row and column sums exists if and only if the maximum flow in this network saturates all edges adjacent to the source and sink. If so, the matrix elements are $a_{i,j} =$ flow in edge (x_i, y_j) $(i = 1, m; j = 1, n)$.

The list of examples could go on, but in Ford and Fulkerson the interested reader will find many more. In the cases above, the fact that the algorithm produces the effects claimed is in each case a by-product of a network flow proof of, respectively, the marriage theorem, P. Hall's theorem on *SDR*, Dilworth's theorem, Menger's theorem, and the Gale–Ryser theorem.

To implement the algorithm in a FORTRAN program we work with the following arrays, only the first of which is involved in input:

ENDPT, a $4 \times$ E matrix (E = number of edges); on input, the first three entries of each column are p, q, $C_{p,q}$; only nonzero $C_{p,q}$ need to be thus listed. On output, the last entry of the column contains $\varphi(p, q)$, the flow from p to q.

CAP, an N × N matrix which is the capacity matrix and which is updated during execution.

VERT, an N × N matrix whose Ith row contains a list of all vertices adjacent to I. The last entry of that row, VERT(I,N), contains the number of neighbors of I. The entries in each row of VERT are permuted during the labeling process, so the useable edges from I are listed first.

CUT, an N-vector, contains, upon return, values 0 and 1; CUT(I) is 1 or 0 according as I does or does not belong to the set S which determines a minimal cut S × S̄. In the labeling process, CUT(I) contains either the label of I or the number of useable edges from I; to distinguish, the labels have negative signs (the value $-N - 1$ denotes "unlabeled"). The useable-edge counts are used in the path-tracing part.

AUX, an N-vector, holds during the labeling process the list of vertices to be scanned, in order. During the path-tracing process, it holds a partially constructed path from source to sink.

When very large networks have to be processed, storage limitations may not permit the square arrays CAP and VERT. We outline, but do not program, some modifications for that case. On input all triples p, q, $C_{p,q}$ and q, p, $C_{q,p}$ are to be supplied even if one of $C_{p,q}$ or $C_{q,p}$ is zero. The program places the columns of ENDPT in lexicographic order with respect to the first two rows, for example, by a radix sort first on row 2 and then on row 1. Row 1 would then be a set of N segments; after the beginning of the segment of P's is stored in R(P) (a new array) for P=1,N, row 1 is redundant. It would then hold pointers from (P,Q) to (Q,P) after performing E binary searches.

Row 3 is then copied into row 4. The labeling and path-tracing would be done as in the present version: row 2 of ENDPT would replace VERT, row 4 replaces CAP, and when columns of ENDPT are permuted, the pointers are adjusted.

SUBROUTINE SPECIFICATIONS

(1) *Name of subroutine:* NETFLO.
(2) *Calling statement:* CALL NETFLO(N,E,ENDPT, SOURCE,SINK,FLOVAL,CUT,CAP,VERT,AUX).
(3) *Purpose of subroutine:* Find maximum flow in a network.
(4) *Description of variables in calling statement:*

Name	Type	I/O/W/B	Description
N	INTEGER	I	Number of vertices.
E	INTEGER	I	Number of input capacities.
ENDPT	INTEGER(4,E)	I/O	In each column are the row index, the column index, the input capacity, the output flow.
SOURCE	INTEGER	I	The designated source vertex.
SINK	INTEGER	I	The designated sink vertex.
FLOVAL	INTEGER	O	The maximum value of a flow.
CUT	INTEGER(N)	O	CUT(I)=1 is 1 if I is in a minimal cut set, 0 otherwise.
CAP	INTEGER(N,N)	W	Working storage.
VERT	INTEGER(N,N)	W	Working storage.
AUX	INTEGER(N)	W	Working storage.

(5) *Other routines which are called by this one:* None.
(6) *Approximate number of* FORTRAN *instructions:* 87.
(7) *Remarks:* Required input data are N;E;(ENDPT(I,J), I=1,3),J=1,E;SOURCE;SINK.

```
      SUBROUTINE NETFLO(N,E,ENDPT,SOURCE,SINK,FLOVAL,
     *CUT,CAP,VERT,AUX)
      IMPLICIT INTEGER(A-Z)
      DIMENSION ENDPT(4,E),CUT(N),CAP(N,N),VERT(N,N),
     *AUX(N)
C
C***   INITIALIZATION
C
      DO 1 I=1,N
      DO 1 J=1,N
```

```
1       CAP(I,J)=0
        DO 2 I=1,E
2       CAP(ENDPT(1,I),ENDPT(2,I))=ENDPT(3,I)
        DO 3 I=1,N
        K=0
        DO 4 J=1,N
        IF(CAP(I,J)+CAP(J,I).EQ.0) GO TO 4
        K=K+1
        VERT(I,K)=J
4       CONTINUE
3       VERT(I,N)=K
        NMIN=-N-1
        FLOVAL=0
C
C***    SCANNING AND LABELING
C
10      LBLSNK=N
        DO 14 I=1,N
14      CUT(I)=NMIN
        RD=0
        WR=0
        P=SOURCE
        LABEL=-1
15      M=VERT(P,N)
        I=1
20      IF(I.GT.M) GO TO 25
        Q=VERT(P,I)
        IF(CAP(P,Q).EQ.0) GO TO 23
        IF(Q.EQ.SINK) LBLSNK=-LABEL
        IF(CUT(Q)-LABEL) 21,22,23
21      CUT(Q)=LABEL
        WR=WR+1
        AUX(WR)=Q
22      I=I+1
        GO TO 20
23      VERT(P,I)=VERT(P,M)
        VERT(P,M)=Q
        M=M-1
        GO TO 20
25      CUT(P)=M
        RD=RD+1
        IF(RD.GT.WR) GO TO 50
```

```
      P=AUX(RD)                          .
      IF(CUT(P)+LBLSNK.EQ.0) GO TO 30
      LABEL=CUT(P)-1
      GO TO 15
C
C***  CONSTRUCTION OF PATH FROM SOURCE TO SINK
C
30    Q=SOURCE
      K=0
35    K=K+1
      AUX(K)=Q
      IF(K.GT.LBLSNK) GO TO 42
40    P=AUX(K)
41    M=CUT(P)
      IF(M.EQ.0) GO TO 43
      Q=VERT(P,M)
      GO TO 35
43    K=K-1
      IF(K.EQ.0) GO TO 10
      P=AUX(K)
      CUT(P)=CUT(P)-1
      GO TO 41
42    IF(Q.NE.SINK) GO TO 43
      DELTA=CAP(P,Q)
      DO 45 I=2,K
45    DELTA=MINO(DELTA,CAP(AUX(I-1),AUX(I)))
46    K=K-1
      IF(K.EQ.0) GO TO 47
      P=AUX(K)
      C=CAP(P,Q)-DELTA
      IF(C.GT.0) GO TO 48
      CUT(P)=CUT(P)-1
      KO=K
48    CAP(P,Q)=C
      CAP(Q,P)=CAP(Q,P)+DELTA
      Q=P
      GO TO 46
47    FLOVAL=FLOVAL+DELTA
      K=KO
      GO TO 40
C
C***  EXIT PROCEDURE
C
```

```
50      DO 51   I=1,N
51      CUT(I)=MINO(1,CUT(I)-NMIN)
        DO 52   I=1,E
52      ENDPT(4,I)=ENDPT(3,I)-CAP(ENDPT(1,I),ENDPT(2,I))
        RETURN
        END
```

SAMPLE OUTPUT

The program NETFLO was called to solve the network shown in Fig. 18.1, in which edge capacities are shown in **bold** type.

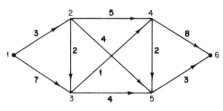

Figure 18.1

On input, the ENDPT array was

$$
\begin{array}{cccccccccc}
1 & 1 & 2 & 2 & 2 & 3 & 3 & 4 & 4 & 5 \\
2 & 3 & 3 & 4 & 5 & 4 & 5 & 5 & 6 & 6 \\
3 & 7 & 2 & 5 & 4 & 1 & 4 & 2 & 8 & 3 \\
- & - & - & - & - & - & - & - & - & -
\end{array}
$$

along with N=6, E=10, SOURCE=1, SINK=6.
On output, the fourth row of ENDPT held the maximum flow

$$3 \quad 4 \quad 0 \quad 3 \quad 0 \quad 1 \quad 3 \quad 0 \quad 4 \quad 3$$

The CUT array was

$$1 \quad 0 \quad 1 \quad 0 \quad 1 \quad 0$$

which describes a cut of capacity 7, and FLOVAL was 7.

19

The Permanent Function (PERMAN)

Let

$$(1) \qquad A = (a_{ij})_{i,j=1}^{n}$$

be an $n \times n$ square matrix. As is well known, the *determinant* of A is the number

$$(2) \qquad \det(A) = \sum_{\sigma} \text{sgn}(\sigma) a_{1,\sigma(1)} a_{2,\sigma(2)} \cdots a_{n,\sigma(n)}$$

where the sum is over all permutations σ of $\{1, 2, \ldots, n\}$. We contrast this with the *permanent* of A, which is instead,

$$(3) \qquad \text{per}(A) = \sum_{\sigma} a_{1,\sigma(1)} a_{2,\sigma(2)} \cdots a_{n,\sigma(n)}$$

The distinction lies solely in the omission of the $\pm$ sign of the permutation σ. This omission causes the permanent not to share many of the nice properties of determinants. For instance, we have generally,

$$(4) \qquad \text{per}(AB) \neq \text{per}(A)\,\text{per}(B)$$

The permanent is of considerable combinatorial importance, however. If A, for instance, is a matrix all of whose entries are $+1$, then from (3), per $A = n!$ is the number of permutations of n letters. More generally, let A be a matrix all of whose entries are either 0 or 1. Then in (3) each term is 0 or 1, and the value of per A is just the number of permutations σ which hit only 1's in the matrix A. This fact can be exploited for various combinatorial purposes.

Let A_n be given by

$$(5) \qquad a_{ij} = \begin{cases} 0 & \text{if} \quad i = j \\ 1 & \text{if} \quad i \neq j \end{cases} \quad (i, j = 1, \ldots, n)$$

Then, a term in the sum (3) is 1 if and only if

$$a_{1, \sigma(1)} = 1 \quad \text{and} \quad a_{2, \sigma(2)} = 1 \quad \text{and} \quad \cdots \quad \text{and} \quad a_{n, \sigma(n)} = 1$$

which in the case (5) means that

$$\sigma(1) \neq 1 \quad \text{and} \quad \sigma(2) \neq 2 \quad \text{and} \quad \cdots \quad \text{and} \quad \sigma(n) \neq n$$

which, in turn, is so if and only if the permutation σ leaves no letter fixed. Hence, for the matrix A_n of (5),

$$(6) \qquad D_n = \text{per}(A_n)$$

is the number of fixed-point free permutations of n letters. These "rencontres" numbers are well known to be given by

$$(7) \qquad D_n = n! \left\{ 1 - 1 + \frac{1}{2!} - \frac{1}{3!} + \cdots + \frac{(-1)^n}{n!} \right\}$$

Again, let $S_1, \ldots, S_n$ be a collection of sets whose union U consists of objects $a_1, a_2, \ldots, a_n$. By a *system of distinct representatives* of the collection $S_1, \ldots, S_n$ we mean a list $y_1, y_2, \ldots, y_n$ of all of the objects in U arranged in sequence so that $y_i \in S_i$ $(i = 1, \ldots, n)$. The permanent function counts systems of distinct representatives: Let a matrix A be defined by $a_{ij} = 1$ if $a_i \in S_j$ and $a_{ij} = 0$ otherwise. This matrix A is called the *incidence matrix* of the objects in the sets. A single term in the sum (3) is $= 1$ or 0 according to whether $a_{\sigma(1)}, \ldots, a_{\sigma(n)}$ is or is not, respectively, a system of distinct representatives for the sets $S_1, \ldots, S_n$. The permanent of A is therefore equal to the number of such systems.

As another application of the permanent function, by an $r \times n$ *Latin rectangle* we mean a rectangular array of r rows and n columns, whose entries are letters chosen from $\{1, 2, \ldots, n\}$ such that (a) the entries in each row constitute a permutation of $\{1, 2, \ldots, n\}$ *and* (b) the entries in each column are all different. We show a 3×5 Latin rectangle in Fig. 19.1. Our question is: In how many ways can we adjoin a new row to a given $r \times n$ Latin rectangle in such a way that the result is an $(r + 1) \times n$ Latin rectangle? To see this question as one about permanents, define n sets $S_1, \ldots, S_n$ as follows: $i \in S_j$ if i does not appear in column j of the

I	2	3	4	5
3	I	5	2	4
2	4	I	5	3

Figure 19.1

given Latin rectangle $(i = 1, \ldots, n; j = 1, \ldots, n)$. Hence, S_j is the set of letters which might possibly appear in the jth column of any new row which is adjoined.

It is easy to check that $|S_j| = n - r$ $(j = 1, \ldots, n)$, and that each letter i appears in exactly $n - r$ of the S_j's. As above, let A be the incidence matrix of the objects $1, 2, \ldots, n$ in the sets $S_1, \ldots, S_n$. Then A is an $n \times n$ matrix of 0's and 1's which has exactly $n - r$ 1's in each row and column. The permanent of A is equal to the number of systems of distinct representations of the family of sets $S_1, \ldots, S_n$, and each system of distinct representations is a way of adjoining a new row. Hence, per(A) is equal to the number of possible extensions. This idea can be used, for example, to prove that an extension is *always* possible. This is so because the permanent of a matrix of nonnegative entries, with constant nonzero row and column sums, is always strictly positive. Thus per $A > 0$ and an extension always exists.

Because of such applications as the above, great interest attaches to the question of estimating the size of the permanent of a square nonnegative matrix in terms of its row and column sums. First, if the entries of A are 0's and 1's, then a conjecture ‡ of Ryser and Minc holds that

$$(8) \qquad \text{per}(A) \leq \prod_{j=1}^{n} (r_j!)^{1/r_j}$$

where r_j is the number of 1's in the jth row of A. If true, (8) would be the best possible. Nijenhuis and Wilf have shown that

$$(9) \qquad \text{per}(A) \leq \prod_{j=1}^{n} \{(r_j!)^{1/r_j} + \tau\}$$

where $\tau = 0.14 \cdots$ is a universal constant.

‡ *Note added in proof:* This has recently been proved by L. M. Bregman, *Dokl. Akad. Nauk. SSSR* **211** (1973), No. 1; *Soviet Math. Dokl.* **14** (1973), 945–949.

In the other direction, if $a_{ij} \geqq 0$ $(i, j = 1, \ldots, n)$ and

(10)
$$\sum_{j=1}^{n} a_{ij} = 1 \quad (i = 1, \ldots, n)$$

$$\sum_{i=1}^{n} a_{ij} = 1 \quad (j = 1, \ldots, n)$$

then an unproven conjecture of van der Waerden states that

(11)
$$\operatorname{per}(A) \geqq \frac{n!}{n^n}$$

which, if true, would also be the best possible.

Observe, for instance, that if (8) were known to be true, then by the construction outlined above we would have at *most*

$$(n - r)!^{n/(n-r)}$$

extensions of an r-rowed Latin rectangle to an $(r + 1)$-rowed one. On the other hand, if (11) were true, then by dividing our incidence matrix by $n - r$, we would satisfy (10) and thereby learn that a Latin rectangle has at *least*

$$(n - r)^n n! / n^n$$

extensions to one of order $r + 1$. The number L_n of $n \times n$ Latin *squares* would then satisfy

(12)
$$\left\{ \prod_{\nu=1}^{n-1} \nu!^{1/\nu} \right\}^n \geqq L_n \geqq \frac{n!^{2n-1}}{n^{n^2}}$$

which would be an improvement over known bounds.

COMPUTATION OF THE PERMANENT FUNCTION

Observe that a direct application of (3) to an $n \times n$ matrix would require about $n \cdot n!$ operations for the calculation of $\operatorname{per}(A)$. We reduce this labor in three steps.

(1) A method due to Ryser evaluates $\operatorname{per}(A)$ in about $n^2 2^{n-1}$ operations. It requires an average of $n^2/2$ calculations for each of the 2^n subsets of $\{1, 2, \ldots, n\}$. Ryser's method is derived below and appears in Eqs. (17) and (18).

(2) We reduce the above by a factor of 2 by a method which makes it necessary to process only the subsets of $\{1, 2, \ldots, n - 1\}$.

Thus in Eq. (24) we do about $n^2/2$ calculations for each of the 2^{n-1} subsets of $\{1, 2, \ldots, n-1\}$, or $(n^2/4)\, 2^n$ operations altogether.

(3) A further reduction by a factor of $n/2$ is accomplished by arranging the sequence of subsets so as to follow a Hamilton walk on an $(n-1)$-cube (see Chapter 1). If this is done, only a slight change in the calculation for a set S will yield the result of the calculation for the successor of S. In this way, our final algorithm PERMAN does about n calculations for each of the 2^{n-1} subsets of $\{1, 2, \ldots, n-1\}$, for a total of $n2^{n-1}$ operations (multiplication and addition) to compute the permanent of an $n \times n$ matrix.

We first describe Ryser's formula. Suppose, for the moment, that A is an $n \times m$ matrix; let $f: \{1, \ldots, n\} \to \{1, \ldots, m\}$ denote a mapping, and let the *weight* of f be

$$(13) \qquad w(f) = \prod_{i=1}^{n} a_{i, f(i)}$$

for each of the n^m mappings f. Then we can define the permanent of such a rectangular matrix by

$$(14) \qquad \mathrm{per}(A) = \sum_{f}{}' w(f)$$

where the prime indicates that the sum is over only whose f such that

$$\forall j \in \{1, \ldots, m\} : f^{-1}(j) \neq \varnothing$$

Note that if $m > n$, $\mathrm{per}(A) = 0$.

Now consider the n^m objects as our mappings f, and let the jth property of one of these objects be

$$P_j : f^{-1}(j) = \phi \quad (j = 1, \ldots, m)$$

Then by the principle of inclusion–exclusion, the total weight of those objects which have none of the properties is

$$(15) \qquad \mathrm{per}\, A = \sum_{T} (-1)^{|T|} N(T)$$

where T runs over all subsets of properties, and $N(T)$ is the weight of those objects which have the set T of properties. But the weight $N(T)$ of those objects is

$$(16) \qquad N(T) = \prod_{i=1}^{n} \left\{ \sum_{j \in T^c} a_{ij} \right\}$$

since the weight of every mapping with properties T occurs once in the expansion of the right-hand side. If we substitute (16) into (15), we find

$$\text{per}(A) = \sum_T (-1)^{|T|} \prod_{i=1}^n \left\{ \sum_{j \in T^c} a_{ij} \right\}$$

and, finally, if we sum over $S = T^c$, instead of T,

(17)
$$\text{per } A = (-1)^n \sum_S (-1)^{|S|} \sigma_S$$

where

(18)
$$\sigma_S = \prod_{i=1}^n \sum_{j \in S} a_{ij}$$

(17) is Ryser's formula. We observe that (17) requires about $2^n \cdot (n^2/2)$ operations for the computation of the permanent.

A variation which saves half of the labor will now be described. Suppose A is $n \times n$. Adjoin to A a new column $[x_1, x_2, \ldots, x_n]^T$, obtaining an $n \times (n + 1)$ matrix A', and number the columns $0, 1, 2, \ldots, n$. If we apply (17) to A', we obtain

(19) $\quad 0 = -\text{per } A' = (-1)^n \sum_{S'} (-1)^{|S'|} \sigma_{S'} + (-1)^n \sum_{S''} (-1)^{|S''|} \sigma_{S''}$

where S' and S'' run, respectively, through all the subsets of $\{0, 1, \ldots, n\}$ which do (respectively, do not) contain 0. Hence

(20)
$$0 = (-1)^n \sum_{S'} (-1)^{|S'|} \sigma_{S'} + \text{per } A$$

But

(21)
$$\sigma_{S'} = \prod_{i=1}^n \left\{ x_i + \sum_{j \in S'} a_{ij} \right\}$$

Let $(S')^c$ be the complementary set of $(S' - \{0\})$. Then

(22)
$$\sigma_{(S')^c} = \prod_{i=1}^n \left[x_i + \left(\sum_{j=1}^n a_{ij} \right) - \sum_{\substack{j \neq 0 \\ j \in S'}} a_{ij} \right]$$
$$= \prod_{i=1}^n \left[x_i + r_i - \sum_{\substack{j \neq 0 \\ j \in S'}} a_{ij} \right]$$

where r_i is the ith-row sum of A. Now choose $x_i = -\frac{1}{2} r_i$. Then

(23)
$$\sigma_{(S')^c} = (-1)^n \sigma_{S'}$$

and the contributions of S' and $(S')^c$ to the sum in (20) are equal. We can, for example, compute only the terms in the sum (20) corresponding to S' which contain both 0 and n, and double the result.

Ryser's method, together with this modification, can be summarized as

$$(24a) \qquad x_i = a_{i,n} - \frac{1}{2} \sum_{j=1}^{n} a_{ij} \quad (i = 1, \ldots, n)$$

$$(24b) \quad \mathrm{per}(A) = (-1)^{n-1} 2 \sum_{S}'' (-1)^{|S|} \prod_{i=1}^{n} \left\{ x_i + \sum_{j \in S} a_{ij} \right\}$$

where S runs only over the subsets of $1, 2, \ldots, n-1$.

To save our final factor of $n/2$ in the amount of computation required, observe that for each subset $S \subseteq \{1, 2, \ldots, n-1\}$ we have to calculate

$$(25) \qquad\qquad f(S) = \prod_{i=1}^{n} \lambda_i(S)$$

where

$$(26) \qquad \lambda_i(S) = x_i + \sum_{j \in S} a_{ij} \quad (i = 1, \ldots, n)$$

Suppose that our current subset S differs from its predecessor S' by a single element, j. Then

$$(27) \qquad \lambda_i(S) = \lambda_i(S') \pm a_{ij} \quad (i = 1, \ldots, n)$$

Thus, instead of requiring $n(|S| + 1)$ operations to compute $\lambda_1, \ldots, \lambda_n$ in (26), we can find them in just n operations by (27). The key to the saving is, then, generating the subsets of $1, 2, \ldots, n-1$ in such a sequence that each set S differs from its predecessor only in a single element. In Chapter 1, this question was discussed in detail, and we produced Algorithm NEXSUB for doing the generation of the subsets. Hence in our present problem, Algorithm PERMAN will simply call NEXSUB to get its next subset of $1, \ldots, n-1$, calculate the λ_i as in (27), $f(S)$ as in (25), and per A from (24). The program is very short, just 26 instructions.

The question of significant digits merits some attention. It is characteristic of inclusion–exclusion calculations that the terms get larger for a while (as $|S|$ increases) then smaller, that there is a good deal of cancellation between terms, and that the final answer may be much smaller than many of the individual terms in the sum. It is tempting to consider using integer arithmetic when calculating with an integer matrix. Yet, in the present situation, one may find that even though per(A) is small enough to fit comfortably into an integer word, intermediate quantities in the calculation may overflow. For these reasons our program is in double-precision mode.

ALGORITHM PERMAN

(**A**) $p \leftarrow 0$; $x_i \leftarrow a_{in} - \dfrac{1}{2} \sum\limits_{j=1}^{n} a_{ij}\ (i = 1, n)$; sgn $\leftarrow -1$.

(**B**) sgn $\leftarrow -$sgn; $P \leftarrow$ sgn; Get next subset of $\{1, 2, \ldots, n-1\}$ from NEXSUB (see Chapter 1); If empty, to (**C**); If j was deleted, $z \leftarrow -1$; Otherwise, $z \leftarrow 1$; $x_i \leftarrow x_i + za_{ij}\ (i = 1, n)$.

(**C**) $P \leftarrow P \cdot x_i\ (i = 1, n)$; $p \leftarrow p + P$; If more subsets remain, to (**B**); Permanent $\leftarrow 2(-1)^{n-1}p$; Exit ■

SUBROUTINE SPECIFICATIONS

(1) *Name of subroutine:* PERMAN.
(2) *Calling statement:* CALL PERMAN(N,A,IN,X,PERMN).
(3) *Purpose of subroutine:* Calculate permanent of square matrix.
(4) *Descriptions of variables in calling statement:*

Name	Type	I/O/W/B	Description
N	INTEGER	I	Size of input matrix.
A	DOUBLE PRECISION(N,N)	I	A(I,J) is the I,J entry of the input matrix.
IN	INTEGER(N)	W	Working storage.
X	DOUBLE PRECISION(N)	W	Working storage.
PERMN	DOUBLE PRECISION	O	Calculated value of the permanent of A.

(5) *Other routines which are called by this one:* NEXSUB.
(6) *Approximate number of* FORTRAN *instructions:* 26.
(7) *Remarks:* Will not work correctly in integer arithmetic by merely changing type declarations.

```
SUBROUTINE PERMAN(N,A,IN,X,PERM)
IMPLICIT DOUBLE PRECISION(A-H,O-Z)
LOGICAL MTC
DIMENSION A(N,N),IN(N),X(N)
```

```
10   P=0
     N1=N-1
     DO 11   I=1,N
     SUM=0
     DO 15   J=1,N
15   SUM=SUM+A(I,J)
11   X(I)=A(I,N)-SUM/2.DO
     SGN=-1
20   SGN=-SGN
     PROD=SGN
30   CALL NEXSUB(N1,IN,MTC,NCARD,J)
     IF(NCARD.EQ.0) GO TO 38
     Z=2*IN(J)-1
     DO 35   I=1,N
35   X(I)=X(I)+Z*A(I,J)
38   DO 39   I=1,N
39   PROD=PROD*X(I)
     P=P+PROD
     IF(MTC) GO TO 20
40   PERM=2.*(2*MOD(N,2)-1)*P
     RETURN
     END
```

SAMPLE OUTPUT

For each $n = 2, 3, \ldots, 12$, PERMAN was asked for the permanent of the $n \times n$ matrix of diagonal 0's and off-diagonal 1's. The output is reproduced below.

```
2     0.10000000D+01
3     0.20000000D+01
4     0.90000000D+01
5     0.44000000D+02
6     0.26500000D+03
7     0.18540000D+04
8     0.14833000D+05
9     0.13349600D+06
10    0.13349610D+07
11    0.14684570D+08
12    0.17621484D+09
```

20

Invert a Triangular Array (INVERT)

This little routine is combinatorial only in its proposed use. In fact it is simple linear algebra. We suppose that there is given an $n \times n$ matrix A which has 1's on the main diagonal and 0's below the main diagonal. If b_{ij} ($i, j = 1, n$) are the entries of A^{-1}, then it is simple to verify that

$$(1) \qquad b_{ij} = \begin{cases} -\sum\limits_{i < k \leq j} a_{ik}b_{kj} & (i < j) \\ 1 & (i = j) \\ 0 & (i > j) \end{cases}$$

We have, then, a simple recurrence formula for calculating the b_{ij} in the following order

$$b_{jj}, \; b_{j-1,j}, \; b_{j-2,j}, \; \ldots, \; b_{1,j} \quad (j = n, \ldots, 1)$$

The computation is so straightforward that we omit the flow chart and its discussion. It is important to notice that the columns are processed in reverse order to permit storage of A and A^{-1} in the same memory space if desired.

ALGORITHM INVERT

(A) $b_{ii} \leftarrow 1$ ($i = 1, n$).

(B) $(b_{ij} \leftarrow -\sum\limits_{i<k\leq j} a_{ik}b_{kj}, \; (i = j-1, \; j-2, \ldots, 1), \; j = n, \ldots, 2)$;

Exit ■

SUBROUTINE SPECIFICATIONS

(1) *Name of subroutine:* INVERT.
(2) *Calling statement:* CALL INVERT(A,AINV,N).
(3) *Purpose of subroutine:* Invert upper triangular matrix.
(4) *Descriptions of variables in calling statement:*

Name	Type	I/O/W/B	Description
A	INTEGER(N,N)	I	Input array.
AINV	INTEGER(N,N)	O	Output, inverse of A.
N	INTEGER	I	Size of A.

(5) *Other routines which are called by this one:* None.
(6) *Approximate number of* FORTRAN *instructions:* 17.
(7) *Remarks:* If this subroutine is called with AINV=A, then the matrix A will be correctly inverted *in place.*

```
      SUBROUTINE INVERT (N,A,AINV)
      IMPLICIT INTEGER(A-Z)
      DIMENSION A(N,N),AINV(N,N)
      J=N
10    I=N
20    SUM=0
      IF (I.EQ.J) SUM=1
      K=I+1
25    IF (K.GT.J) GO TO 30
      SUM=SUM-A(I,K)*AINV(K,J)
      K=K+1
      GO TO 25
30    AINV (I,J)=SUM
      I=I-1
      IF (I.GT.0) GO TO 20
      J=J-1
      IF (J.GT.0) GO TO 10
      RETURN
      END
```

21

Triangular Numbering in Partially Ordered Sets (TRIANG)

Let $\mathscr{P}$ be a finite partially ordered set, say

$$\mathscr{P} = \{1, 2, \ldots, n\}$$

and let $\leqslant$ be the partial-order relation defined on $\mathscr{P}$. By the *zeta matrix* of $\mathscr{P}$ we mean the incidence matrix ζ of the relation $\leqslant$ i.e.,

(1)
$$\zeta_{ij} = \begin{bmatrix} 1 & \text{if} & i \leqslant j \\ 0 & \text{otherwise} \end{bmatrix}$$

We claim that it is always possible to renumber the rows and columns of ζ (i.e., relabel the elements of $\mathscr{P}$) in such a way that ζ becomes an upper-triangular matrix. In terms of the original partially ordered set $\mathscr{P}$, we are claiming that there is a permutation

$$\sigma: \{1, \ldots, n\} \to \{1, \ldots, n\}$$

such that

(2)
$$\sigma^{-1}(i) \leqslant \sigma^{-1}(j) \Rightarrow i \leq j \quad (i, j = 1, \ldots, n)$$

where the $\leq$ on the right side of (2) is the natural order of the positive integers. Such renumbering will be used in Chapter 22 to construct the Möbius function and is useful in many combinatorial situations where computation must be sequenced consistently with some natural partial order in the problem.

We prove the claim by describing an algorithm which accomplishes the desired renumbering. Choose an element $x \in \mathscr{P}$. If there is no $y \prec x$ ($y \in \mathscr{P}$), then assign to x the next available label. If there is such a y, replace x by y and repeat. Since $\mathscr{P}$ is finite, we surely will reach an element with no predecessor after a finite number of steps.

As is so often the case, the most obvious algorithm is not the best one.‡ In the algorithm described above, we descend a chain in the partial-order relation until we reach a minimal element. Next we search for a new unlabeled element and repeat the process. However, we have lost a good deal of useful information because the element which preceded the minimal element just labeled is a better place to start the search for the next element to label. This is so because we would thereby start lower down in the partially ordered set and would be nearer to our next minimal element.

To recover this information we must make better use of our array σ_i ($i = 1, n$) which carries the labels of the points. This array is set to zero initially, and if a point is labeled, then σ_i carries the label. However, we will now put σ_i to work at intermediate stages also. Precisely, as we go down a chain $i_1 \succ i_2 \succ \cdots \succ i_{\mu-1} \succ i_\mu$ we write in each σ_{i_k} its predecessor i_{k-1} ($k = 2, \mu$). Then, when we reach i_μ, we save σ_{i_μ} temporarily, in q, say, insert the label of i_μ into σ_{i_μ}, and then resume the search at q.

If q is zero then we have just labeled a point which was the largest element i_1 in some chain of $\mathscr{P}$, all of whose elements are now labeled. Therefore, we resume our search for the next unlabeled point at $1 + i_1$. If q is not zero, then q is indeed the predecessor of the point which was just labeled, and we climb down a chain hanging below q. The nature of the numbering process is such that when we are searching below q to find a minimal element, the search can begin at the next integer larger than the last i below q which was labeled. If we begin the search below q, we may start at $i_1 + 1$ because all points before i_1 have already been labeled.

We give below the formal algorithm which describes the process in detail. This algorithm is designed so that the partial-order relation can be described on input by its full zeta matrix, or else by just the matrix of its covering relation, or more generally, by any matrix

‡ One considerably more efficient method for this problem, called "topological sorting," appears in [K1, Vol. 1, p. 262]. It is assumed there that the input is given as a set of related ordered pairs. For our purposes we need a square incidence matrix of input.

whose (i, j) entry is nonzero if j covers i and 0 if $j \prec i$. In fact, if one is assured that the full zeta matrix will be used for input, then certain further economies become possible: In step (**B**) we can delete "$t \leftarrow m + 1$," and step (**C**) can be replaced by "$r \leftarrow m + 1$" which will start the searches lower down in the structure.

ALGORITHM TRIANG

(**A**) $m \leftarrow 0; l \leftarrow 0; \sigma_i \leftarrow 0 \ (i = 1, n)$.

(**B**)   [*To next unlabeled*] $m \leftarrow m + 1$; If $\sigma_m \neq 0$, to (**E**); $t \leftarrow m + 1$.

(**C**)   [*Start climb down*] $r \leftarrow t$.

(**D**)   If $r \leq n$, to (**F**); [*Label m*] $l \leftarrow l + 1$; $q \leftarrow \sigma_m$; $\sigma_m \leftarrow l$; [*Climb up to predecessor*] If $q = 0$, to (**E**); $r \leftarrow m + 1$; $m \leftarrow q$; To (**D**).

(**E**)   [*Done?*] If $m = n$, exit; To (**B**).

(**F**)   [*Is r an unlabeled element below m?*] If $\sigma_r \neq 0$ or $\zeta(r, m) \neq 1$, set $r \leftarrow r + 1$ and return to (**D**); [*Go down from m to r*] $\sigma_r \leftarrow m$; $m \leftarrow r$; To (**C**) ∎

SUBROUTINE SPECIFICATIONS

(1)   *Name of subroutine:*   TRIANG.

(2)   *Calling statement:*   CALL TRIANG(N,ZETA,SIG).

(3)   *Purpose of subroutine:*   Discover consistent labeling of elements of partially ordered set.

(4)   *Descriptions of variables in calling statement:*

Name	Type	I/O/W/B	Description
N	INTEGER	I	Number of elements in partially ordered set.
ZETA	INTEGER(N,N)	I	ZETA(I,J)=1 if I≼J, 0 otherwise
SIG	INTEGER(N)	O	SIG(I) is the new label assigned to I ($1 \leq SIG(I) \leq N; 1 \leq I \leq N$)

(5)   *Other routines which are called by this one:*   None.

(6)   *Approximate number of* FORTRAN *instructions:*   20.

(7)   *Remarks:* Input matrix can be any matrix which generates the partial order.

```
      SUBROUTINE TRIANG(N,ZETA,SIG)
      IMPLICIT INTEGER(A-Z)
      DIMENSION SIG(N), ZETA(N,N)
10    M=0
      L=0
      DO 11 I=1,N
11    SIG(I)=0
20    M=M+1
30    IF (SIG(M).EQ.0) GO TO 40
130   IF (M.EQ.N) RETURN
      GO TO 20
40    T=M+1
50    R=T
60    IF (R.GT.N) GO TO 100
70    IF (SIG(R).NE.0.OR.ZETA(R,M).EQ.0) GO TO 90
80    SIG(R)=M
      M=R
      GO TO 50
90    R=R+1
      GO TO 60
100   L=L+1
      Q=SIG(M)
      SIG(M)=L
110   IF (Q.EQ.0) GO TO 130
      R=M+1
120   M=Q
      GO TO 60
      END
```

SAMPLE OUTPUT

The partially ordered set in our example is the set of divisors of 48 ordered by divisibility. The divisors are arranged, on input, in the order

$$16, \quad 3, \quad 8, \quad 24, \quad 1, \quad 6, \quad 2, \quad 12, \quad 48, \quad 4$$

The zeta matrix corresponding to this input ordering is shown as the following 10×10 array. The output permutation σ, which also follows, rearranges the divisors in the order

$$1, \quad 2, \quad 4, \quad 8, \quad 16, \quad 3, \quad 6, \quad 12, \quad 24, \quad 48$$

in which the zeta matrix is triangular.

```
1  0  0  0  0  0  0  0  1  0
0  1  0  0  0  1  0  1  1  0
1  0  1  1  0  0  0  0  1  0
0  0  0  1  0  0  0  0  1  0
1  1  1  1  1  1  1  1  1  1
0  0  0  1  0  1  0  1  1  0
1  0  1  1  0  1  1  1  1  1
0  0  0  1  0  0  0  1  1  0
0  0  0  0  0  0  0  0  1  0
1  0  1  1  0  0  0  1  1  1

5  6  4  9  1  7  2  8  10  3
```

22

The Möbius Function (MOBIUS)

Let $\mathscr{P}$ be a partially ordered set, and let f be a function defined on $\mathscr{P}$ to the real numbers. Then we can define a new function g on $\mathscr{P}$ by

$$(1) \qquad g(x) = \sum_{y \preccurlyeq x} f(y) \quad (x \in \mathscr{P})$$

As we noted in Chapter 21, if $\mathscr{P}$ contains a 0 element and is locally finite (which we henceforth assume), then the sum in (1) has only a finite number of terms in it for each $x \in \mathscr{P}$. We can rewrite (1) as

$$(2) \qquad g(x) = \sum_{y} \zeta_{x,y} f(y) \quad (x \in \mathscr{P})$$

where the sum is now over all $y \in \mathscr{P}$, and ζ is the zeta function (see Chapter 21) of $\mathscr{P}$. In simple vector–matrix form we could write (2) as

$$(3) \qquad g = \zeta f$$

We now ask how to invert the relation (1). That is, if $g(x)$ is given, for all $x \in \mathscr{P}$, how can we find $f(x)$ $(x \in \mathscr{P})$ such that (1) is true? The importance of this question rests on the fact that in many combinatorial situations where we want f, f and g are related by (1), and g is relatively easy to find.

Now (3) suggests that the inverse relation is

$$(4) \qquad f = \zeta^{-1} g$$

provided ζ has an inverse. Our discussion in Chapter 21, however, showed that, under the present hypotheses, the elements of $\mathscr{P}$ can be relabeled so that ζ is upper-triangular with 1's on the diagonal. Such a matrix can always be inverted (see Chapter 20).

The *Möbius function* $\mu(x, y)$ $(x, y \in \mathscr{P})$ is defined as the inverse of the zeta function $\zeta_{x,y}$ $(x, y \in \mathscr{P})$ of $\mathscr{P}$. Our problem in this chapter concerns the efficient computation of $\mu(x, y)$ for a "given" set $\mathscr{P}$.

First we ask for an efficient way to describe the given set $\mathscr{P}$. Certainly the zeta matrix completely describes $\mathscr{P}$. On the other hand, it contains a good deal of redundant information. If we are told, for example, that $\zeta_{1,3} = 1$ and $\zeta_{3,7} = 1$, we do not need to be told that $\zeta_{1,7} = 1$ since that follows from the transitivity of the $\leqslant$ relation.

To describe a more economical method, we define the "covering" relation. We say that, in a partially ordered set $\mathscr{P}$, b *covers* a, written a c b, if

(i) $a \prec b$

and

(ii)   there is no $z \in \mathscr{P}$ such that $a \prec z \prec b$.

We denote by $H(x, y)$ the incidence matrix of the covering relation

$$H(x, y) = \begin{cases} 1 & \text{if } x \text{ c } y \\ 0 & \text{otherwise} \end{cases}$$

The H matrix describes the complete partial-order relation in $\mathscr{P}$, for if $x \alpha y$, then there is a chain

$$x \text{ c } x_1 \text{ c } x_2 \text{ c } \cdots \text{ c } x_p \text{ c } y$$

in which each element is covered by its successor joining x to y. By finding the totality of such chains, we can therefore deduce the totality of relations $x \prec y$, and thereby find the full zeta matrix from its "skeleton" H.

Let us describe this process more formally. Let $\mathscr{P}$ be a finite partially ordered set. Then

$$H^2(x, y) = \sum_z H(x, z) H(z, y)$$

according to the rules of matrix multiplication. A term on the right side is 0 unless z covers x and is covered by y. The sum therefore counts the number of maximal chains of length 2 (Fig. 22.1) which join x to y. Similarly, $H^k(x, y)$ counts the number of maximal chains of length k

Fig. 22.1

$$x \text{ c } z_1 \text{ c } z_2 \text{ c } \cdots \text{ c } z_{k-1} \text{ c } y$$

which join x to y, in which each element is covered by its successor.

Now if $x \prec y$ in $\mathscr{P}$, there surely is a chain of *some* length which joins x to y, with each element covered by its successor. Hence, at least one of the numbers

$$H^k(x, y) \quad (k = 1, 2, 3, \ldots)$$

must be positive. Since the others are nonnegative, it follows that

(5) $$H(x, y) + H^2(x, y) + H^3(x, y) + \cdots$$

will have positive entries precisely where $x \prec y$, or, equivalently,

(6) $$\delta(x, y) + H(x, y) + H^2(x, y) + \cdots$$

has positive entries precisely where $x \leqslant y$ (δ is the Kronecker delta).

The apparently infinite series (6) actually terminates. Indeed, since $\mathscr{P}$ is finite, there is only a finite number of different covering chains in $\mathscr{P}$, and if N is the length of the largest one, then $H^m(x, y) = 0$ for all $m > N$ and all $(x, y) \in \mathscr{P}$. The series (6) therefore represents $(I - H)^{-1}$, where I is the identity matrix, and we have shown the

Proposition *In a finite partially ordered set $\mathscr{P}$ with covering matrix H, we have $x \leqslant y$ if and only if*

(7) $$(I - H)^{-1}_{x, y} > 0$$

This relation remains true if H is any nonnegative matrix which generates the partial order.

More precisely, this proposition is true if we have only

(a) $\quad\quad\quad H_{x, y} = 0 \quad$ when $\quad x \leqslant y$ is false
(b) $\quad\quad\quad H_{x, y} > 0 \quad$ when $\quad x \text{ c } y$
(c) $\quad\quad\quad H_{x, y} \geqq 0 \quad$ always

For notational convenience, let us define for any matrix Q of nonnegative entries a new matrix $\psi(Q)$ according to

(8) $$\psi(Q)_{i, j} = \begin{cases} 1 & \text{if } Q_{i, j} > 0 \\ 0 & \text{if } Q_{i, j} = 0 \end{cases}$$

According to the proposition above, then, the zeta matrix of a finite partially ordered set can be generated from the covering matrix H by means of the relation

$$(9) \qquad \zeta = \psi((I - H)^{-1})$$

Finally, the Möbius function μ is the inverse of ζ, and so it can be obtained from the covering matrix by

$$(10) \qquad \mu = \psi((I - H)^{-1})^{-1}$$

The covering matrix H can be obtained from the zeta matrix in a similar manner because $x \, c \, y$ if and only if there is precisely one chain

$$x = x_0 \prec x_1 \prec \cdots \prec x_p = y$$

In that case, p must be 1. It is easily seen that the (i, j) entry in

$$(\zeta - I) + (\zeta - I)^2 + \cdots$$

counts the number of chains from i to j.

Define for any matrix Q a new matrix $\omega(Q)$ according to

$$\omega(Q)_{i,j} = \begin{cases} 1 & \text{if } i \neq j \text{ and } Q_{i,j} = 1 \\ 0 & \text{otherwise} \end{cases}$$

then we have

$$H = \omega((2I - \zeta)^{-1})$$

We hereby summarize the calculation. Beginning with the incidence matrix H of the a covers b relation, we perform the following operations:

(1) Find the permutation SIGMA such that when the rows and columns of H are renumbered according to SIGMA, H becomes triangular (use subroutine TRIANG, Chapter 21).

(2) Apply the permutation SIGMA to the rows and columns of H (use subroutine RENUMB, Chapter 13).

(3) Invert $I - H$ (use subroutine INVERT, Chapter 20).

(4) Replace all nonzero elements by 1's, yielding the zeta matrix of the partial order.

(5) Invert the resulting matrix (use subroutine. INVERT,

Chapter 20). This gives the Möbius function MU but according to the renumbering SIGMA.

(6) Find the inverse permutation SIG1 of SIGMA. Renumber the rows and columns of MU according to SIG1 (use subroutine RENUMB, Chapter 13). We now have the Möbius matrix MU consistent with the initial ordering of the rows and columns of H. Output MU. Exit.

Another procedure for doing the above would be to ignore the renumbering and simply invert the matrices as they are. If this were done, we would need to use general matrix inversion programs because the triangularity would no longer be exploited. Thus, instead of INVERT, which requires $\frac{1}{6}n^3 + O(n^2)$ operations to invert a triangular matrix, we would use a program which, at best, might need $\frac{1}{2}n^3$ operations plus the inconvenience of dealing with real numbers, or three times the computational effort. The cost of triangularizing, renumbering, and unrenumbering is $O(n^2)$, which gives an economic advantage to the procedure outlined above.

An additional noteworthy feature is that the entire calculation can be done with just one integer matrix array because each matrix can be written over its predecessor.

SUBROUTINE SPECIFICATIONS

(1) *Name of subroutine:* MOBIUS.

(2) *Calling statement:* CALL MOBIUS(N,H,MU,SIGMA,SIG1).

(3) *Purpose of subroutine:* Find Möbius matrix from covering relation.

(4) *Descriptions of variables in calling statement:*

Name	Type	I/O/W/B	Description
N	INTEGER	*I*	Number of elements in partially ordered set P.
H	INTEGER(N,N)	*I*	H(I,J)=1 if I is covered by J, 0 otherwise (I,J=1,N).
MU	INTEGER(N,N)	*O*	MU(I,J) is Möbius matrix element (I,J=1,N).
SIGMA	INTEGER(N)	*W*	Working storage.
SIG1	INTEGER(N)	*W*	Working storage.

(5) *Other routines which are called by this one:* TRIANG, RENUMB, INVERT.

(6) *Approximate number of* FORTRAN *instructions:* 20.

(7) *Remarks:* If called with MU and H being the same array, the correct output will be obtained, and the input H will of course be lost. Then the routine requires only a single square integer array of storage.

```
     SUBROUTINE MOBIUS(N,H,MU,SIGMA,SIG1)
     IMPLICIT INTEGER(A-Z)
     DIMENSION H(N,N),SIGMA(N),MU(N,N),SIG1(N)
     CALL TRIANG(N,H,SIGMA)
     DO 1 I=1,N
     DO 1 J=1,N
1    MU(I,J)=H(I,J)
     CALL RENUMB(N,N,SIGMA,SIGMA,MU)
     N1=N-1
     DO 11  I=1,N1
     J1=I+1
     DO 11  J=J1,N
11   MU(I,J)=-MU(I,J)
     CALL INVERT(MU,MU,N)
     DO 12  I=1,N
     DO 12  J=I,N
12   IF(MU(I,J).NE.0)MU(I,J)=1
     CALL INVERT (MU,MU,N)
     DO 20  I=1,N
20   SIG1(SIGMA(I))=I
     CALL RENUMB(N,N,SIG1,SIG1,MU)
     RETURN
     END
```

SAMPLE OUTPUT

On the following page we show the input H matrix and the output μ matrix in the case of the set of partitions of the integer 6, partially ordered by refinement. The order is: (1) $4 + 1 + 1$, (2) $2 + 1 + 1 + 1 + 1$, (3) $3 + 1 + 1 + 1$, (4) $2 + 2 + 1 + 1$, (5) $2 + 2 + 2$, (6) $4 + 2$, (7) 6, (8) $1 + 1 + 1 + 1 + 1 + 1$, (9) $3 + 2 + 1$, (10) $5 + 1$, (11) $3 + 3$.

For example,

$$\mu(2 + 2 + 1 + 1, 4 + 2) = 2 = \mu(3 + 2 + 1, 6)$$

and all other entries of the μ matrix are at most 1, in absolute value.

0	0	0	0	0	1	0	0	0	1	0
0	0	1	1	0	0	0	0	0	0	0
1	0	0	0	0	0	0	0	1	0	0
1	0	0	0	1	0	0	0	1	0	0
0	0	0	0	0	1	0	0	0	0	0
0	0	0	0	0	0	1	0	0	0	0
0	0	0	0	0	0	0	0	0	0	0
0	1	0	0	0	0	0	0	0	0	0
0	0	0	0	0	1	0	0	0	1	1
0	0	0	0	0	0	1	0	0	0	0
0	0	0	0	0	0	1	0	0	0	0

1	0	0	0	0	-1	1	0	0	-1	0
1	1	-1	-1	0	-1	1	0	1	-1	0
-1	0	1	0	0	1	-1	0	-1	1	0
-1	0	0	1	-1	2	-1	0	-1	1	0
0	0	0	0	1	-1	0	0	0	0	0
0	0	0	0	0	-1	1	0	0	0	0
0	0	0	0	0	0	1	0	0	0	0
0	-1	0	0	0	0	0	1	0	0	0
0	0	0	0	0	-1	2	0	1	-1	-1
0	0	0	0	0	0	-1	0	0	1	0
0	0	0	0	0	0	-1	0	0	0	1

23

The Backtrack Method (BACKTR)

(A) GENERAL (BACKTR)

The backtrack method is a reasonable approach to use on problems of exhaustive search when all possibilities must be enumerated or processed. The precise mathematical setting is that we are required to find all vectors

$$(a_1, a_2, \ldots, a_l)$$

of given length l, whose entries $a_1, \ldots, a_l$ satisfy a certain condition $\mathscr{C}$. In the most naive approach, we might first make a list of all possible vectors whose entries a_i lie within the range of the problem; then, from this list we could strike out all vectors which do not satisfy our condition $\mathscr{C}$.

In the backtrack procedure, we "grow" the vector from left to right, and we test at each stage to see if our partially constructed vector has any chance to be extended to a vector which satisfies $\mathscr{C}$. If not, we immediately reject the partial vector, and go to the next one, thereby saving the effort of constructing the descendants of a clearly unsuitable partial vector.

Thus, at the kth stage ($k = 1, l$), we have before us a partial vector

$$(a_1, a_2, \ldots, a_{k-1})$$

which is not inconsistent with $\mathscr{C}$. We construct from it the list of all candidates for the kth position in our vector. To say that a particular element x is a candidate is just to say that the new partial vector

$$(a_1, a_2, \ldots, a_{k-1}, x)$$

does not yet show any irretrievable inconsistency with our condition $\mathscr{C}$.

If there are no candidates for the kth position, i.e., if for every x, the extended vector $(a_1, a_2, \ldots, a_{k-1}, x)$ is inconsistent with $\mathscr{C}$, we "backtrack" by reducing k by 1, deleting a_{k-1} from the list of candidates for position $k-1$, and choosing the new occupant of the $(k-1)$th position from the reduced list of candidates.

If and when we reach $k = l$, we exit with $a_1, \ldots, a_l$. Upon reentry, we delete a_l from the list of candidates for position l and proceed as before.

We now discuss the computer implementation of this procedure. Our aim is to split off the universal aspects of the backtrack method as a subroutine which will be useful in most, or all, applications, and to leave the part of the application which differs from one situation to the next to the user, as a program which he must prepare within certain guidelines. Our approach is that we suppose that the user wishes to prepare a program which will exhibit one vector at a time which satisfies his condition $\mathscr{C}$, and inform him when no more such vectors exist.

Although it would be simplest to have BACKTR produce one vector (or a negative message) on each call, we do not do so because such a program would have to (a) call the subroutine which provides the list of candidates for each position and hence know the name of this routine, and (b) pass along to this subroutine all the variables, arrays, dimensions, etc., that it needs to operate. These will differ from one application to another.

Instead, the method we have adopted involves the following principles (four examples follow in Sections (B)–(E) of this chapter, which should make the ideas much clearer):

(1) The complete calculation is carried out by three programs: MAIN, BACKTR, CANDTE, of which BACKTR is universal (and appears below) and the other two are prepared by the user.

(2) Communication between the programs is as shown in Fig. 23.1. Note that BACKTR and CANDTE do not speak to each other directly.

(3) MAIN receives input data from the "outside world," and asks BACKTR to inaugurate the search for complete vectors by calling

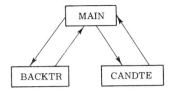

Figure 23.1

BACKTR with INDEX=0.

(4) When BACKTR needs a list of all candidates for the Kth component of the output vector, having already found $A(1),\ldots,A(K-1)$, it asks for this list by RETURN-ing to MAIN with INDEX=2.

(5) MAIN responds to this request by a call to CANDTE, telling CANDTE the value of K, the predecessors $A(1),\ldots A(K-1)$, and whatever auxiliary arrays are needed for the construction.

(6) CANDTE finds the list of candidates and places them at the end of a STACK, i.e., a linear array containing all candidates for all positions up to the Kth, along with a count of the candidates, which becomes the last word in the stack.

(7) MAIN tells BACKTR this information, and the search continues. When K=L, so that the search is successfully completed, BACKTR returns to MAIN with INDEX=1. If there are no more vectors of the type sought, the search terminates with a return to MAIN with INDEX=3.

The above description is a general one. Specific recipes for writing the two routines MAIN and CANDTE will now be given.

The structure of MAIN is as follows:

```
      . . .
      DIMENSION A(100), STACK(1000),...
         Obtain input data

      INDEX=0
1     CALL BACKTR(L,A,INDEX,K,M,STACK,NSTK)
      GO TO (10,20,30), INDEX
10    ⌠ Process output vector A(1),....,A(L)
      ⌡ but do not change it!
      GO TO 1
20    CALL CANDTE(A,K,M,STACK,...)
      GO TO 1
30    . . .
```

The variables and arrays mentioned play very precise roles:

L is the desired length of a complete output vector.

A is the output vector.

INDEX is explained above.

K is the length of a partially constructed vector: A call to CANDTE is a request for position A(K); K is set by BACKTR.

M is the location of the last item on the stack; it is changed by both BACKTR and CANDTE.

STACK is a linear array, of maximal length NSTK, whose appearance at a typical intermediate stage in the calculation is shown in Fig. 23.2.

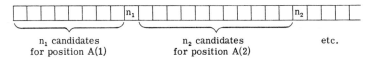

n_1 candidates for position A(1) n_2 candidates for position A(2)   etc.

Figure 23.2

More precisely, let the lists of candidates for A(1), ..., A(K−1), A(K) be stored in STACK, each list followed by its length. Let NC=STACK(M) be the last item on STACK. Then the items STACK(M−1), ..., STACK(M−NC) are the candidates for A(K), given the current values of A(1), ..., A(K−1). When one candidate is needed, NC=STACK(M) is examined; if it is zero, we set M←M−1, K←K−1, and repeat. Otherwise, we set M←M−1, A(K)← STACK(M), STACK(M)←NC−1. If K=L, we return A. Otherwise, we set K←K+1 and ask CANDTE to place the candidates for A(K) in locations M+1, ..., M+Q of STACK, to enter Q into STACK(M+Q+1), and to set M←M+Q+1. Then BACKTR takes over again.

From this discussion, the precise mission of CANDTE emerges, which we state as follows: *Given* K, A(1), ..., A(K−1), M. *Find all candidates for* A(K), *insert them in locations* M+1, ..., M+Q *of* STACK, *insert* Q *into* STACK(M+Q+1), *set* M←M+Q+1, *and return to* MAIN.

DESCRIPTION OF FLOW CHART

Box 10 Start a new sequence (or first sequence)?

Boxes 20, 30 Initialization to pass information to auxiliary routine.

Box 50 Read length NC of list of candidates for A(K) from stack.

Boxes 60, 70   If NC=0, backtrack to Box 70.

Boxes 80, 90   If K=0, list is complete, exit.

Box 100   Read A(K) from stack, reduce list count.

Boxes 110–130   Vector complete? Set K and INDEX accordingly; exit.

FLOW CHART BACKTR

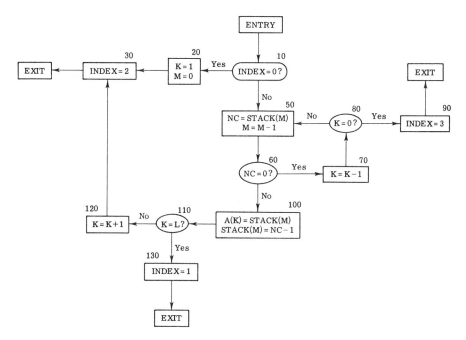

The relationship of backtracking to *random* selection is worth a few remarks. Suppose we have a backtrack situation in which we want a single random choice of an admissible vector, rather than a sequential search for all such vectors. Then, instead of choosing a particular candidate from the list of all possible candidates at the Kth stage, we might envision choosing one of the candidates at random from the list. Unfortunately, if the choice is made uniformly, then not all of the final objects will have equal a priori probability, in general.‡ Thus, this process will, at best, serve as an inadequate substitute for genuine random selection if nothing better suggests itself in a particular situation.

‡ In addition, if there are "few" admissible vectors but many partial vectors, the method may be hard put to find a single admissible vector!

SUBROUTINE SPECIFICATIONS

(1) *Name of subroutine:* BACKTR.

(2) *Calling statement:* CALL BACKTR(L,A,INDEX,K,M,STACK, NSTK).

(3) *Purpose of subroutine:* Supervise backtrack search.

(4) *Descriptions of variables in calling statement:*

Name	Type	I/O/W/B	Description
L	INTEGER	I	Length of completed vector.
A	INTEGER(L)	O	A(1),...,A(L) is an output vector.
INDEX	INTEGER	I/O	=0 to start a search; =1 with a complete output vector; =2 if candidates are needed; =3 if no more vectors exist.
K	INTEGER	I/O	Current length of partial vector.‡
M	INTEGER	I/O	Current length of STACK.‡
STACK	INTEGER(NSTK)	I/O	List‡ of candidates for positions 1,...,K.
NSTK	INTEGER	I	Maximum length of STACK.

‡ Input variables supplied by CANDTE routine.

(5) *Other routines which are called by this one:* None.

(6) *Approximate number of* FORTRAN *instructions:* 23.

```
        SUBROUTINE BACKTR(L,A,INDEX,K,M,STACK,NSTK)
        IMPLICIT INTEGER(A-Z)
        DIMENSION A(L),STACK(NSTK)
10      IF(INDEX.NE.0) GO to 50
20      K=1
        M=0
30      INDEX=2
        RETURN
50      NC=STACK(M)
        M=M-1
60      IF(NC.NE.0) GO TO 100
70      K=K-1
80      IF(K.NE.0) GO TO 50
90      INDEX=3
        RETURN
100     A(K)=STACK(M)
        STACK(M)=NC-1
110     IF(K.NE.L) GO TO 120
        INDEX=1
```

```
        RETURN
120     K=K+1
        GO TO 30
        END
```

(B) COLORING THE VERTICES OF A GRAPH
(COLVRT)

As our first application of backtracking, let G be a graph of n vertices, and let λ be a given positive integer. A proper coloring of the vertices of G in λ colors is an assignment of a color a_i $(1 \leq a_i \leq \lambda)$ to each vertex $i = 1, n$ in such a way that for each edge e of G, the two endpoints of e have different colors.

The vector

$$(a_1, a_2, \ldots, a_n)$$

will be the output of our backtrack program, and we will prepare, in this section, the subroutine CANDTE, in this case called COLVRT, which will cause all possible proper colorings of G in λ colors to be delivered sequentially.

We observed in the discussion of Section (A) that the key question for the user of BACKTR is the determination of all candidates for position K of the output vector if a partially constructed vector

$$(A(1), \ldots, A(K-1))$$

is given.

In the present case, our answer is as follows: If K=1, A(1)=1 is the only candidate (for normalization). If K>1, the list of candidates is the set of those integers J such that

(1) $1 \leq J \leq \lambda$

and

(2)   there is no I$\leq$K−1, such that A(I)=J and vertex I is connected to vertex K in the graph G.

Suppose that the graph G is specified by means of its vertex-adjacency matrix in LOGICAL form, i.e.,

$$\text{ADJ}(I,J) = \begin{cases} .\text{TRUE}. & \text{if } I<J, \text{ and vertex I connected to J} \\ .\text{FALSE}. & \text{if } I<J, \text{ otherwise} \quad (1 \leq I, J \leq N) \end{cases}$$

Then the set of candidates for position K, if K>1, is precisely

$$\{1,2,\ldots,\lambda\}-\{A(I)\,|\,I\leq K-1 \text{ and } ADJ(I,K)=.TRUE.\}$$

The actual program adheres exactly to the format described in Section (A).

SUBROUTINE SPECIFICATIONS

(1) *Name of subroutine:* COLVRT.
(2) *Calling statement:* CALL COLVRT(N,A,K,M,STACK,NSTK, LAMBDA,ADJ,COL).
(3) *Purpose of subroutine:* Find possible colors of vertex K.
(4) *Descriptions of variables in calling statement:*

Name	Type	I/O/W/B	Description
N	INTEGER	I	Number of vertices in the graph.
A	INTEGER(N)	I	A(I) is the color of vertex I(I=1,N).‡
K	INTEGER	I	Vertex whose color-candidates are to be found.‡
M	INTEGER	I/O	Current length of stack.‡
STACK	INTEGER(NSTK)	I/O	Candidates for positions A(1),...,A(K-1).‡
NSTK	INTEGER	I	Maximum length of STACK.
LAMBDA	INTEGER	I	Number of colors available (1≤A(I)≤LAMBDA for I=1,N).
ADJ	LOGICAL(N,N)	I	ADJ(I,J)=.TRUE. if vertices I,J are joined by an edge; =.FALSE. otherwise.
COL	LOGICAL(N)	W	Working storage.

‡ Input values are supplied by BACKTR.

(5) *Other routines which are called by this one:* None.
(6) *Approximate number of* FORTRAN *instructions:* 24.

```
SUBROUTINE COLVRT(N,A,K,M,STACK,NSTK,LAMBDA,ADJ,COL)
IMPLICIT INTEGER(A-Z)
LOGICAL ADJ,COL
DIMENSION A(N),STACK(NSTK),ADJ(N,N),COL(N)
IF(K.GT.1) GO TO 10
STACK(1)=1
STACK(2)=1
M=2
RETURN
```

```
10   K1=K-1
     DO 20   I=1,LAMBDA
20   COL(I)=.TRUE.
     DO 30   I=1,K1
30   IF(ADJ(I,K)) COL(A(I))=.FALSE.
     M1=M
     DO 40   I=1,LAMBDA
     IF(.NOT.COL(I)) GO TO 40
     M1=M1+1
     STACK(M1)=I
40   CONTINUE
     STACK(M1+1)=M1-M
     M=M1+1
     RETURN
     END
```

SAMPLE OUTPUT

The following output shows the six possible proper colorings of a 4-cycle (Fig. 23.3) in which the color of vertex 1 is fixed at color 1.

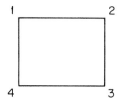

Figure 23.3

The input ADJ array was

$$ADJ = \begin{pmatrix} - & T & F & T \\ T & - & T & F \\ F & T & - & T \\ T & F & T & - \end{pmatrix}$$

```
1   3   2   3
1   3   1   3
1   3   1   2
1   2   3   2
1   2   1   3
1   2   1   2
```

(C) EULER CIRCUITS (EULCRC)

Let G be a (directed or undirected) graph of n vertices and e edges. By an *Euler circuit* on G we mean a walk along the edges of G which visits each edge exactly once, returning to the starting point, and following the direction of each edge if G is directed.

A celebrated theorem of Euler holds that an undirected graph has such a circuit if and only if every vertex of G has even valence. A directed graph has such a circuit if and only if at each vertex there are an equal number of ingoing and outgoing edges. In either case G is called *Eulerian.*

If G is Eulerian we can ask for a program which will list all of the Euler circuits of G in the fashion of our "next" subroutines, i.e., producing one circuit each time called, until no more remain.

The backtrack program provides a ready-made tool for such a task, and so we now describe the utilization of BACKTR in our desired subroutine. As usual, we suppose given a partially constructed Euler circuit

$$(A(1),A(2),\ldots,A(K-1))$$

and we ask for the list of candidates for the Kth edge A(K) in the circuit.

We first need to define the idea of a "terminal vertex." If G is undirected, we choose one of the endpoints of edge A(1) and declare it to be the terminal vertex of A(1). Then, for I=2,3,...the terminal vertex Z1(I) is that vertex of A(I) which is not the terminal vertex of A(I-1). If G is directed, the terminal vertex of A(I) is prescribed.

To return now to the question of candidates for A(K), if G is undirected, an edge e' is a candidate for A(K) if

(1) e' does not appear among A(1),...,A(K-1)

and

(2)   the terminal vertex Z1(K-1) of edge A(K-1) is an endpoint of e'.

If G is directed, condition (2) is replaced by

(2')   the terminal vertex Z1(K-1) of edge A(K-1) is the initial vertex of e'.

Euler's theorem guarantees that such a path must return to its starting point, if G is Eulerian.

Many of the interesting applications of our subroutine occur with graphs G which have loops and multiple edges. We therefore permit these in the input graph. Hence input data will consist of ENDPT(1,I),ENDPT(2,I), and the two ends of edge I (I=1,E), where the two endpoints may be equal, and the same pair may appear several times. If G is directed, ENDPT(1,I) is the initial vertex and ENDPT(2,I) is the terminal vertex of edge I.

For an undirected G (OPTION=1), the algorithm for determining the list of candidates for A(K) is

ALGORITHM EULCRC

(A) K=1? If so, set Z1(1)←ENDPT(2,1); Candidate is edge 1, only; Exit.
(B) K=2? If so, to (**D**).
(C) Z1(K–1)←ENDPT(1,A(K–1))+ENDPT(2,A(K–1))–Z1(K–2).
(D) ED(I)←.FALSE. (I=1,E).
(E) For I=1,E: {If Z1(K–1) is one of the endpoints of edge I, set ED(I)←.TRUE.}.
(F) ED(A(I))←.FALSE. (I=1,K–1) ∎

The candidates are then the edges I such that ED(I)=.TRUE.. If G is directed (OPTION=2), step (**E**) above is replaced by

(E') For I=1,E: {If Z1(K–1) is the initial vertex of edge I, set ED(I)←.TRUE.} ∎

A brief comment about step (**C**) above seems warranted. If we have three numbers x, y, z, and if z is known to be one of x, y, but it is not known which one, and if we wish to set w equal to the other one of x, y (i.e., the one which is not z), then the quickest program is

$$w = x + y - z$$

which is done in step (**C**).

Program CANDTE (called EULCRC) for listing Euler circuits appears on the following two pages.

SUBROUTINE SPECIFICATIONS

(1) *Name of subroutine:* EULCRC.
(2) *Calling statement:* CALL EULCRC(E,A,K,M,STACK,NSTK, OPTION,ENDPT,Z1,ED).

(3) *Purpose of subroutine:* Find candidates for Kth edge of Euler circuit.

(4) *Descriptions of variables in calling statement:*

Name	Type	I/O/W/B	Description
E	INTEGER	I	Number of edges in graph G.
A	INTEGER(E)	I	A(I) is the Ith edge in the circuit (I=1,E).‡
K	INTEGER	I	Index of next edge to be determined in circuit.‡
M	INTEGER	I/O	Current length of stack.‡
STACK	INTEGER(NSTK)	I/O	Candidates for all positions 1,...,K−1.‡
NSTK	INTEGER	I	Maximum length of stack.
OPTION	INTEGER	I	=1 if G is undirected; =2 if G is directed.
ENDPT	INTEGER(2,E)	I	ENDPT(1,I), ENDPT(2,I) are the two ends of edge I(I=1,E).
Z1	INTEGER(E)	W	Working storage.
ED	LOGICAL(E)	W	Working storage.

‡ Input supplied by BACKTR.

(5) *Other routines which are called by this one:* None.
(6) *Approximate number of* FORTRAN *instructions:* 32.

```
      SUBROUTINE EULCRC(E,A,K,M,STACK,NSTK,OPTION,
     *ENDPT,Z1,ED)
      IMPLICIT INTEGER(A-Z)
      LOGICAL ED(E)
      DIMENSION A(E),STACK(NSTK),ENDPT(2,E),Z1(E)
10    IF(K.NE.1) GO TO 30
20    Z1(1)=ENDPT(2,1)
      STACK(1)=1
      STACK(2)=1
      M=2
      RETURN
30    IF(K.EQ.2) GO TO 60
40    Z1(K-1)=ENDPT(1,A(K-1))+ENDPT(2,A(K-1))-Z1(K-2)
60    T=Z1(K-1)
      IF(OPTION.EQ.2) GO TO 80
61    DO 62 I=1,E
62    ED(I)=T.EQ.ENDPT(1,T).OR.T.EQ.ENDPT(2,I)
64    K1=K-1
65    DO 66 I=1,K1
```

```
66   ED(A(I))=.FALSE.
70   M1=M
     DO 71   I=1,E
     IF(.NOT.ED(I)) GO TO 71
     M1=M1+1
     STACK(M1)=I
71   CONTINUE
     STACK(M1+1)=M1-M
     M=M1+1
     RETURN
80   DO 81   I=1,E
81   ED(I)=T.EQ.ENDPT(1,I)
     GO TO 64
     END
```

SAMPLE OUTPUT

The complete graph K_5 on 5 vertices has 132 different Euler circuits. On the following pages there appear, first of all, the ENDPT array which describes K_5, and then the full list of 132 circuits as obtained, successively, from the program.

1	1	1	1	2	2	2	3	3	4
2	3	4	5	3	4	5	4	5	5

1	7	10	8	9	4	3	6	5	2
1	7	10	8	9	4	2	5	6	3
1	7	10	8	5	6	3	4	9	2
1	7	10	8	5	6	3	2	9	4
1	7	10	8	2	4	9	5	6	3
1	7	10	8	2	3	6	5	9	4
1	7	10	6	5	9	4	3	8	2
1	7	10	6	5	9	4	2	8	3
1	7	10	6	5	8	3	4	9	2
1	7	10	6	5	8	3	2	9	4
1	7	10	6	5	2	4	9	8	3
1	7	10	6	5	2	3	8	9	4
1	7	10	3	4	9	8	6	5	2
1	7	10	3	4	9	5	6	8	2
1	7	10	3	2	8	6	5	9	4

1	7	10	3	2	5	6	8	9	4
1	7	9	8	10	4	3	6	5	2
1	7	9	8	10	4	2	5	6	3
1	7	9	8	6	5	2	4	10	3
1	7	9	8	6	5	2	3	10	4
1	7	9	8	3	4	10	6	5	2
1	7	9	8	3	2	5	6	10	4
1	7	9	5	6	10	4	3	8	2
1	7	9	5	6	10	4	2	8	3
1	7	9	5	6	8	2	4	10	3
1	7	9	5	6	8	2	3	10	4
1	7	9	5	6	3	4	10	8	2
1	7	9	5	6	3	2	8	10	4
1	7	9	2	4	10	8	5	6	3
1	7	9	2	4	10	6	5	8	3
1	7	9	2	3	8	5	6	10	4
1	7	9	2	3	6	5	8	10	4
1	7	4	3	10	9	8	6	5	2
1	7	4	3	10	9	5	6	8	2
1	7	4	3	8	9	10	6	5	2
1	7	4	3	8	5	6	10	9	2
1	7	4	3	6	5	9	10	8	2
1	7	4	3	6	5	8	10	9	2
1	7	4	2	9	10	8	5	6	3
1	7	4	2	9	10	6	5	8	3
1	7	4	2	8	10	9	5	6	3
1	7	4	2	8	6	5	9	10	3
1	7	4	2	5	6	10	9	8	3
1	7	4	2	5	6	8	9	10	3
1	6	10	9	8	3	4	7	5	2
1	6	10	9	8	3	2	5	7	4
1	6	10	9	5	7	4	3	8	2
1	6	10	9	5	7	4	2	8	3
1	6	10	9	2	4	7	5	8	3
1	6	10	9	2	3	8	5	7	4
1	6	10	7	5	9	4	3	8	2
1	6	10	7	5	9	4	2	8	3
1	6	10	7	5	8	3	4	9	2
1	6	10	7	5	8	3	2	9	4
1	6	10	7	5	2	4	9	8	3
1	6	10	7	5	2	3	8	9	4
1	6	10	4	3	8	9	7	5	2

1	6	10	4	3	8	5	7	9	2
1	6	10	4	2	9	7	5	8	3
1	6	10	4	2	5	7	9	8	3
1	6	8	9	10	3	4	7	5	2
1	6	8	9	10	3	2	5	7	4
1	6	8	9	7	5	2	4	10	3
1	6	8	9	7	5	2	3	10	4
1	6	8	9	4	3	10	7	5	2
1	6	8	9	4	2	5	7	10	3
1	6	8	5	7	10	3	4	9	2
1	6	8	5	7	10	3	2	9	4
1	6	8	5	7	9	2	4	10	3
1	6	8	5	7	9	2	3	10	4
1	6	8	5	7	4	3	10	9	2
1	6	8	5	7	4	2	9	10	3
1	6	8	2	4	9	5	7	10	3
1	6	8	2	4	7	5	9	10	3
1	6	8	2	3	10	9	5	7	4
1	6	8	2	3	10	7	5	9	4
1	6	3	4	10	8	9	7	5	2
1	6	3	4	10	8	5	7	9	2
1	6	3	4	9	8	10	7	5	2
1	6	3	4	9	5	7	10	8	2
1	6	3	4	7	5	9	10	8	2
1	6	3	4	7	5	8	10	9	2
1	6	3	2	9	10	8	5	7	4
1	6	3	2	9	7	5	8	10	4
1	6	3	2	8	10	9	5	7	4
1	6	3	2	8	10	7	5	9	4
1	6	3	2	5	7	10	8	9	4
1	6	3	2	5	7	9	8	10	4
1	5	9	10	8	2	4	7	6	3
1	5	9	10	8	2	3	6	7	4
1	5	9	10	6	7	4	3	8	2
1	5	9	10	6	7	4	2	8	3
1	5	9	10	3	4	7	6	8	2
1	5	9	10	3	2	8	6	7	4
1	5	9	7	6	10	4	3	8	2
1	5	9	7	6	10	4	2	8	3
1	5	9	7	6	8	2	4	10	3
1	5	9	7	6	8	2	3	10	4
1	5	9	7	6	3	4	10	8	2

1	5	9	7	6	3	2	8	10	4
1	5	9	4	3	10	7	6	8	2
1	5	9	4	3	6	7	10	8	2
1	5	9	4	2	8	10	7	6	3
1	5	9	4	2	8	6	7	10	3
1	5	8	10	9	2	4	7	6	3
1	5	8	10	9	2	3	6	7	4
1	5	8	10	7	6	3	4	9	2
1	5	8	10	7	6	3	2	9	4
1	5	8	10	4	3	6	7	9	2
1	5	8	10	4	2	9	7	6	3
1	5	8	6	7	10	3	4	9	2
1	5	8	6	7	10	3	2	9	4
1	5	8	6	7	9	2	4	10	3
1	5	8	6	7	9	2	3	10	4
1	5	8	6	7	4	3	10	9	2
1	5	8	6	7	4	2	9	10	3
1	5	8	3	4	10	6	7	9	2
1	5	8	3	4	7	6	10	9	2
1	5	8	3	2	9	10	6	7	4
1	5	8	3	2	9	7	6	10	4
1	5	2	4	10	8	9	7	6	3
1	5	2	4	10	6	7	9	8	3
1	5	2	4	9	8	10	7	6	3
1	5	2	4	9	8	6	7	10	3
1	5	2	4	7	6	10	9	8	3
1	5	2	4	7	6	8	9	10	3
1	5	2	3	10	9	8	6	7	4
1	5	2	3	10	7	6	8	9	4
1	5	2	3	8	9	10	6	7	4
1	5	2	3	8	9	7	6	10	4
1	5	2	3	6	7	10	8	9	4
1	5	2	3	6	7	9	8	10	4

(D) HAMILTON CIRCUITS (HAMCRC)

In a graph G of n vertices, a Hamilton circuit is a sequence

$$V_1, V_2, V_3, \ldots, V_n$$

of vertices of G such that the V_i are some rearrangement of all of the vertices of G, each V_i is connected by an edge to V_{i+1} ($i = 1, \ldots, n-1$), and V_n is connected to V_1.

More pictorially, a Hamilton circuit is a round-trip walk on the edges of G which visits every *vertex* once entering and once leaving (following the directions of the edges if G is a directed graph). Many graphs do not have Hamilton circuits, and there are no simple criteria for deciding whether a given G has such a circuit and, if so, how many different such circuits it has.

The program in this section presents to the calling routine, each time it is called, a Hamilton circuit of G until no more exist, at which time it will so inform the main routine in the usual manner by setting INDEX=3.

We have here a simple exercise in backtracking, in which, if

$$A(1), A(2), \ldots, A(K-1)$$

is the vertex sequence in a partially constructed circuit, the set of candidates for A(K) is the set of all vertices x in G such that

(1) If K=1: $x = 1$.
(2) If K>1: (a) A(K−1) is joined to x by an edge of G
                    and
              (b) x is distinct from A(1), ..., A(K−1).
(3) If K=N: (c) x is joined to A(1) by an edge of G
                    and
              (d) $x < $ A(2),
                    and
              (a) *and* (b) above.

We ensure that each Hamilton circuit occurs exactly once by the normalization conditions in (1) and (3d) above, which require that A(1)=1 and A(N)<A(2).

If G is a directed graph we omit condition (3d). The program will handle an undirected (OPTION=1) or directed (OPTION=2) graph. Program CANDTE (here called HAMCRC) for this purpose appears on the following pages.

SUBROUTINE SPECIFICATIONS

(1) *Name of subroutine:* HAMCRC.
(2) *Calling statement:* CALL HAMCRC(N,A,K,M,STACK,NSTK, ADJ,VERT,OPTION).
(3) *Purpose of subroutine:* Find candidates for Kth vertex in a Hamilton circuit.
(4) *Descriptions of variables in calling statement:*

Name	Type	I/O/W/B	Description
N	INTEGER	I	Number of vertices in graph G.
A	INTEGER(N)	I	A(I) is the Ith vertex in the circuit.‡
K	INTEGER	I	Index of next step on current partial circuit.‡
M	INTEGER	I/O	Current length of stack.‡
STACK	INTEGER(NSTK)	I/O	Candidates for steps 1,...,K-1 (see text).‡
NSTK	INTEGER	I	Maximum length of stack.
ADJ	LOGICAL(N,N)	I	ADJ(I,J)=TRUE if edge (I,J) is in G; FALSE otherwise.
VERT	LOGICAL(N)	W	Working storage.
OPTION	INTEGER	I	=1 if G is undirected; =2 if G is directed.

‡ Input supplied by BACKTR.

(5) *Other routines which are called by this one:* None.
(6) *Approximate number of* FORTRAN *instructions:* 38.

```
     SUBROUTINE HAMCRC(N,A,K,M,STACK,NSTK,ADJ,VERT,OPTION)
     IMPLICIT INTEGER(A-Z)
     LOGICAL ADJ(N,N),VERT(N)
     DIMENSION A(N),STACK(NSTK)
10   IF(K.NE.1) GO TO 30
20   STACK(1)=1
     STACK(2)=1
     M=2
     RETURN
30   K1=K-1
     A1=A(K1)
     DO 31 I=1,N
31   VERT(I)=ADJ(A1,I)
     DO 32 I=1,K1
     M1=A(I)
32   VERT(M1)=.FALSE.
```

```
      M1=M
      IF(K.EQ.N) GO TO 50
40    DO 41   I=1,N
      IF(.NOT.VERT(I)) GO TO 41
      M1=M1+1
      STACK(M1)=I
41    CONTINUE
44    STACK(M1+1)=M1-M
      M=M1+1
      RETURN
50    DO 51   I=1,N
      IF(.NOT.VERT(I)) GO TO 51
      IF(OPTION.EQ.2) GO TO 52
      IF(I.GT.A(2)) GO TO 44
52    IF(.NOT.ADJ(I,1)) GO TO 44
      M=M+2
      STACK(M-1)=I
      STACK(M)=1
      RETURN
51    CONTINUE
      GO TO 44
      END
```

SAMPLE OUTPUT 1

The graph in Fig. 23.4, on 20 vertices, was one of those originally studied by Hamilton. There are 30 Hamilton circuits in the graph,

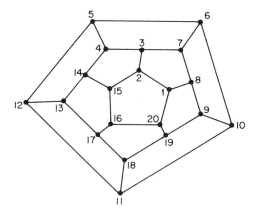

Figure 23.4

and they are shown in the following output, one circuit per line. Elapsed computer time was less than one minute on a relatively slow and small machine.

The vertices of this graph are numbered consecutively following one of the circuits found by Hamilton, which appears as the first one below.

```
1 20 19 18 17 16 15 14 13 12 11 10  9  8  7  6  5  4  3 2
1 20 19 18 17 16 15  2  3  7  6  5  4 14 13 12 11 10  9 8
1 20 19 18 11 12 13 17 16 15 14  4  5  6 10  9  8  7  3 2
1 20 19 18 11 12  5  6 10  9  8  7  3  4 14 13 17 16 15 2
1 20 19 18 11 12  5  4 14 13 17 16 15  2  3  7  6 10  9 8
1 20 19 18 11 10  9  8  7  6  5 12 13 17 16 15 14  4  3 2
1 20 19  9 10 11 18 17 16 15  2  3  4 14 13 12  5  6  7 8
1 20 19  9 10  6  5  4 14 13 12 11 18 17 16 15  2  3  7 8
1 20 19  9  8  7  6 10 11 18 17 16 15 14 13 12  5  4  3 2
1 20 19  9  8  7  3  4 14 13 12  5  6 10 11 18 17 16 15 2
1 20 16 17 18 19  9 10 11 12 13 14 15  2  3  4  5  6  7 8
1 20 16 17 18 19  9  8  7  3  4  5  6 10 11 12 13 14 15 2
1 20 16 17 13 14 15  2  3  4  5 12 11 18 19  9 10  6  7 8
1 20 16 17 13 12 11 18 19  9 10  6  5  4 14 15  2  3  7 8
1 20 16 17 13 12  5  6 10 11 18 19  9  8  7  3  4 14 15 2
1 20 16 17 13 12  5  4 14 15  2  3  7  6 10 11 18 19  9 8
1 20 16 15 14 13 17 18 19  9  8  7  6 10 11 12  5  4  3 2
1 20 16 15 14  4  5  6 10 11 12 13 17 18 19  9  8  7  3 2
1 20 16 15  2  3  7  6 10 11 12  5  4 14 13 17 18 19  9 8
1 20 16 15  2  3  4 14 13 17 18 19  9 10 11 12  5  6  7 8
1  8  9 19 20 16 17 18 11 10  6  7  3  4  5 12 13 14 15 2
1  8  9 19 20 16 15 14  4  5 12 13 17 18 11 10  6  7  3 2
1  8  9 10 11 18 19 20 16 17 13 12  5  6  7  3  4 14 15 2
1  8  9 10 11 12 13 17 18 19 20 16 15 14  4  5  6  7  3 2
1  8  9 10 11 12  5  6  7  3  4 14 13 17 18 19 20 16 15 2
1  8  9 10  6  7  3  4  5 12 11 18 19 20 16 17 13 14 15 2
1  8  7  6 10  9 19 20 16 15 14 13 17 18 11 12  5  4  3 2
1  8  7  6  5 12 13 17 18 11 10  9 19 20 16 15 14  4  3 2
1  8  7  3  4 14 13 17 18 11 12  5  6 10  9 19 20 16 15 2
1  8  7  3  4  5  6 10  9 19 20 16 17 18 11 12 13 14 15 2
```

SAMPLE OUTPUT 2

Consider the graph G whose 24 vertices correspond to the permu-tations of 4 letters, where each permutation σ is connected to the three other permutations which can be obtained from σ by a single interchange of two *adjacent* letters. Thus *abcd* is connected to *bacd*, *acbd*, and *abdc*. A Hamilton circuit in G is then a sequencing of the 24 permutations so that each is obtainable from its predecessor by such an interchange.

With the aid of NEXPER, BACKTR, HAMCRC and a main program, we found that there are 44 such Hamilton circuits in G, which are listed on the next page, one to a line, in the following format: To go from permutation I to I+1 in the circuit, we exchange the Jth letter with the (J+1)th letter ($1 \leq J \leq 3$). The sequence of values of J, for I=1,23 is shown in each line.

For example, in the tenth line of the output we find the sequence

$$3212 \quad 1232 \quad 3212 \quad 1232 \quad 3212 \quad 123$$

of values of J, which yields the list of 24 permutations in the follow-ing order:

1	1234	9	2314	17	3124
2	1243	10	2341	18	3142
3	1423	11	2431	19	3412
4	4123	12	4231	20	4312
5	4213	13	4321	21	4132
6	2413	14	3421	22	1432
7	2143	15	3241	23	1342
8	2134	16	3214	24	1324

A further examination of this list of Hamilton circuits was carried out in order to find equivalence classes with respect to action of the group generated by (a) replacing each J in a sequence by 3−J and (b) cyclically permuting a sequence. This examination showed that there are just five equivalence classes of circuits among the 44 cir-cuits which were printed out, representatives of which are

3121	2131	2121	3123	2121	232
3123	1321	3123	1321	3123	132
3132	3231	3212	3232	1231	323
3212	1232	3212	3212	1232	321
3212	1232	3212	1232	3212	123

```
3 1 2 1 2 1 3 1 2 1 2 1 3 1 2 3 2 1 2 1 2 3 2
3 1 2 1 2 1 3 1 2 3 2 1 2 1 2 3 2 1 3 1 2 1 2
3 1 2 3 2 1 2 1 2 3 2 1 3 1 2 1 2 1 3 1 2 1 2
3 1 2 3 1 3 2 1 3 1 2 3 1 3 2 1 3 1 2 3 1 3 2
3 1 3 2 3 2 3 1 3 2 3 2 3 1 3 2 1 2 3 2 3 2 1
3 1 3 2 3 2 3 1 3 2 1 2 3 2 3 2 1 2 3 1 3 2 3
3 1 3 2 1 3 1 2 3 1 3 2 1 3 1 2 3 1 3 2 1 3 1
3 1 3 2 1 2 3 2 3 2 1 2 3 1 3 2 3 2 3 1 3 2 3
3 2 1 2 1 2 3 2 3 2 1 2 3 2 1 2 1 2 3 2 3 2 1
3 2 1 2 1 2 3 2 3 2 1 2 1 2 3 2 3 2 1 2 1 2 3
3 2 1 2 1 2 3 2 1 3 1 2 1 2 1 3 1 2 1 2 1 3 1
3 2 1 2 1 2 3 2 1 2 3 2 3 2 1 2 1 2 3 2 1 2 3
3 2 1 2 3 1 3 2 3 2 3 1 3 2 3 2 3 1 3 2 1 2 3
3 2 1 2 3 2 3 2 1 2 1 2 3 2 1 2 3 2 3 2 1 2 1
3 2 1 2 3 2 3 2 1 2 3 1 3 2 3 2 3 1 3 2 3 2 3
3 2 1 2 3 2 1 2 1 2 3 2 3 2 1 2 3 2 1 2 1 2 3
3 2 1 3 1 2 1 2 1 3 1 2 1 2 1 3 1 2 3 2 1 2 1
3 2 1 3 1 2 3 1 3 2 1 3 1 2 3 1 3 2 1 3 1 2 3
3 2 3 1 3 2 1 2 3 2 3 2 1 2 3 1 3 2 3 2 3 1 3
3 2 3 1 3 2 3 2 3 1 3 2 1 2 3 2 3 2 1 2 3 1 3
3 2 3 2 1 2 1 2 3 2 1 2 3 2 3 2 1 2 1 2 3 2 1
3 2 3 2 1 2 1 2 3 2 3 2 1 2 1 2 3 2 3 2 1 2 1
3 2 3 2 1 2 3 2 1 2 1 2 3 2 3 2 1 2 3 2 1 2 1
3 2 3 2 1 2 3 1 3 2 3 2 3 1 3 2 3 2 3 1 3 2 1
3 2 3 2 3 1 3 2 1 2 3 2 3 2 1 2 3 1 3 2 3 2 3
3 2 3 2 3 1 3 2 3 2 3 1 3 2 1 2 3 2 3 2 1 2 3
2 3 2 3 2 1 2 1 2 3 2 1 2 3 2 3 2 1 2 1 2 3 2
2 3 2 3 2 1 2 1 2 3 2 3 2 1 2 1 2 3 2 3 2 1 2
2 3 2 3 2 1 2 3 2 1 2 1 2 3 2 3 2 1 2 3 2 1 2
2 3 2 3 2 1 2 3 1 3 2 3 2 3 1 3 2 3 2 3 1 3 2
2 3 2 1 3 1 2 1 2 1 3 1 2 1 2 1 3 1 2 3 2 1 2
2 3 2 1 2 1 2 3 2 3 2 1 2 3 2 1 2 1 2 3 2 3 2
2 3 2 1 2 1 2 3 2 1 3 1 2 1 2 1 3 1 2 1 2 1 3
2 3 2 1 2 3 2 3 2 1 2 1 2 3 2 1 2 3 2 3 2 1 2
2 3 1 3 2 3 2 3 1 3 2 3 2 3 1 3 2 1 2 3 2 3 2
2 3 1 3 2 1 3 1 2 3 1 3 2 1 3 1 2 3 1 3 2 1 3
2 1 3 1 2 3 2 1 2 1 2 3 2 1 3 1 2 1 2 1 3 1 2
2 1 3 1 2 1 2 1 3 1 2 3 2 1 2 1 2 3 2 1 3 1 2
2 1 2 3 2 3 2 1 2 3 2 1 2 1 2 3 2 3 2 1 2 3 2
2 1 2 3 2 3 2 1 2 1 2 3 2 3 2 1 2 1 2 3 2 3 2
2 1 2 3 2 1 3 1 2 1 2 1 3 1 2 1 2 1 3 1 2 3 2
2 1 2 3 2 1 2 3 2 3 2 1 2 1 2 3 2 1 2 3 2 3 2
2 1 2 1 3 1 2 3 2 1 2 1 2 3 2 1 3 1 2 1 2 1 3
2 1 2 1 3 1 2 1 2 1 3 1 2 3 2 1 2 1 2 3 2 1 3
```

(E) SPANNING TREES (SPNTRE)

Our final example of a backtrack routine will, each time it is called, exhibit one spanning tree of a given graph G and inform the user when no more exist.

Suppose, then, that

$$A(1),A(2),\ldots,A(K-1)$$

are the edges of a partially constructed spanning tree of G. What are the candidates for $A(K)$? Suppose we were to adopt the condition that for $A(K)$ we use any edge I such that exactly one endpoint of I is incident with the subgraph spanned by $A(1),\ldots,A(K-1)$. We would surely generate all spanning trees, but a given tree T could be generated many times. This is because the present problem is fundamentally different from the preceding applications in that the order of the components in the output vector is immaterial. A given tree T might appear with several different edge orderings, and we want each one to be generated just once.

To avoid this problem, we might require not only that edge I have exactly one vertex in the previous partial tree, but also that $I>A(K-1)$. This would insure that the edges would be in ascending order, so each tree T would then be generated no more than once. Unfortunately, some trees would not be generated at all! Indeed T could be so generated if and only if when the edges of T are arranged in increasing order of their numbers, each edge $A(I)$ is incident with the subgraph spanned by $A(1),\ldots,A(I-1)$, and this is clearly a special property not shared by all T.

In order to insure that each tree appears at most once, we continue the requirement that $A(K)>A(K-1)$. To insure that all trees appear, we ask only that edge $A(K)$ not form any circuits in the subgraph spanned by $A(1),\ldots,A(K-1)$, but we do not insist that it be incident with that subgraph. Our partially constructed trees $\{A(1),\ldots,A(K-1)\}=T_K$ will actually be forests, i.e., will have several connected components, each of them a tree. To determine whether or not an edge e completes a circuit in T_K we ask if both endpoints of e lie in the same connected component of T_K. Finally, observe that the complete tree T will have $N-1$ edges, and if these edges are to be numbered in ascending order, then we must have $A(K)\leqq E-N+K+1$ $(K=1,\ldots,N-1)$.

To summarize, edge I *is a candidate for position* K, *given*

$A(1), \dots, A(K-1)$ *if*

(1) $A(K-1)+1 \leq I \leq E-N+K+1$

and

(2) $ENDPT(1,I)$ *and* $ENDPT(2,I)$ *are in different connected components of the subgraph whose vertices are all of the vertices of* G *and whose edges are* $A(1), \dots, A(K-1)$.

Subroutine SPANFO of Chapter 14 will assume the task of determining the connected component $X(J)$ in which each vertex $J=1,N$ lives.

SUBROUTINE SPECIFICATIONS

(1) *Name of subroutine:* SPNTRE.

(2) *Calling statement:*
CALL SPNTRE(E,N,A,K,M,STACK,NSTK,ENDPT,END,X,NV,Y).

(3) *Purpose of subroutine:* Find candidates for Kth edge of spanning tree.

(4) *Descriptions of variables in calling statement:*

Name	Type	I/O/W/B	Description
E	INTEGER	I	Number of edges of graph G.
N	INTEGER	I	(Number of vertices of graph G) $- 1$ (!!!)
A	INTEGER(N)	I	A(I) is Ith edge of spanning tree (I=1,N).‡
K	INTEGER	I	Index of position for which candidates are needed.‡
M	INTEGER	I/O	Current size of stack.‡
STACK	INTEGER(NSTK)	I/O	List of candidates for all positions (see text).‡
NSTK	INTEGER	I	Maximum length of stack.
ENDPT	INTEGER(2,E)	I	ENDPT(1,I), ENDPT(2,I) are the two ends of vertex *I* in G (I=1,E).
END	INTEGER(2,N)	W	Working storage.
X	INTEGER(N)	W	Working storage.
NV	INTEGER(N)	W	Working storage.
Y	INTEGER(N)	W	Working storage.

‡ Input supplied by BACKTR.

(5) *Other routines which are called by this one:* SPANFO, RENUMB.

(6) *Approximate number of* FORTRAN *instructions:* 28.

```
      SUBROUTINE SPNTRE(N,A,K,M,STACK,NSTK,ENDPT,END,
     *X,NV,Y)
```

```
      IMPLICIT INTEGER(A-Z)
      DIMENSION A(N),STACK(NSTK),ENDPT(2,E),END(2,N),
     *NV(N),Y(N),X(N)
10    IF(K.NE.1) GO TO 30
20    N2=E-N+1
      DO 21  I=1,N2
21    STACK(I)=I
      M=N2+1
      STACK(M)=N2
      RETURN
30    K1=K-1
      DO 31  I=1,K1
      END(1,I)=ENDPT(1,A(I))
31    END(2,I)=ENDPT(2,A(I))
      N3=N+1
      CALL SPANFO(N3,K1,END,COMP,X,NV,Y)
      I1=A(K1)+1
      I2=E-N+K
      M1=M
32    DO 35  I=I1,I2
      IF(X(ENDPT(1,I)).EQ.X(ENDPT(2,I))) GO TO 35
      M1=M1+1
      STACK(M1)=I
35    CONTINUE
      STACK(M1+1)=M1-M
      M=M1+1
      RETURN
      END
```

SAMPLE OUTPUT

Suppose that five cities A, B, C, D, E are situated as shown in the "map" in Fig. 23.5 in which the numbers are the distances between cities. We ask for the shortest length of telephone cable which would connect all of the cities together. Evidently, we seek the spanning tree of the graph of shortest total length (Fig. 23.6). The output of our program shows for each of the 125 spanning trees of the graph, first its total length, and then the four edges which comprise the tree. It is seen that the shortest connection is 235 miles long. There are much more efficient ways of handling this problem (see Chapter 28) and this example is intended only to illustrate the operation of SPNTRE.

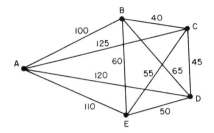

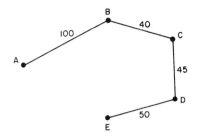

Figure 23.5 The map.

Figure 23.6 The shortest connection.

455	4	7	9	10	290	3	5	6	7
395	4	7	8	10	400	3	4	7	9
385	4	7	8	9	340	3	4	7	8
375	4	6	9	10	320	3	4	6	9
315	4	6	8	10	260	3	4	6	8
305	4	6	8	9	330	3	4	5	9
380	4	6	7	9	270	3	4	5	8
320	4	6	7	8	345	3	4	5	7
385	4	5	9	10	265	3	4	5	6
325	4	5	8	10	415	2	7	9	10
315	4	5	8	9	355	2	7	8	10
400	4	5	7	10	345	2	7	8	9
330	4	5	7	8	335	2	6	9	10
320	4	5	6	10	275	2	6	8	10
310	4	5	6	9	265	2	6	8	9
325	4	5	6	7	340	2	6	7	9
420	3	7	9	10	280	2	6	7	8
360	3	7	8	10	345	2	5	9	10
350	3	7	8	9	285	2	5	8	10
340	3	6	9	10	275	2	5	8	9
280	3	6	8	10	360	2	5	7	10
270	3	6	8	9	290	2	5	7	8
345	3	6	7	9	280	2	5	6	10
285	3	6	7	8	270	2	5	6	9
350	3	5	9	10	285	2	5	6	7
290	3	5	8	10	405	2	4	7	10
280	3	5	8	9	335	2	4	7	8
365	3	5	7	10	325	2	4	6	10
295	3	5	7	8	255	2	4	6	8
285	3	5	6	10	330	2	4	6	7
275	3	5	6	9	335	2	4	5	10

265	2	4	5	8	295	1	4	6	9
260	2	4	5	6	235	1	4	6	8
370	2	3	7	10	315	1	4	5	10
360	2	3	7	9	245	1	4	5	8
290	2	3	6	10	240	1	4	5	6
280	2	3	6	9	335	1	3	9	10
295	2	3	6	7	275	1	3	8	10
300	2	3	5	10	265	1	3	8	9
290	2	3	5	9	340	1	3	7	9
305	2	3	5	7	280	1	3	7	8
350	2	3	4	7	280	1	3	5	10
270	2	3	4	6	270	1	3	5	9
280	2	3	4	5	285	1	3	5	7
395	1	7	9	10	315	1	3	4	9
335	1	7	8	10	255	1	3	4	8
325	1	7	8	9	260	1	3	4	5
315	1	6	9	10	330	1	2	9	10
255	1	6	8	10	270	1	2	8	10
245	1	6	8	9	260	1	2	8	9
320	1	6	7	9	345	1	2	7	10
260	1	6	7	8	275	1	2	7	8
325	1	5	9	10	265	1	2	6	10
265	1	5	8	10	255	1	2	6	9
255	1	5	8	9	270	1	2	6	7
340	1	5	7	10	320	1	2	4	10
270	1	5	7	8	250	1	2	4	8
260	1	5	6	10	245	1	2	4	6
250	1	5	6	9	285	1	2	3	10
265	1	5	6	7	275	1	2	3	9
370	1	4	9	10	290	1	2	3	7
310	1	4	8	10	265	1	2	3	4
300	1	4	8	9					

24

Random Tree (RANTRE)

We have observed in Chapter (23) that the backtrack method is not suitable for choosing random combinatorial objects because uniform probability density is in general not achieved. We therefore must find special methods for each such problem. Here we consider the question of selecting a random labeled tree on n vertices. A celebrated theorem of Cayley asserts that there are exactly n^{n-2} such trees, and so we want an algorithm to select one of these in such a way that, a priori, each tree has probability $n^{-(n-2)}$ of being selected.

The idea for the algorithm is based on a proof, due to Prüfer, of Cayley's theorem. Prüfer gave an explicit construction which associates with each labeled tree on n vertices a unique $(n-2)$-tuple of integers $a_1, a_2, \ldots, a_{n-2}$ in the range

$$(1) \qquad\qquad 1 \leqq a_i \leqq n \quad (i = 1, \ldots, n - 2)$$

in a 1–1 way. Since there are obviously n^{n-2} sequences $a_1, \ldots, a_{n-2}$ which satisfy (1), Cayley's result is an immediate consequence of the construction which we now describe.

Given a tree T on n labeled vertices $1, 2, \ldots, n$. By an *endpoint* of T we mean a vertex of valence 1. It is easy to see that every tree has at least one endpoint.

Let x be the endpoint of T of smallest index. Let a_1 be the unique vertex of T to which x is connected. Delete the vertex x and the edge (x, a_1) from T, to obtain a new tree T'. Again, let x' be the endpoint

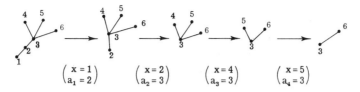

$$\left(\begin{array}{c} x = 1 \\ a_1 = 2 \end{array}\right) \qquad \left(\begin{array}{c} x = 2 \\ a_2 = 3 \end{array}\right) \qquad \left(\begin{array}{c} x = 4 \\ a_3 = 3 \end{array}\right) \qquad \left(\begin{array}{c} x = 5 \\ a_4 = 3 \end{array}\right)$$

Figure 24.1

of T' of smallest index, and let a_2 be the unique vertex of T' to which x' is connected. Delete x' and edge (x', a_2) from T' to obtain T'', etc. The process halts when we have found $a_1, a_2, \ldots, a_{n-2}$ and the tree has been reduced to a single edge.

For example, we have the sequence of Fig. 24.1. The tree at the left is associated with the sequence $(2, 3, 3, 3)$ of integers in the range $[1, 6]$.

Prüfer's construction goes both ways. Given a sequence $(a_1, \ldots, a_{n-2})$ in the range $[1, n]$, make two lists. List$_1$ initially contains the numbers $1, 2, \ldots, n$ in order. List$_2$ initially contains $a_1, \ldots, a_{n-2}$. List$_1$ has length 2 greater than List$_2$. Hence, there are numbers in List$_1$ which are not in List$_2$. Let x be the smallest of these $(1 \leq x \leq n)$. Connect vertex x and vertex a_1 by an edge. Delete x from List$_1$ and a_1 from List$_2$. Again, let x be the smallest number in List$_1$, which is not in List$_2$. Connect (x, a_2) by an edge. Delete x and a_2 from their respective lists, etc.

The process terminates when List$_2$ is empty and List$_1$ contains two elements x, y. Connect (x, y) by an edge, and the tree is now complete. For example, if $n = 6$, we have the sequence shown in Fig. 24.2.

The argument actually is useful for a good deal more than a proof of Cayley's theorem. For instance, given an n-tuple $a = (a_1, \ldots, a_{n-2})$ satisfying (1); what is the valence $\rho(i)$ of vertex i in the tree

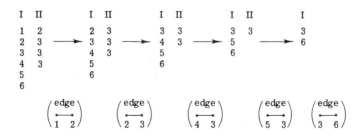

Figure 24.2

which corresponds to a? The construction shows that $\rho(i) = 1 + \mu(i)$ where $\mu(i)$ is the number of appearances of i in a $(i = 1, \ldots, n)$.

Hence, if the number of trees on n labeled vertices with valences $\rho(1), \ldots, \rho(n)$ (given) is denoted by $F_n(\boldsymbol{\rho})$, we know that $F_n(\boldsymbol{\rho})$ is the number of $(n-2)$-tuples a which satisfy both (1) and the additional condition that

$$(2) \qquad \mu(i) = \rho(i) - 1 \quad (i = 1, \ldots, n)$$

Since evidently

$$(3) \qquad \sum_{i=1}^{n} \mu(i) = n - 2$$

we have from (2)

$$(4) \qquad \sum_{i=1}^{n} \rho(i) = 2n - 2$$

as a necessary condition on the $\boldsymbol{\rho}$ if $F_n(\boldsymbol{\rho}) > 0$. If (3) holds, then $F_n(\boldsymbol{\rho})$ is the number of ways of arranging $\rho(1) - 1$ 1's, $\rho(2) - 1$ 2's, $\ldots$, $\rho(n) - 1$ n's in an $(n-2)$-vector; i.e.,

$$(5) \qquad F_n(\boldsymbol{\rho}) = \frac{(n-2)!}{(\rho(1) - 1)! \cdots (\rho(n) - 1)!}$$

is the number of trees with valence vector $\boldsymbol{\rho}$. Summation of (5) over all $\boldsymbol{\rho}$ which satisfy (4) yields Cayley's theorem again, but (5) is considerably more precise.

How many labeled trees on n vertices have exactly t endpoints? We can select which t vertices shall be the endpoints in

$$\binom{n}{t}$$

ways. The number of trees in which vertices $1, 2, \ldots, t$ are the endpoints is the number of ways of placing $n - 2$ labeled balls into $n - t$ labeled boxes with no box empty. To see this, let the balls be labeled $1, 2, \ldots, n - 2$, and let the boxes be labeled $t + 1, t + 2, \ldots, n$. For any arrangement of the balls in the boxes with no box empty, interpret the set of labels on the balls in box i as the set of subscripts j such that $a_j = i$ $(j = 1, \ldots, n - 2; i = t + 1, \ldots, n)$. The arrangement therefore leads uniquely to a vector $(a_1, \ldots, a_{n-2})$ in which $a_i \geq t + 1$ $(i = 1, \ldots, n - 2)$, and therefore to a tree in which vertices $1, 2, \ldots, t$ are endpoints. We have proved the

Theorem The number of labeled trees on n vertices which have exactly t endpoints is

(6)
$$\frac{n!}{t!} \left\{ \begin{matrix} n-2 \\ n-t \end{matrix} \right\} \quad (2 \leqq t \leqq n-1)$$

in which the quantity in braces is a Stirling number of the second kind.

A consequence of (6) is the identity

(7)
$$\sum_{t=2}^{n-1} \frac{n!}{t!} \left\{ \begin{matrix} n-2 \\ n-t \end{matrix} \right\} = n^{n-2}$$

which is well-known in the theory of Stirling numbers. The average number of endpoints over all trees on n vertices is

$$\bar{t} = n^{-(n-2)} \sum_{t=2}^{n-1} t \frac{n!}{t!} \left\{ \begin{matrix} n-2 \\ n-t \end{matrix} \right\} = n^{-(n-2)} \sum_{r=1}^{n-2} (n-r) \frac{n!}{(n-r)!} \left\{ \begin{matrix} n-2 \\ r \end{matrix} \right\}$$

$$= n^{-(n-2)} \cdot n \sum_{r=1}^{n-2} \binom{n-1}{r} r! \left[\begin{matrix} n-2 \\ r \end{matrix} \right] = n^{-(n-2)} \cdot n \cdot (n-1)^{n-2}$$

$$= n \left(1 - \frac{1}{n} \right)^{n-2} \sim \frac{n}{e} \quad (n \to \infty)$$

Hence an average tree has about n/e endpoints.

We return now to the main purpose of the discussion, which is to describe an algorithm for generating a random tree. Evidently what we need to do is just

(a) Select $n-2$ integers $a_1, \ldots, a_{n-2}$ at random in $[1, n]$.
(b) Carry out Prüfer's construction to get the tree.

The formal algorithm utilizes arrays as follows:

A(J)	(J=1,N-2)	The $n-2$ numbers $a_1, \ldots, a_{n-2}$ (this is List$_2$).
B(J)	(J=1,N)	=.TRUE. if J is on List$_1$; .FALSE. otherwise.
M(J)	(J=1,N)	The number of appearances of J in List$_2$.
$\left\{ \begin{matrix} \text{END}(1,\text{M1}) \\ \text{END}(2,\text{M1}) \end{matrix} \right.$	(M1=1,N-1)	The two endpoints of the M1th edge in the output tree.

FLOW CHART RANTRE

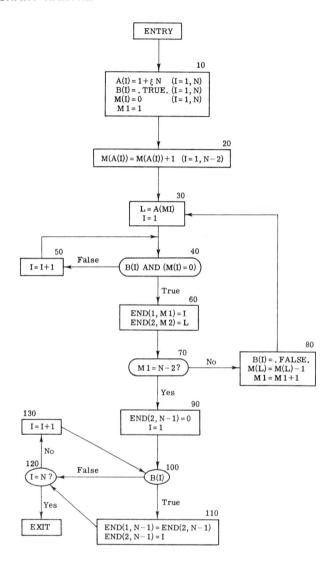

DESCRIPTION OF FLOW CHART

Box 10 Select $A(1),\dots,A(N-2)$ at random in $[1,N]$; set all $B(I)=.TRUE.$; initialize $M(I)$, the multiplicity of I in List$_2$, to 0.

Box 20 Count $M(I)$ in List$_2$, for all I.

Boxes 30–50   Find smallest I which is in List₁ (B(I)=.TRUE.) but not in List₂ (M(I)=0).

Box 60   Set endpoints of next (M1th) edge of tree equal to I and A(M1).

Box 70   Is List₂ now empty?

Box 80   If not, delete I from List₁, decrease multiplicity of A(M1) in List₂, and increase M1, the initial entry of the current List₂.

Box 90   If List₂ is empty, set END(1,N−1),END(2,N−1) to be the last two entries in List₁ and exit.

SUBROUTINE SPECIFICATIONS

(1)   *Name of subroutine:*   RANTRE.
(2)   *Calling statement:*   CALL RANTRE (N,END,A,B,M).
(3)   *Purpose of subroutine:*   Generate a random tree on *n* labeled vertices.
(4)   *Descriptions of variables in calling statement:*

Name	Type	I/O/W/B	Description
N	INTEGER	I	Number of vertices in desired tree.
END	INTEGER(2,N)	O	END(1,I), END(2,I) are the two vertices at the Ith edge of the output tree (I=1,N−1).
A	INTEGER(N)	W	Working storage.
B	LOGICAL(N)	W	Working storage.
M	INTEGER(N)	W	Working storage.

(5)   *Other routines which are called by this one:*
FUNCTION RAND(I) (Random number generator).
(6)   *Approximate number of* FORTRAN *instructions:*   32.

```
       SUBROUTINE RANTRE(N,END,A,B,M)
       IMPLICIT INTEGER(A-Z)
       REAL RAND
       LOGICAL B(N)
       DIMENSION END(2,N),A(N),M(N)
       N2=N-2
10     DO 11  I=1,N
       A(I)=1+RAND(1)*N
       B(I)=.TRUE.
11     M(I)=0
       M1=1
       DO 20  I=1,N2
```

```
20     M(A(I))=M(A(I))+1
30     L=A(M1)
40     DO 50   I=1,N
       IF(B(I).AND.(M(I).EQ.0)) GO TO 60
50     CONTINUE
60     END(1,M1)=I
       END(2,M1)=L
70     IF(M1.EQ.N2) GO TO 90
80     B(I)=.FALSE.
       M(L)=M(L)-1
       M1=M1+1
       GO TO 30
90     END(2,N-1)=0
       DO 130   I=1,N
100    IF(.NOT.B(I)) GO TO 130
110    END(1,N-1)=END(2,N-1)
       END(2,N-1)=I
130    CONTINUE
       RETURN
       END
```

SAMPLE OUTPUT

The program RANTRE was called 60 times with N=6. The sixty resulting labeled trees which follow are shown, one per printed line, each line containing (END(1,I), END(2,I), I=1,5).

Thus, for example, the first five trees which appear are, respectively, those shown in Fig. 24.3.

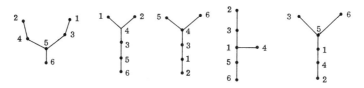

Figure 24.3

Note that of the $6^4 = 1296$ different labeled trees on 6 vertices, there are 360 of the type shown in Fig. 24.4. Hence, in our list of 60 there should be $16\frac{2}{3}$ trees of this form, and, in fact, there are 17.

Figure 24.4

1	3	2	4	3	5	4	5	5	6
1	4	2	4	4	3	3	5	5	6
2	1	1	3	5	4	4	3	4	6
2	3	3	1	4	1	5	1	5	6
2	4	3	5	4	1	5	1	5	6
1	4	2	4	3	5	5	4	5	6
2	4	3	6	5	1	1	4	4	6
3	4	5	2	2	4	4	1	4	6
1	5	2	5	5	3	3	4	4	6
1	6	2	6	5	3	3	4	4	6
1	3	2	6	4	3	3	5	5	6
2	6	5	1	1	3	3	4	4	6
2	3	4	3	3	1	1	6	5	6
4	3	3	2	2	1	1	5	5	6
3	2	2	4	4	1	5	1	5	6
5	4	4	3	3	1	1	2	2	6
1	6	2	4	3	6	4	6	5	6
4	1	1	3	3	2	2	6	5	6
1	5	2	4	4	6	5	3	5	6
3	2	4	2	5	1	1	2	2	6
3	1	4	2	2	5	5	1	5	6
1	5	2	3	3	5	4	5	5	6
1	4	3	5	5	4	4	2	4	6
1	3	2	3	4	5	5	3	5	6
1	3	3	6	5	2	2	4	4	6
1	6	4	3	3	2	2	5	5	6
2	1	3	1	1	5	4	6	5	6
3	6	5	4	4	1	1	2	2	6
3	5	4	1	1	2	2	5	5	6
1	6	3	4	5	2	2	4	4	6
1	4	4	3	3	6	5	2	5	6
1	4	3	6	5	2	2	4	4	6
2	1	1	4	3	6	4	6	5	6

1	5	2	3	5	4	4	3	4	6
1	5	5	4	4	3	3	2	3	6
1	2	2	4	3	5	4	5	5	6
3	5	4	1	1	2	5	2	5	6
1	2	4	3	3	5	5	2	5	6
1	6	3	4	4	2	2	6	5	6
1	3	3	5	4	2	2	5	5	6
3	6	5	2	2	1	1	4	4	6
2	1	1	5	3	5	5	4	5	6
2	5	3	6	4	5	5	1	5	6
1	6	2	6	4	6	5	3	5	6
1	4	2	6	4	3	5	3	5	6
1	3	3	2	2	6	4	5	5	6
1	6	4	3	3	6	5	2	5	6
3	2	2	6	5	1	1	4	4	6
1	4	2	6	3	5	4	5	5	6
3	2	2	1	1	6	4	6	5	6
1	6	3	2	4	6	5	2	5	6
2	1	4	5	5	1	1	3	3	6
1	2	2	3	3	4	4	5	5	6
4	2	5	1	1	2	2	3	3	6
1	6	2	5	3	5	4	5	5	6
4	2	2	5	5	1	1	3	3	6
2	4	3	1	4	1	5	1	5	6
4	1	1	2	2	3	3	5	5	6
3	1	5	4	4	2	2	1	2	6
1	5	2	4	3	4	4	5	5	6

25

Random Unlabeled Rooted Trees (RANRUT)

The algorithms for finding random partitions of an integer (Ranpar, Chapter 10) and random equivalence classes on a set (Ranequ, Chapter 12) were both based on recurrence relations of the approximate form

$$(1) \qquad na_n = \sum_{m<n} c_{n-m} a_m$$

where a_n is the number of objects of order n and where the c's were known or easy to compute. A combinatorial proof of (1) was essential, which then gave rise to an inductive construction by dividing both sides of (1) by the left side and interpreting the terms on the right as a sum of probabilities that add up to one.

The situation for random unlabeled rooted trees (briefly called "trees" for the remainder of this chapter) is similar since it is also a special case of the ideas in the Postscript to Chapter 10 pp. 77–80, although more complicated. The essential formula which t_n, the number of trees on n vertices, satisfies is now

$$(2) \qquad (n-1)t_n = \sum_{1 \leq m < n} t_{n-m} \sum_{d \mid m} dt_d \quad (n > 1, \, t_1 = 1)$$

For n fixed, select an integer m, $1 \leq m < n$, a divisor d of m, a tree T' of $n - m$ vertices, and a tree T'' of d vertices. Make $j = m/d$ copies of T''. Join the root R of T' to the roots of each of the copies of

T''. There results a tree T of n vertices rooted at R. This operation is symbolized by $T \leftarrow T' + j \otimes T''$.

To prove (2), take d copies of T. We claim that, thus, every rooted tree on n vertices is created exactly $n - 1$ times. Indeed, if T is such a tree, let k be the valence of the root R of T. Delete these k edges and also R, and root each component at the vertex which was connected to R. Suppose the resulting k trees consist of μ_1 copies of a tree τ_1 on l_1 vertices, . . . , μ_s copies of a tree τ_s, on l_s vertices, where, of course, $\mu_1 l_1 + \cdots + \mu_s l_s = n - 1$, and the trees $\tau_1, \ldots, \tau_s$ are nonisomorphic. From these data the tree T can be obtained in the following way: let $1 \le j \le s$, $1 \le r \le \mu_j$, and let T' be the tree obtained by deleting from T r copies of τ_j, including the edges joining their roots to R. Then T is obtained as $T' + r \otimes \tau_j$. We count this construction l_j times; then T is counted $\mu_1 l_1 + \cdots + \mu_s l_s = n - 1$ times, as claimed in (2). See the Postscript to Chapter 10, pp. 77–80, where the general principles underlying such constructions are described.

Formula (2) is well known. The usual proof, which we do not present here, is based on the generating function $T(x) = \sum_{n=1}^{\infty} t_n x^n$ which satisfies the identity

$$(3) \qquad T(x) = x \exp\left\{ \sum_{r=1}^{\infty} \frac{T(x^r)}{r} \right\}$$

Indeed, our construction proves (3), because (2) and (3) are equivalent after logarithmic differentiation of (3).

Most important for our present purposes, we can now use (2) to construct random trees. First the numbers $t_1, t_2, \ldots, t_n$ are to be computed using (2), or the equivalent form (set $m = jd$; take $t_k = 0$ when $k \le 0$)

$$(4) \qquad (n - 1) t_n = \sum_{j=1}^{\infty} d t_{n-1-jd} t_d, \quad t_1 = 1$$

then divide by the left side

$$1 = \sum_{d=1}^{\infty} \frac{d t_{n-jd} t_d}{(n - 1) t_n}$$

and interpret the right side as a sum of probabilities: Choose a pair (j, d), with $j \ge 1$, $d \ge 1$, with a priori probability

$$(5) \qquad \mathrm{prob}(j, d) = \frac{d t_{n-jd} t_d}{(n - 1) t_n}$$

then choose (inductively) a random tree T' on $n - jd$ vertices (with probability $\dfrac{1}{t_{n-jd}}$) and a random tree T'' on d vertices (with probability $\dfrac{1}{t_d}$). Carry out the construction described above to yield a rooted tree T. To calculate the a priori probability of T, observe that the present single construction yields T with probability

$$\frac{dt_{n-jd}t_d}{(n-1)t_n} \cdot \frac{1}{t_{n-jd}} \cdot \frac{1}{t_d} = \frac{d}{(n-1)t_n}$$

Suppose now, as before, that T can be constructed from μ_1 copies of a rooted tree $\tau_1, \ldots, \mu_s$ copies of τ_s; then T could have been constructed with τ_1 taking the part of T'' for $j = 1, \ldots, \mu_1$ (so $d = l_1$) with τ_s taking the part of T'' for $j = 1, \ldots, \mu_s$ (so $d = l_s$). The total a priori probability of T is therefore

$$\sum_{m=1}^{s} \sum_{j=1}^{\mu_m} \frac{l_m}{(n-1)t_n} = \frac{1}{(n-1)t_n} \sum_{m=1}^{s} \mu_m l_m = \frac{1}{t_n}$$

and it follows that all trees of n vertices are equally likely to occur.

The actual inductive construction of random rooted unlabeled trees is complicated by the nonlinearity of (2) and (4): the construction of T requires the construction of *two* other random trees, T' and T''; they in their turn require two trees, etc. This does not end until we hit a random tree with 1 or 2 vertices, which we know how to construct.

As an illustration, let $n = 11$. A random selection based on Eq. (5) with $n = 11$ produces, e.g., $(j, d) = (2, 3)$; so $n - jd = 5$. We draw again, now for $n = 5$ (yielding, e.g., $(3, 1)$) and $n = 2$ (yielding $(1, 2)$). We represent the results in a diagram (actually, a binary tree) in which, for each n, the $n - jd$ is written below n, the d to the right of $n - jd$; and the j along the arrow connecting n to d. The bottom row of Fig. 25.1 now gives rise to the trees in Fig. 25.2 (roots drawn

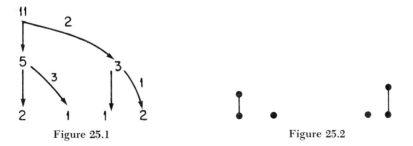

Figure 25.1   Figure 25.2

on top). By joining these according to the line above in Fig. 25.1, we obtain Fig. 25.3. Finally, join these again, and obtain Fig. 25.4.

Figure 25.3   Figure 25.4

Algorithm RANRUT is based on the idea of constructing the tree in Fig. 25.1 in parts, going downward whenever possible, and to the right only when needed. Then, we save what can be constructed and combine pieces as quickly as possible. Figure 25.5 shows, in each column, the part of Fig. 25.1 that has at any moment been determined, and under it a list of relevant graphs from Figs. 25.2–25.4, which are being constructed at the same time. Each column constitutes one step of progress over the previous one. The thin arrows indicate transitions. The numerical codes 1 and 2 are translated into trees because there is only one tree with that number of vertices. Pairs (j, d) are split up into a pair $(j, 0)$ which serves as a reminder on how to combine two trees once they have been constructed, and d which indicates the size of the tree which is to be worked on next.

The pairs of integers (j, d) are stored in one list and are retrieved as needed, on a "last-in, first-out" basis (a so-called "stack"). The partial graphs are stored similarly, and constitute a second stack. The graph is finished when the first stack is empty; the tree T just constructed is the desired output.

An examination of the Figs. 25.1–4 indicates that the stack of pairs

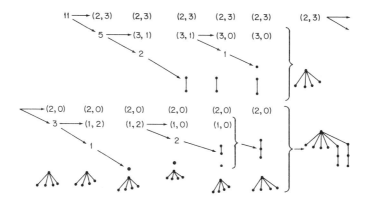

Figure 25.5

of integers never contains more than n elements. Similarly, the stack of trees contains a total of no more than n vertices.

Comment. The notion of unlabeled rooted tree means "equivalence class under isomorphisms of trees in which roots correspond to roots." In more practical terms, the present algorithm claims to produce each equivalence class of rooted n-trees with equal probability, but that does not necessarily hold for each of the inevitable labelings of the vertices in a computer output with which a tree of one type can occur. It is in that sense that the trees here are unlabeled even though the computer forces each one to carry a labeling.

To implement these ideas, the structure of the stacks has to be described more precisely. The first stack, named STACK, will contain pairs (j, d) or $(j, 0)$, and its members are therefore ordered pairs of integers. The second stack, named OUT (because it will hold the final tree) has to contain entire trees of different sizes. Each tree is a collection of edges; i.e., of pairs of vertices, one less in number than the vertices of the tree. OUT therefore also consists of pairs of positive integers, followed by the pair $(N, *)$ ($*$ is irrelevant information) to indicate the size of the tree which is listed before it. (As stacks are read backward, this information actually precedes the edges.) A tree of m vertices occupies $m - 1$ spaces in OUT for its edges, followed by $(m, *)$, a total of m spaces. Counters IS1, IS2 keep track of the content of the stacks. The operation $T' + j \otimes T'' \to T$ is performed in the array OUT itself, in which the final tree is also left as output.

ALGORITHM RANRUT

[*Note:* T_1, T_2 denote the (unique) rooted unlabeled trees on 1, 2 vertices respectively; T', T'' denote generic trees; $T' + j \otimes T''$ denotes the tree constructed from one copy of T' and j copies of T''.]

(A) $n \leftarrow N$; STACK and OUT empty.
(B)   If $n \leq 2$, OUT $\leftarrow T_n$; to (C);
      Else, find (j, d) by (5);
          STACK $\leftarrow (j, d)$; $n \leftarrow n - jd$;
          To (B).
(C) $(j, d) \leftarrow$ STACK;
      If $d = 0$: $\begin{cases} T'' \leftarrow \text{OUT} \\ \\ T' \ \leftarrow \text{OUT} \end{cases}$ $T \leftarrow T' + j \otimes T''$; OUT $\leftarrow T$;

If STACK is empty, T is OUTput: exit;
Else, to (**C**);
Else STACK $\leftarrow (j, 0)$;
$n \leftarrow d$
To (**B**) ■

FLOW CHART RANRUT

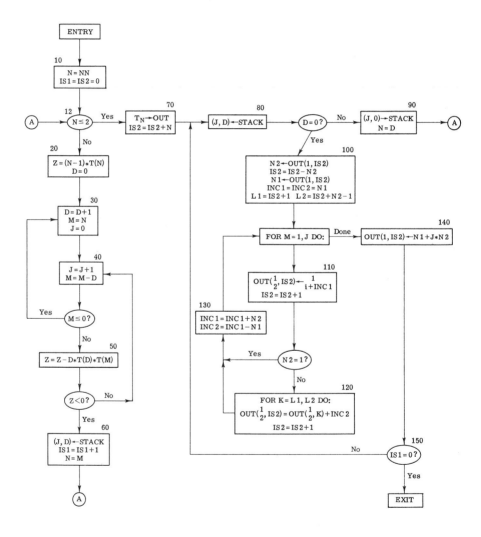

DESCRIPTION OF FLOW CHART

Box 10   Input number of vertices = NN; STACK and OUT are initialized.

Boxes 20–60   Pair (J,D) is determined according to formula (5). D and J are cycling to take all pairs of values for which D*J≤N−1. Pair (J,D) stored in STACK in Box 60.

Box 70   If N=2, IS1←IS1+1; the pair (1,2) is stored in location IS1 of STACK. Then, for all N≤2, IS1←IS1+1; (N,*) is stored in location IS1 of STACK. (* means the content is irrelevant.)

Boxes 80, 90   The following sequence of instructions performs these functions very efficiently:
  N←STACK(2,IS1).
  If N≠0, set STACK(2,IS1)←0; If N≤2, to Box 70; To Box 20. Else, J← STACK(1,IS1), IS1←IS1−1. Proceed with Box 100.

Boxes 100–130   In these boxes, the tree $T' + j \otimes T''$ is constructed in detail. Note that the vertex count N2 of T'' is stored in OUT(1,IS2), and the vertex count N1 of T' in OUT(1,IS2−N2). In the graph $T = T' + j \otimes T''$, the edge listing of T' is left completely unchanged. Box 110 creates for each of the J copies of T'' an edge connecting its root to R(=1). The first copy of T'' (with vertex numbers increased by N1) is written on top of the old one; following copies are then made with vertex numbers increased by another N2 each time. There are special checks for the case N2=1 [skip Box 120]. The variables INC1 and INC2 reset the increments appropriately; first INC1 is set equal N1 (Box 100), then N2 is added each succeeding time (Box 130). INC2 starts off as N1 (Box 100), but then stays N1 units behind NC1 (Box 130) to reflect the fact that it is the already incremented T'' which is being copied after the first time.

SUBROUTINE SPECIFICATIONS

(1)   *Name of subroutine:*   RANRUT.
(2)   *Calling statement:*   CALL RANRUT(NN,OUT,STACK,T).
(3)   *Purpose of subroutine:*   Generate random unlabeled rooted tree.
(4)   *Descriptions of variables in calling statement:*

Name	Type	I/O/W/B	Description
NN	INTEGER	*I*	Number of vertices in desired tree.
OUT	INTEGER(2,NN)	*O*	OUT(1,I), OUT(2,I) are the two end points of the Ith edge of the output tree (I=1,...,NN−1).
STACK	INTEGER(2,NN)	*W*	Working storage.
T	INTEGER(NN)	*B*	T(I) is the number of rooted unlabeled trees of I vertices (I=1,2,...) (universal constants).

(5) *Other routines which are called by this one:*
FUNCTION RAND(I) (random numbers).

(6) *Approximate number of* FORTRAN *instructions:* 73.

```
      SUBROUTINE RANRUT(NN,OUT,STACK,T)
      IMPLICIT INTEGER(A-Z)
      REAL RAND,FLOAT
      DIMENSION OUT(2,NN),STACK(2,NN),T(NN)
      DATA NLAST/1/
      T(1)=1
1     IF(NN.LE.NLAST) GO TO 10
      SUM=0
      DO 2  D=1,NLAST
      I=NLAST+1
      TD=T(D)*D
      DO 3  J=1,NLAST
      I=I-D
      IF(I.LE.0) GO TO 2
3     SUM=SUM+T(I)*TD
2     CONTINUE
      NLAST=NLAST+1
      T(NLAST)=SUM/(NLAST-1)
      GO TO 1
10    N=NN
      IS1=0
      IS2=0
12    IF(N.LE.2) GO TO 70
20    Z=FLOAT((N-1)*T(N))*RAND(1)
      D=0
30    D=D+1
      TD=D*T(D)
      M=N
      J=0
40    J=J+1
      M=M-D
      IF(M.LT.1) GO TO 30
50    Z=Z-T(M)*TD
      IF(Z.GE.0) GO TO 40
60    IS1=IS1+1
      STACK(1,IS1)=J
      STACK(2,IS1)=D
      N=M
```

```
      GO TO 12
70    IF(N.LE.1) GO TO 71
      IS2=IS2+1
      OUT(1,IS2)=1
      OUT(2,IS2)=2
71    IS2=IS2+1
      OUT(1,IS2)=N
80    N=STACK(2,IS1)
      IF(N.EQ.0) GO TO 90
      STACK(2,IS1)=0
      GO TO 12
90    J=STACK(1,IS1)
      IS1=IS1-1
100   N2=OUT(1,IS2)
      IS2=IS2-N2
      N1=OUT(1,IS2)
      INC1=N1
      INC2=N1
      L1=IS2+1
      L2=IS2+N2-1
      DO 110  M=1,J
      OUT(1,IS2)=1
      OUT(2,IS2)=1+INC1
      IS2=IS2+1
      IF(N2.EQ.1) GO TO 130
      DO 120  K=L1,L2
      OUT(1,IS2)=OUT(1,K)+INC2
      OUT(2,IS2)=OUT(2,K)+INC2
120   IS2=IS2+1
130   INC1=INC1+N2
110   INC2=INC1-N1
140   OUT(1,IS2)=N1+J*N2
150   IF(IS1.EQ.0) RETURN
      GO TO 80
      END
```

SAMPLE OUTPUT

Subroutine RANRUT was called 450 times with NN=5. There are 9 different rooted unlabeled trees of 5 vertices (Fig. 25.6). The

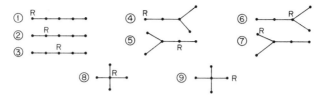

Figure 25.6

frequency with which each of these 9 trees was constructed by RANRUT is shown in the output below.

The value of χ^2 (not shown) is $\chi^2 = 5.6$ with 8 degrees of freedom. In 95% of such experiments the value of χ^2 would lie between 2.03 and 18.17 if the choice of the trees were truly uniform.

1	58
2	48
3	44
4	52
5	52
6	50
7	40
8	58
9	48

26

The Sign of a Permutation (SIGNUM)

Let σ be a permutation of n letters, and suppose that

$$(1) \qquad \sigma = t_1 t_2 \cdots t_p$$

where the t_i are transpositions. Then, by the *sign of* σ we mean $+1$ or -1 depending on whether p is even or odd, respectively. It is well known that the sign of σ depends only on σ and not on the particular representation (1), i.e., no matter how we exhibit σ in the form (1), the parity of p is constant.

Computationally, there are better ways of calculating the sign of than the above. We have, indeed the following

Theorem Let σ be a permutation of n letters, with q cycles. Then

$$(2) \qquad \text{sign}(\sigma) = (-1)^{n-q}$$

To prove this, decompose σ into disjoint cyclic permutations

$$(3) \qquad \sigma = C(n_1)C(n_2) \cdots C(n_q), \qquad n_1 + \cdots + n_q = n$$

and observe that each cyclic permutation

$$C(m): i_1 \to i_2 \to \cdots \to i_m \to i_1$$

can be written as a product of $m-1$ transpositions

$$t_{ij}: i \to j \to i$$

as follows

$$(4) \qquad C(m) = t_{i_1 i_m} \cdots t_{i_1 i_3} t_{i_1 i_2}$$

Now, substitute (4), with $m = n_1, \ldots, n_q$, in (3). We then see σ written as a product of

$$(n_1 - 1) + \cdots + (n_q - 1) = n - q \text{ transpositions}$$

The program is very short. It follows the cycles of σ around, increasing CYCLES by 1 each time it encounters a new cycle, employing the sign bit of SIGMA(I) (I=1,N) to hold the information as to whether I has already appeared in some cycle.

ALGORITHM SIGNUM

(A) $c \leftarrow 0$; $\sigma(i) \leftarrow -\sigma(i)$ $(i = 1, n)$; $i \leftarrow 1$.
(B) If $\sigma(i) > 0$, to (D); $c \leftarrow c + 1$; $m \leftarrow i$.
(C) $\sigma(m) \leftarrow -\sigma(m)$; $m \leftarrow \sigma(m)$; If $m \neq i$, to (C).
(D) If $i < n$: $\{i \leftarrow i + 1$; to (B)$\}$; Sign $\leftarrow (-1)^{n+c}$; Exit ■

SUBROUTINE SPECIFICATIONS

(1) *Name of subroutine:* SIGNUM.
(2) *Calling statement:* CALL SIGNUM(SIGMA,N,SIGN,CYCLES).
(3) *Purpose of subroutine:* Count cycles and find sign of a permutation.
(4) *Descriptions of variables in calling statement:*

Name	Type	I/O/W/B	Description
SIGMA	INTEGER(N)	I	SIGMA(I) is the value of the input permutation $\sigma(I)$ (I=1,N).
N	INTEGER	I	The number of letters being permuted.
SIGN	INTEGER	O	+1 if σ is even, −1 if σ is odd.
CYCLES	INTEGER	O	Number of cycles of the input permutation σ.

(5) *Other routines which are called by this one:* None.
(6) *Approximate number of* FORTRAN *instructions:* 16.

```
SUBROUTINE SIGNUM(SIGMA,N,SIGN,CYCLES)
INTEGER SIGMA(N),SIGN,CYCLES
```

```
     CYCLES=0
     DO 5   I=1,N
5    SIGMA(I)=-SIGMA(I)
     DO 10   I=1,N
     IF(SIGMA(I).GT.0) GO TO 10
     CYCLES=CYCLES+1
     M=I
15   SIGMA(M)=-SIGMA(M)
     M=SIGMA(M)
     IF(M.NE.I) GO TO 15
10   CONTINUE
     SIGN=1-2*MOD(N+CYCLES,2)
     RETURN
     END
```

SAMPLE OUTPUT

If a sequence of edges $e_1, e_2, \ldots, e_E$ is an Euler circuit of a graph G, we call the circuit *even* or *odd* depending on whether the permutation σ of E letters

$$\sigma: i \to e_i \quad (i = 1, E)$$

is an even or odd permutation. For the graph G (Fig. 26.1) we used

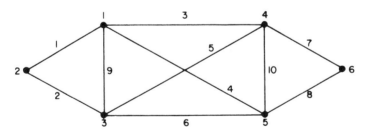

Figure 26.1

the BACKTR subroutine of Chapter 23(C) to generate all Euler circuits, and then used SIGNUM to determine if each circuit was even or odd, and the number of cycles in the corresponding permutation.

On the next page we see, for each of the 44 circuits, the sign of the circuit, the number of cycles in the permutation, and its sequence of edges. Twenty-two circuits are even, and 22 are odd.

-1	5	1	2	9	4	10	7	8	6	5	3
-1	5	1	2	9	4	10	5	6	8	7	3
1	4	1	2	9	4	8	7	10	6	5	3
-1	5	1	2	9	4	8	7	5	6	10	3
1	6	1	2	9	4	6	5	10	8	7	3
-1	7	1	2	9	4	6	5	7	8	10	3
1	4	1	2	9	3	10	8	7	5	6	4
1	4	1	2	9	3	10	6	5	7	8	4
-1	3	1	2	9	3	7	8	10	5	6	4
1	4	1	2	9	3	7	8	6	5	10	4
-1	5	1	2	9	3	5	6	10	7	8	4
1	6	1	2	9	3	5	6	8	7	10	4
-1	3	1	2	6	10	7	8	4	9	5	3
1	4	1	2	6	10	7	8	4	3	5	9
-1	5	1	2	6	10	5	9	4	8	7	3
-1	5	1	2	6	10	5	9	3	7	8	4
1	4	1	2	6	10	3	9	5	7	8	4
1	4	1	2	6	10	3	4	8	7	5	9
1	4	1	2	6	8	7	10	4	9	5	3
-1	3	1	2	6	8	7	10	4	3	5	9
1	4	1	2	6	8	7	5	9	4	10	3
-1	3	1	2	6	8	7	5	9	3	10	4
1	4	1	2	6	8	7	3	9	5	10	4
1	4	1	2	6	8	7	3	4	10	5	9
-1	5	1	2	6	4	9	5	10	8	7	3
1	6	1	2	6	4	9	5	7	8	10	3
-1	5	1	2	6	4	3	10	8	7	5	9
1	4	1	2	6	4	3	7	8	10	5	9
1	4	1	2	5	10	8	7	3	9	6	4
-1	3	1	2	5	10	8	7	3	4	6	9
1	4	1	2	5	10	6	9	4	8	7	3
1	4	1	2	5	10	6	9	3	7	8	4
-1	5	1	2	5	10	4	9	6	8	7	3
-1	5	1	2	5	10	4	3	7	8	6	9
-1	3	1	2	5	7	8	10	3	9	6	4
1	4	1	2	5	7	8	10	3	4	6	9
1	4	1	2	5	7	8	6	9	4	10	3
-1	5	1	2	5	7	8	6	9	3	10	4
-1	3	1	2	5	7	8	4	9	6	10	3
-1	3	1	2	5	7	8	4	3	10	6	9
1	4	1	2	5	3	9	6	10	7	8	4
-1	5	1	2	5	3	9	6	8	7	10	4
1	6	1	2	5	3	4	10	7	8	6	9
-1	5	1	2	5	3	4	8	7	10	6	9

27

Sorting (HPSORT)

A frequently occurring problem in combinatorial work is the *sorting* of an array. One is given b_1, b_2, . . . , b_n, and it is required to permute the members of the array so that the output is in nondecreasing order of size. This is an intensively studied subject, but, even so, important advances continue to be made.

There are various criteria by which one may evaluate the effectiveness of a sorting method, such as (a) the *average* amount of labor (pairwise comparisons or displacements of position) required to sort an array of length n; (b) the *maximum* amount of labor required by *some* sequence of length n; (c) the amount of array storage required; (d) the amount by which the method takes advantage of whatever order is already present in the input list; (e) elegance, compactness, universality, etc.

A comprehensive survey of sorting is given by Knuth [K1, Volume III]. We note here only that the best methods now available require about cn to $cn(\log n)^2$ units of labor on the average, and about $cn(\log n)$ to cn^2 at worst. Furthermore, the best methods will need n to $n + O(\log n)$ storage registers (including the input) and, in the case of merging methods, will speed up operation if considerable order is present on input.

No single sorting method optimizes all departments at once. Our selection here is, we think, a good choice if just one general-purpose sort is to be available for combinatorial applications. It requires an

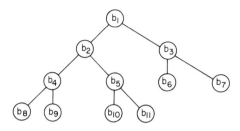

Figure 27.1

average of $cn \log n$ operations, a *maximum* of $cn \log n$ operations, *no* array storage other than the input array, and it is extremely elegant, compact, and universal. Its only unfortunate aspect is that in category (d) above, not only does it fail to take advantage of whatever order is already present, it is actually embarrassingly clumsy when the input list is already sorted! More about this later (see Sample Output p. 231).

Our choice is the "Heapsort" method of Williams and Floyd, which is of quite recent origin (1964).

First, by a *heap* we mean an array $b_1, b_2, \ldots, b_n$ which has the property that

$$(1) \qquad b_{\lfloor j/2 \rfloor} \geq b_j \quad (1 \leq \lfloor j/2 \rfloor < j \leq n)$$

The importance of this idea rests in the fact that if we imagine the elements $b_1, \ldots, b_n$ as being placed at the successive vertices of a binary tree, as in Fig. 27.1 where $n = 11$, then the sequence is a heap if and only if *every "parent" is at least as large as its two "children."* The reader would study this figure and its relationship to (1) carefully before proceeding. The main properties of the parental relationship which we will use are that

$$(2) \qquad \text{The } parent \text{ of } b_j \text{ is } b_{\lfloor j/2 \rfloor} \quad (2 \leq j \leq n)$$

and

$$(3) \qquad \text{The } children \text{ of } b_j \text{ are } \begin{cases} b_{2j} \text{ and } b_{2j+1}, & \text{if } 2j + 1 \leq n \\ b_{2j} \text{ only}, & \text{if } 2j = n \\ \varnothing, & \text{if } 2j > n \end{cases}$$

The Heapsort algorithm is divided into two phases as follows: First, the input array is transformed into a heap, and, second, the heap is sorted into nondecreasing order.

The first problem, then, concerns the transformation of a given array into a heap by rearrangement of its elements. The vertices of the tree are processed in reverse order beginning with the first parent which is $b_{\lfloor n/2 \rfloor}$. Inductively, suppose that we have arrived at a certain parent b_l, and that the left subtree at b_l and the right subtree at b_l have already been transformed into heaps, as shown in Fig. 27.2. How can we make the tree rooted at b_l into a heap?

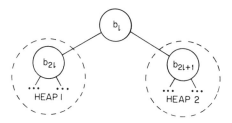

Figure 27.2

We first move b_l to a "safe place," say b^*, thereby creating a vacancy in the tree. Next we begin a "percolating-up" process (Fig. 27.3). The larger of the two descendants of the now-vacant space

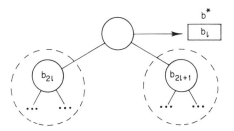

Figure 27.3

moves up if it is larger than b^* and fills the vacancy, but thereby creates another empty slot. Next, the larger of the two descendants of the newly vacated space moves up, if it is larger than b^*, and fills that vacancy but creates another one, and so forth.

The upward motion ceases when the current vacancy has no descendant larger than b^*, and, in particular, it halts if the vacancy has no descendants at all. When it halts, the contents of b^* are moved into the current vacant slot and the upward percolation is complete. At this time the situation in Fig. 27.2 will have been processed, and the full tree shown, including b_l, will constitute a heap. We next go to process b_{l-1} in a similar way.

It is important to break off this piece of the Heapsort as a separate algorithm, which we do as follows:

Definition $\mathscr{F}(l, n)$ is the operation which, given a vertex l in a binary tree of n vertices, and given also that the left subtree at l and the right subtree at l are heaps, carries out an upward percolation process until the entire tree rooted at l is a heap.

ALGORITHM $\mathscr{F}(l, n)$

(A) $l_1 \leftarrow l;\ b^* \leftarrow b_l.$
(B) $m \leftarrow 2l_1;$ If $m > n$, to **(E)**; If $m = n$, to **(D)**.
(C) If $b_{m+1} > b_m,\ m \leftarrow m + 1.$
(D) If $b^* \geqq b_m$, to **(E)**; $b_{l_1} \leftarrow b_m;\ l_1 \leftarrow m;$ to **(B)**.
(E) $b_{l_1} \leftarrow b^*;$ Exit ■

In terms of this Algorithm, the entire transformation of a linear array $b_1, \ldots, b_n$ to a heap is done by

ALGORITHM TOHEAP

(A) For $l = \lfloor n/2 \rfloor, \lfloor n/2 \rfloor - 1, \ldots, 1:$ Do $\mathscr{F}(l, n)$ ■

We now consider the second phase of Heapsort, in which we sort a heap into nondecreasing order. Here, the reason for dealing with operation $\mathscr{F}(l, n)$ as a separate algorithm will become clear because we will use the same algorithm in a different way in this phase.

First, since $b_1, \ldots, b_n$ now constitute a heap, surely b_1 is the largest of all of the array elements. We therefore exchange b_1 and b_n, at which point the nth array element has its final form. Future operations will therefore leave b_n untouched, and we must now contend with the fact that the reduced tree $b_1, \ldots, b_{n-1}$ no longer is a heap because we just ruined everything by moving the last element to b_1. However, the left subtree at vertex 1 is still a heap, and the right subtree at vertex 1 is still a heap. Hence if we apply operation $\mathscr{F}(1, n - 1)$, then all will be well again!

After doing $\mathscr{F}(1, n - 1)$, the largest of $b_1, \ldots, b_{n-1}$ will now occupy position 1. We exchange b_1 with b_{n-1}, apply $\mathscr{F}(1, n - 2)$, etc., after which the input array appears in sorted order.

The algorithm for sorting a heap is therefore

ALGORITHM SORTHEAP

(A) $n_1 \leftarrow n$.

(B) Exchange b_1, b_{n_1}; If $n_1 \leq 2$, exit; $n_1 \leftarrow n_1 - 1$; Do $\mathscr{F}(1, n_1)$; To **(B)** ■

We can observe that Algorithm $\mathscr{F}(l, n)$ is used by both of the phases of Heapsort. It will therefore be written as a subroutine within a subroutine and will be called by the other phases.

The labor involved in $\mathscr{F}(l, n)$ is, at most, one comparison and one displacement for each level of the tree below the level of the lth element. The lth element is at level $1 + \lfloor \log_2 l \rfloor$ in the tree, so $\mathscr{F}(l, n)$ involves, at most,

$$(1 + \lfloor \log_2 n \rfloor) - (1 + \lfloor \log_2 l \rfloor) = O\left(\log \frac{n}{l}\right)$$

comparisons and a like number of displacements of position.

It follows, by summation, that phase Toheap entails at most $O(n)$ operations. Sortheap takes $O(n \log n)$ operations. The full algorithm Heapsort, therefore, is accomplished with at most $O(n \log n)$ comparisons and displacements.

The program is very simply related to the algorithms: Instructions in lines 3–7 are Toheap, 8–10 are Sortheap, and 11–21 do operation $\mathscr{F}(\text{L}, \text{N1})$. The entire program requires just 23 FORTRAN instructions.

SUBROUTINE SPECIFICATIONS

(1) *Name of subroutine:* HPSORT.

(2) *Calling statement:* CALL HPSORT(N,B).

(3) *Purpose of subroutine:* Sort a linear array into nondecreasing order.

(4) *Descriptions of variables in calling statement:*

Name	Type	I/O/W/B	Description
N	INTEGER	I	Length of input array.
B	INTEGER(N)	I/O	B(I) is the Ith element of the input array, and then is the Ith element of the sorted array (I=1,N).

(5) *Other routines which are called by this one:* None.

(6) *Approximate number of* FORTRAN *instructions:* 23.

(7) *Remarks:* If B is a REAL array, change type declaration of B,BSTAR to REAL.

```
      SUBROUTINE HPSORT(N,B)
      INTEGER B(N),BSTAR
      N1=N
      L=1+N/2
11    L=L-1
      BSTAR=B(L)
      GO TO 30
25    BSTAR=B(N1)
      B(N1)=B(1)
29    N1=N1-1
30    L1=L
31    M=2*L1
      IF(M-N1) 32,33,37
32    IF(B(M+1).GE.B(M)) M=M+1
33    IF(BSTAR.GE.B(M)) GO TO 37
      B(L1)=B(M)
      L1=M
      GO TO 31
37    B(L1)=BSTAR
      IF(L.GT.1) GO TO 11
      IF(N1.GE.2) GO TO 25
      RETURN
      END
```

SAMPLE OUTPUT

We illustrate the workings of HPSORT by showing it in the case where, on input, $B(I)=I$ ($I=1,10$), so that no sorting is really required at all. The first nine lines of output show the status of the array B on input, and then after each displacement. At the ninth step the input array has been transformed into a heap, which concludes the TOHEAP part of the operation. In each line the appearance of a box □ indicates the position of the vacancy in the percolation-up process, and the number within the box is the current content of the "safekeeping" register b^*.

The next 22 lines of output show the transformation of the heap into a fully sorted array. Note how the final output appears from right to left starting from the last array element.

```
 1   2   3   4  [5]  6   7   8   9  10
 1   2   3  [4] 10   6   7   8   9   5
 1   2  [3]  9  10   6   7   8   4   5
 1  [2]  7   9  10   6   3   8   4   5
 1  10   7   9  [2]  6   3   8   4   5
 1  10   7   9   5   6   3   8   4  [2]
10  [1]  7   9   5   6   3   8   4   2
10   9   7  [1]  5   6   3   8   4   2
10   9   7   8   5   6   3  [1]  4   2

 2   9   7   8   5   6   3   1   4  10
 9  [2]  7   8   5   6   3   1   4  10
 9   8   7  [2]  5   6   3   1   4  10
 9   8   7   4   5   6   3   1  [2] 10
 2   8   7   4   5   6   3   1   9  10
 8  [2]  7   4   5   6   3   1   9  10
 8   5   7   4  [2]  6   3   1   9  10
 1   5   7   4   2   6   3   8   9  10
 7   5  [1]  4   2   6   3   8   9  10
 7   5   6   4   2  [1]  3   8   9  10
[3]  5   6   4   2   1   7   8   9  10
 6   5  [3]  4   2   1   7   8   9  10
[1]  5   3   4   2   6   7   8   9  10
 5  [1]  3   4   2   6   7   8   9  10
 5   4   3  [1]  2   6   7   8   9  10
[2]  4   3   1   5   6   7   8   9  10
 4  [2]  3   1   5   6   7   8   9  10
[1]  2   3   4   5   6   7   8   9  10
 3   2  [1]  4   5   6   7   8   9  10
[1]  2   3   4   5   6   7   8   9  10
 2  [1]  3   4   5   6   7   8   9  10
 1   2   3   4   5   6   7   8   9  10
```

28

Tree of Minimal Length (MINSPT)

Suppose we are given n "cities" which are to be interconnected by a communications network by connecting certain pairs of cities, and suppose the network is to be as short as possible. It takes only a moment to observe that the minimal network will be a tree on the n given vertices, namely, that tree T^* whose edges have minimum total length.

For illustrative purposes, at the end of Chapter 23(E) we found such a minimal tree by examining all n^{n-2} possible candidates and choosing the one of minimum length. Yet, the same objective can be attained in $O(n^2)$ calculations, a saving so substantial that the calculation for $n \sim 50$ or 100 is brought from the realm of the unthinkable to the ordinary.

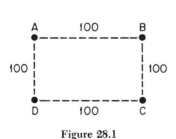

Figure 28.1

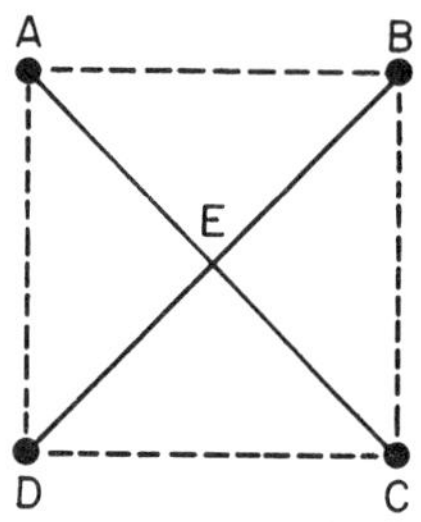

Figure 28.2

Before we discuss the algorithm, let us observe that another, more general, question is actually more "realistic." To connect the four cities A, B, C, D in Fig. 28.1 would require a network 300 units long. But, if we first introduce a new point E at the center of the square (Fig. 28.2), the interconnection can be achieved, as shown, with a network of length only 282^+ units. The reader may wish to see if, by adding *two* extra points, the network can be made still shorter. This more general problem in which we are allowed to add new vertices is called the Steiner tree problem and has an extensive literature, although it remains unsolved. We shall restrict ourselves here to the original problem in which no further points can be adjoined to the configuration.

We claim that the following procedure will generate a tree of minimal length:

Let T_0 denote the tree which consists of the single vertex $\{1\}$. For $j = 1, 2, \ldots, n - 1$ let T_j be obtained by adjoining to T_{j-1} an edge a_j whose length is minimal in the class of all edges with one end in T_{j-1} and one end not in T_{j-1}. Then T_{n-1} is a tree of minimal length.

Indeed, suppose T^* is any tree of minimal length. Let D^*, D be the lengths of T^*, T_{n-1}, respectively. Suppose $D > D^*$. Let a_i be the first edge in the sequence

$$a_1, a_2, \ldots, a_{n-1}$$

of edges of T_{n-1}, which does not appear in T^*. In T^*, let b denote the edge which joins the component C_1 spanned by edges $a_1, \ldots, a_i$ to the component of T^* induced by the vertices of T^* which are not in C_1. Suppose b is larger than a_i. Then we could replace b by a_i in T^* and obtain a shorter tree, contradicting the minimality of T^*. Suppose b is shorter than a_i. Then we would have chosen b instead of a_i at the ith stage of our construction of T_{n-1}. Hence, b and a_i have the same length.

Replace b by a_i in T^*, which leaves its length invariant, and repeat the argument: Let a_k be the first edge of T_{n-1} which is not in T^*, etc. The argument halts after at most $n - 1$ steps with T^* having been transformed into T_{n-1} by a sequence of length-preserving edge-substitutions ■

For the implementation of the algorithm on the computer, we consider first a straightforward approach which costs $O(n^3)$ operations, then a slightly devious one which is executed in only $O(n^2)$ operations.

Suppose a partial minimal tree T_{j-1} has been given. For each of the $n - j$ vertices x not in T_{j-1}, we find the minimum distance from x to the j vertices in T_{j-1}. This requires jn operations. We adjoin the edge of minimal length to T_{j-1}. This requires

$$\sum_{j=1}^{n-1} jn = \frac{n^3}{2} + O(n^2)$$

operations.

An improvement could be made by first sorting the distances into ascending order in $O(n^2 \log n)$ operations, but, to achieve the $O(n^2)$ promised above, suppose at the jth stage we maintain not only a record of the edges in the current partial tree T_{j-1}, but also the auxiliary linear arrays:

y_i = minimum distance from vertex i to current partial tree T_{j-1} (or 0, if vertex $i \in T_{j-1}$) $(i = 1, \ldots, n)$

and

u_i = name of a vertex in the current partial tree to which i is nearest

$(i \notin T_{j-1}; i = 1, \ldots, n)$.

Then to construct T_j from T_{j-1} we (a) find the smallest nonzero y_i, say y_{i^*} (n operations); (b) Let $j^* = u_{i^*}$, and adjoin the edge (i^*, j^*) to T_{j-1}; (c) update the array y_i by putting $y_{i^*} = 0$ and replacing all other nonzero y_i by the smaller of $(y_i$, distance from i to $i^*)$. Further, if y_i is not the smaller of those two numbers, then replace u_i by i^* ($2n$ operations).

Formally, our algorithm for finding a minimal spanning tree is

ALGORITHM MINSPT

(A) [*Initialize*] $y_1 \leftarrow 0$; For $i = 2$; n: $\{u_i \leftarrow 1, y_i \leftarrow \text{dist } (1, i)\}$.

(B) [*Adjoin next edge*] $d_{\min} \leftarrow \min \{y_i | y_i \neq 0\} = y_{i_{\min}}$; Adjoin edge $(i_{\min}, u_{i_{\min}})$.

(C) [*Update arrays*] If tree has $n - 1$ edges, exit; $y_{i_{\min}} \leftarrow 0$; For $i = 2, n$: {If $y_i \neq 0$ and $\text{dist}(i, i_{\min}) < y_i$: $\{u_i \leftarrow i_{\min}; y_i \leftarrow \text{dist}(i, i_{\min})\}\}$; To (B) ∎

FLOW CHART MINSPT

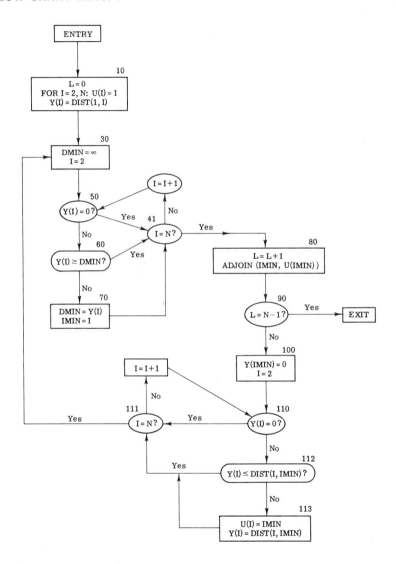

DESCRIPTION OF FLOW CHART

Box 10   L counts the edges in the current tree. Initialize arrays.

Boxes 30–70   Find minimum Y(I) among those which are ≠0, and IMIN=I at which
minimum occurs.

Box 80 Increase L and adjoin IMIN, U(IMIN) as the Lth edge of the output array ENDPT.

Box 90 If L=N-1 we are finished.

Boxes 100–113 Update arrays Y(I), U(I) and go to Box 30 to adjoin next edge.

SUBROUTINE SPECIFICATIONS

(1) *Name of subroutine:* MINSPT.
(2) *Calling statement:* CALL MINSPT(DIST,N,ENDPT,U,Y).
(3) *Purpose of subroutine:* Find spanning tree of minimal length.
(4) *Descriptions of variables in calling statement:*

Name	Type	I/O/W/B	Description
DIST	REAL(N,N)	I	DIST(I,J) = distance from I to J ($1 \leq I, J \leq N$).
N	INTEGER	I	Number of vertices.
ENDPT	INTEGER(2,N)	O	ENDPT(1,I), ENDPT(2,I) are the two ends of the Ith edge in the output minimal tree (I=1,N-1).
U	INTEGER(N)	W	Working storage.
Y	REAL(N)	W	Working storage.

(5) *Other routines which are called by this one:* None.
(6) *Approximate number of* FORTRAN *instructions:* 28.
(7) *Remarks:* If input graph is not complete, put DIST=∞ on missing edges.

```
      SUBROUTINE MINSPT(DIST,N,ENDPT,U,Y)
      INTEGER U(N),ENDPT(2,N)
      DIMENSION Y(N),DIST(N,N)
10    L=0
20    DO 21  I=2,N
      U(I)=1
21    Y(I)=DIST(1,I)
30    DMIN=1.E50
40    DO 41  I=2,N
50    IF(Y(I).EQ.0) GO TO 41
60    IF(Y(I).GE.DMIN) GO TO 41
70    DMIN=Y(I)
      IMIN=I
41    CONTINUE
```

```
80   L=L+1
     ENDPT(1,L)=IMIN
     ENDPT(2,L)=U(IMIN)
90   IF(L.EQ.N-1) RETURN
100  Y(IMIN)=0
110  DO 111  I=2,N
     IF(Y(I).EQ.0) GO TO 111
     D1=DIST(I,IMIN)
112  IF(Y(I).LE.D1) GO TO 111
113  U(I)=IMIN
     Y(I)=D1
111  CONTINUE
     GO TO 30
     END
```

SAMPLE OUTPUT

Refer to sample output of Chapter 23(E), p. 199 for the statement of the problem.

Below we find first the input matrix DIST(I,J) (I,J= 1,5), and then the ENDPT array which is output of MINSPT.

```
  0.   100.   125.   120.   110.
100.     0.    40.    65.    60.
125.    40.     0.    45.    55.
120.    65.    45.     0.    50.
110.    60.    55.    50.     0.

2  3  4  5
1  2  3  4
```

Exercises

[The numbers in brackets are those of the relevant chapters.]

1. Find the first ten Taylor series coefficients, about the origin, of $w(z)$, the solution of the equation $we^{-w} = z$. [17]

2. Statistically estimate, by 1000 random trials, the probability that a shuffled deck of 52 cards contains no "straight," i.e., a set of five cards of consecutive faces values (Ace = 1, Jack = 11, Queen = 12, King = 13). [8]

3. Tabulate the number of labeled trees on n vertices which have exactly j endpoints ($j = 1, 2, \ldots, n$; $n = 2, 3, 4, 5, 6$). [23(E)]

4. Find the average number of endpoints in a sample of 200 random labeled trees on n vertices ($n = 2, 3, 4, 5, 6$). [24]

5. Deal poker hands to k people. [4]

6. The symmetric group S_n is generated by just *two* elements

$$t : 1 \to 2;\; 2 \to 1;\; 3 \to 3;\; \ldots\; ;\; n \to n$$

$$u : 1 \to 2 \to 3 \to \cdots \to n \to 1$$

Sequence the 24 elements of S_4 so that each is obtained from its predecessor by either t or u. Can you do S_5? [7, 23]

7. For some small values of n, estimate by random trials the average number of edges which must be added one at a time to the totally disconnected graph on n vertices in order to connect it. [14]

8. Given A, an $n \times n$ integer matrix. Output a single integer word whose ith bit position is 1 or 0 according to whether the ith row sum of A is odd or even, respectively.

9. For Hamilton's graph of p. 193,

(a) calculate the chromatic polynomial $P(\lambda; G)$
(b) evaluate $P(\lambda; G)$ $(\lambda = 0(1)8)$
(c) find the edge-connectivity of G
(d) what is the chromatic number χ of G?
(e) list all χ-colorings of G.   [16, 15, 18, 23(B)]

10. Modify PERMAN to calculate the permanent of a double-precision complex matrix. Test your program to make sure it works.
[19]

11. (a) Which of the "random" routines in this book do you think would provide a sensitive test of the randomness of a random number generator? Discuss.

(b) Use the program of your choice to compare any three random number generators.

12. Think about how a subroutine can discover how many bits are in a machine word in the machine on which the subroutine is being run.

13. Given blocks of information $B(1), \ldots, B(N)$ (each block could be, e.g., a row of a matrix). Assume a subroutine MOVE(I,J) will move the content of B(I) to B(J). There is one more block B0. Information is moved into and out of B0 by calling MOVE(I,0) or MOVE(0,I).

Permute the blocks so that $B(P(I))$ is moved to $B(I)$ (I=1,N), where P is a given permutation.   [13]

14. (a) Identify the revolving-door algorithm as the unfolding of a Hamilton circuit on a certain graph $G(n, k)$. Describe $G(n, k)$.   [3]

(b) How many vertices does $G(n, k)$ have? How many edges?
(c) What is the valence of each vertex of $G(n, k)$?
(d) Draw $G(5, 3)$.
(e) Use HAMCRC [23(D)] to list all of the Hamilton circuits of $G(5, 3)$. Identify the RD algorithm as one of these circuits.

15. (a)   Determine if two given graphs G, H are isomorphic.   [7]
(b)   Determine all isomorphism types of graphs on six vertices.

16.   Sample a nonnegative integer n at random from the Poisson distribution

$$\text{Prob}(n) = \frac{a^n}{n!}\, e^{-a} \quad (n = 0, 1, \ldots)$$

where $a > 0$ is given.

17.   Determine if the integers from 1 to n, inclusive, can be arranged in three sets that if a and b are in the same set, then $a + b$ is not in that set. Run this program to find the largest n for which it can be done.   [23]

18.   Given a Boolean polynomial f of M terms, in N variables. Determine if f is a tautology (always true), and if not, output a set of values of the variables at which f is false.   [1]

19.   Given two partitions of n: π and π'. Output $+1$ if π is a refinement of π', -1 if π' is a refinement of π, 0 otherwise.   [9]

20.   Find the Möbius function of the set of partitions of n, partially ordered by refinement.   [9, 22]

21.   Can you invert a given permutation of n letters using no additional array storage? (Cheat slightly: Use the left halves of the array words whose right halves contain the given permutation.) Write the program as a subroutine PERINV(N,SIGMA).

22.   (a)   Output the list of edges of a random graph on n labeled vertices, k edges, without loops or multiple edges.
(b)   Estimate, by random trials, the probability that such a graph is connected, for some small values of k, n.   [4, 24]

23.   Show that when the chromatic polynomial is expressed in factorial form, the coefficients are the number of colorings in *exactly m* colors, $m = 0, 1, \ldots$ [15, 16]

24.   To find random subsets of $\{1, \ldots, n\}$, note that 2^{-i} is the probability that i is the smallest element. A random ξ can determine, without a search, a_1 as the smallest i for which $2^{-1} \leq \xi$ (use logarithms!); adjoin this i to the subset; now work on $\{i + 1, \ldots, n\}$, etc. Work out all details and estimate the labor involved per subset.   [2]

25.   What is a rhyme scheme, in poetry? How many rhyme schemes can an n-line poem have? Print all possible rhyme schemes of an

n-line poem, $n = 2, 3, 4, 5, 6$. (Our thanks to John Riordan for this one.) [11]

26. (a) Construct the vertex-adjacency matrix of the n-cube Q_n.
    (b) List the Hamilton circuits of Q_4. [1]

27. Print the multiplication table of S_n. [7]

28. To choose random k-subsets of $\{1, \ldots, n\}$: for each $i = 1, \ldots, k$, choose l at random in $[1, n - i + 1]$; let m be the number among the previously chosen $a_1, \ldots, a_{i-1}$ which are less than l. Set $a_i \leftarrow l + m$.

   (a) Prove that the method works.
   (b) Estimate its operation count.
   (c) Modify it by binary search and insertion to assume the list is in increasing order. [4]

29. Given numbers $k_1, \ldots, k_l$ whose sum is n. Write a subroutine which randomly partitions $\{1, \ldots, n\}$ into subsets $S_1, \ldots, S_l$ with $k_1, \ldots, k_l$ elements, respectively.
   Can you do this with $O(nl)$ operations? With $O(n \log l)$ operations? [12]

30. Work out an algorithm for generating a random k-subset which will select an integer at random from $[1, n]$ and insert it to a linked binary tree or reject it if it was already in the tree. Discuss the labor and array storage involved. [4]

31. Given the edge-list of a tree T on n vertices. Consider vertex 1 to be the root.

   (a) Find, for each vertex, its distance from the root.
   (b) Orient the edges of T "away from the root."
   (c) Rearrange the edge-list of T such that no edge e is preceded in the list by an edge e' which occurs after e on some directed path from the root. [13, 20, 21]

32. Let $a_1, \ldots, a_k$ be given positive integers. For each $n \geq 0$, let $P(n)$ denote the number of representations of n in the form

$$n = \mu_1 a_1 + \mu_2 a_2 + \cdots + \mu_k a_k \quad (\mu_i \geq 0, \forall i)$$

   (a) Show that

$$\frac{1}{(1 - x^{a_1}) \cdots (1 - x^{a_k})} = \sum_{j=0}^{\infty} P(j) x^j$$

(b)   Differentiate logarithmically to show that

$$nP(n) = \sum_{m<n} \tilde{\sigma}(n-m)P(m) \quad (P(0) = 1)$$

Describe $\tilde{\sigma}(m)$.

(c)   Modify RANPAR to select a representation of n in this form at random (p. 70; see also [NW3]).   [10, 17]

33.   Transpose an $m \times n$ matrix A using a minimum of auxiliary array storage.

34.   Devise an algorithm which will generate all compositions of n into k parts, sequenced so that each is obtained from its immediate predecessor by a single jump of one ball from one cell to another.
                                                                          [5]

35.   Devise an algorithm which will generate all partitions of an n-set, sequenced so that each is obtained from its predecessor by changing the class of some single element.   [11]

36.   In many applications, we may want to process the $(\leq k)$-subsets of an n-set and then, as each one is produced, compute some function of the subset. Depending on the outcome, we may designate the subset as "bad" in which case we do not want to see any of *its* subsets.

Think about the design of an algorithm which will go a long way toward this objective.

37.   Write a FORTRAN subroutine of ≤ 25 instructions, which will select at random a binary tree on n vertices and output the edge list.
                                                                          [25]

38.   (a)   Given an array B(1),...,B(N). Describe a method of sorting B into nondecreasing order by constructing the zeta matrix of a certain partial order, then calling TRIANG, then calling RENUMB.

(b)   Why is this a very inefficient sorting method? [13, 21, 27]

39.   Tabulate the number of displacements and the number of comparisons required to sort each of 100 random input vectors B(1),..., B(N). Print the average and the maximum for N=3,4,...,12. Do this for the Heapsort program of Chapter 27, and for two other sorting methods of your choice.   [8, 27]

40. Let $F(n, j)$ denote the number of permutations of n letters such that the Heapsort program requires exactly j exchanges of pairs in order to sort the permutation into ascending order.

Tabulate $F(n, j)$ for $n = 2, 3, 4, 5, 6, 7$ and all j.   [27, 7]

Bibliographic Notes

Chapter 1 This algorithm is well-known. See Gilbert [G1] for further interesting properties of paths on the cube. For a history of the Gray Code, see Gardner [Ga1].

Chapter 3 The lexicographic algorithm is well-known. Lehmer [L1] discusses it and several variations. The revolving-door algorithm was worked out in this form by Peter Freyd and the present authors.

Chapter 4 For combinatorial properties of Stirling numbers, see Feller [F1] and Knuth [K1]. Random number generators are in Ralston and Wilf [RW1] and Knuth [K1, Vol. II].

Chapter 5 Ehrenfest's argument is given in Feller [F1]. Three other algorithms are mentioned in Lehmer [L1].

Chapter 7 Many methods are known for generating permutations. For Wells's see [W1] or his book [W2]. To generate them by a transposition of *adjacent* letters, see Trotter [Tr1]. Other possibilities are in Lehmer [L1].

Chapter 9 To generate partitions with a fixed number of parts, see Lehmer [L1].

Chapter 10 The ideas are due to Nijenhuis and Wilf [NW1]. For elementary properties of partitions, see Liu [Li1].

Postscript   See Bender and Goldman [BG1] for "Prefabs," as well as the earlier work by Foata and Schützenberger [FS1].

Chapter 11   The algorithm is well-known; see e.g. [Ev1].

Chapter 12   This is due to Nijenhuis and Wilf [NW1].

Chapter 16   For elementary properties of the chromatic polynomial, see Read [R1]. The reduction formula (1) goes back at least as far as Whitney [Wh1]. The general method of visiting the vertices of a binary tree is one of those in Knuth [K1]. The arrangement of the chromatic polynomial calculation as a binary tree search, the listing of edges with a spanning tree first, and the reconstruction of the spanning tree after identification all appear here for the first time.

Chapter 17   Faa di Bruno's formula is discussed in Knuth [K1]. The logarithmic differentiation algorithm for $f(z)^n$ is well-known [K1, Vol. II, Section 47]. Its use for a general $g(f(z))$ seems to be new (compare [K1, Exercises 4.7–4.11]).

Chapter 18   The standard and still-excellent reference on network flows is Ford and Fulkerson [FF1]; see also [Be1]. For an in-depth discussion of edge-connectivity, see Tutte [Tu1]. Dinic's algorithm is in [D1]. The work of Even and Tarjan is contained in a paper "Network flow and testing graph connectivity" which was kindly made available to us by the authors.

Chapter 19   Ryser's formula is in Ryser [Ry1]. For the rencontres numbers, see Riordan [Ri1]. The conjecture of Ryser and Minc is enunciated in Ryser [Ry2] and Minc [M1]. The theorem of (9) is due to Nijenhuis and Wilf [NW2]. The factor of 2, as in (24), can also be derived from Eq. (2) of Wilf [Wi1]. The applicability of the Gray code has also been observed by Knuth [K1, Vol. 2, p. 440] who also gives an algorithm as fast as ours, which however requires nearly 2^n storage locations and a more complex program.

Chapter 22   Current interest in the Möbius function is traceable to Rota [Ro1] (though the idea is older) and many interesting properties of the function are developed there.

Chapter 23   The backtrack method in general is discussed in Lehmer [L1] and Walker [Wa1].

Chapter 24   Several proofs of Cayley's theorem are in Moon [Mo1]. The enumerations (5) and (6) are in Moon [Mo2].

Chapter 25   Formula (2) is in standard references such as Knuth [K1]. The algorithm is new here, as is the combinatorial interpretation of (2).

Chapter 26 The theorem (2) can be found in any book on finite groups. The problem of even and odd Euler circuits, and particularly the classification of graphs which have an equal number even and odd, has an interesting literature. See Swan [S1], Kostant [Ko1], Hutchinson [H1].

Chapter 27 A definitive discussion of sorting is in Knuth [K1, Vol. III]. The Heapsort is due to Floyd [Fl1] and Williams [Wl1].

Chapter 28 The more complex Steiner tree problem is reviewed in Gilbert and Pollak [GP1]. The algorithm here is due to Kruskal [Kr1] and Prim [P1]. Our thanks to Dr. Pollak for several informative discussions of this problem.

References

Beckenbach, E.
  [Be1] Network flow problems, in "Applied Combinatorial Mathematics" (E. Beck-
         enbach, ed.). Wiley, New York, 1964.
Bender, E. A., and Goldman, J. R.
  [BG1] Enumerative uses of generating functions, *Indiana Univ. Math. J.* **20**
         (*1971*), 753–765.
Conte, S. I., and de Boor, C.
  [CB1] "Elementary Numerical Analysis" 2nd ed. McGraw-Hill, New York, 1972.
Dinic, E. A.
  [D1]   Algorithms for the solution of a problem of maximum flow in a network with
         power estimation, *Dokl. Nauk. S.S.S.R.* **11** (1970), 1277–1280.
Even, S.
  [Ev1] "Combinatorial Algorithms." Macmillan, New York, 1973.
Feller, W.
  [F1]   "An Introduction to Probability Theory and Its Applications." Wiley, New
         York, 1951.
Floyd, R. W.
  [Fl1] *Comm. ACM.* **7** (1964), 701.
Foata, D., and Schützenberger, M.
  [FS1] "Théorie géométrique des polynomes euleriens" (Lecture Notes in Math.,
         No. 138). Springer-Verlag, Berlin and New York, 1970.
Ford, L. R., and Fulkerson, D. R.
  [FF1] "Flows in Networks." Princeton Univ. Press, Princeton, New Jersey, 1962.
Gardner, M.
  [Ga1] Sci. Amer. (August, 1972), 105–109.

Gilbert, E. N.
[G1] Gray codes and paths on the n-cube, *Bell System Tech. J.* **37** (1958), 815–826.
Gilbert, E. N., and Pollak, H. O.
[GP1] Steiner minimal trees, *SIAM J. Appl. Math.* **16** (1968), 1–29.
Goldman, J. R.
　　　See [BG1].
Hutchinson, J. P.
[H1] Eulerian graphs and polynomial identities for sets of matrices, *Proc. Nat. Acad. Sci. U.S.A.*, 1974.
Knuth, D.
[K1] "The Art of Computer Programming" (3 vols.). Addison-Wesley, Reading, Massachusetts, 1968, 1969, 1973.
Kostant, B.
[Ko1] A theorem of Frobenius, a theorem of Amitsur-Levitzki and cohomology theory, *J. Math. Mech.* **7** (1958) 237–264.
Kruskal, J. B., Jr.
[Kr1] On the shortest spanning subtree of a graph and the travelling salesman problem, *Proc. Amer. Math. Soc.* **7** (1956), 48–50.
Lehmer, D. H.
[L1] The machine tools of combinorics, *in* "Applied Combinatorial Mathematics" (E. Beckenbach, ed.). Wiley, New York, 1964.
Liu, C. L.
[Li1] "Introduction to Combinatorial Mathematics." McGraw-Hill, New York, 1968.
Minc, H.
[M1] Upper bounds for permanents of (0,1) matrices, *Bull. Am. Math. Soc.* **69** (1963), 789–791.
Moon, J. W.
[Mo1] Various proofs of Cayley's formula for counting trees, *in* "A Seminar on Graph Theory" (L. Beineke and F. Harary, eds.). Holt, New York, 1967.
[Mo2] Counting labelled trees, *Canad. Math. Monographs*, No. 1, 1970.
Nijenhuis, A., and Wilf, H. S.
[NW1] A method and two algorithms in the theory of partitions, *J. Combinatorial Theory*, to appear.
[NW2] On a conjecture of Ryser and Minc, *Nederl. Akad. Wetensch., Proc. Ser. A*, **73** (1970), 151–157.
[NW3] Representations of integers by linear forms in nonnegative integers, *J. Number Theory*, **4** (1970), 98–106.
Pollak, H. O.
　　　See [GP1].
Prim, R. C.
[P1] Shortest connection networks and some generalizations, *Bell System Tech. J.* **36** (1957) 1389–1401.
Ralston, A., and Wilf, H. S.
[RW1] "Mathematical Methods for Digital Computers" (2 vols.). Wiley, New York, 1960, 1966.
Read, R. C.
[R1] An introduction to chromatic polynomials, *J. Combinatorial Theory* **4** (1968), 52–71.
Riordan, John
[Ri1] "An Introduction to Combinatorial Analysis." Wiley, New York, 1958.

Rota, G. C.

[Ro1]   On the foundations of combinatorial theory, I. The Möbius function. Z. *Wahrscheinlichkeitstheorie und Verw. Gebiete*, **2** (1964), 340–368.

Ryser, H.

[Ry1]   "Combinatorial Mathematics" (Carus Math. Monographs, No. 14). Wiley, New York, 1963.

[Ry2]   Matrices of zeros and ones, *Bull. Amer. Math. Soc.* **66** (1960), 442–464.

Swan, R. G.

[S1]   An application of graph theory to algebra, *Proc. Amer. Math. Soc.* **14** (1963), 367–373; Correction, **21** (1969), 379–380.

Trotter, H.

[Tr1]   "PERM", Algorithm 115, *Comm. ACM.* **5** (1962), 434–435.

Tutte, W. T.

[T1]   "Connectivity in Graphs." Univ. of Toronto Press, Toronto, 1966.

Walker, R. J.

[Wa1]   An enumerative technique for a class of combinatorial problems, in "Combinatorial Analysis," *Proc. Symp. Appl. Math.* **10** (1960), 91–94 (R. Bellman and M. Hall, eds.). Amer. Math. Soc., Providence, Rhode Island.

Wells, M. B.

[W1]   Generation of permutations by transposition, *Math. Comp.* **15** (1961), 192–195.

[W2]   "Elements of Combinatorial Computing." Pergamon, New York, 1971.

Whitney, H.

[Wh1]   The coloring of graphs, *Ann. of Math.* **33** (1932) 688–718.

Wilf, H. S.

[Wi1]   A mechanical counting method and combinatorial applications, *J. Combinatorial Theory* **4** (1968), 246–258. See also [NW1], [NW2], [NW3], [RW1].

Williams, J. W. J.

[Wl1]   *Comm. ACM.* **7** (1964), 347–348.

Index

Computer Science and Applied Mathematics
A SERIES OF MONOGRAPHS AND TEXTBOOKS

Editor
Werner Rheinboldt
University of Maryland

HANS P. KÜNZI, H. G. TZSCHACH, and C. A. ZEHNDER. Numerical Methods of Mathematical Optimization: With ALGOL and FORTRAN Programs, Corrected and Augmented Edition

AZRIEL ROSENFELD. Picture Processing by Computer

JAMES ORTEGA AND WERNER RHEINBOLDT. Iterative Solution of Nonlinear Equations in Several Variables

AZARIA PAZ. Introduction to Probabilistic Automata

DAVID YOUNG. Iterative Solution of Large Linear Systems

ANN YASUHARA. Recursive Function Theory and Logic

JAMES M. ORTEGA. Numerical Analysis: A Second Course

G. W. STEWART. Introduction to Matrix Computations

CHIN-LIANG CHANG AND RICHARD CHAR-TUNG LEE. Symbolic Logic and Mechanical Theorem Proving

C. C. GOTLIEB AND A. BORODIN. Social Issues in Computing

ERWIN ENGELER. Introduction to the Theory of Computation

F. W. J. OLVER. Asymptotics and Special Functions

DIONYSIOS C. TSICHRITZIS AND PHILIP A. BERNSTEIN. Operating Systems

ROBERT R. KORFHAGE. Discrete Computational Structures

PHILIP J. DAVIS AND PHILIP RABINOWITZ. Methods of Numerical Integration

A. T. BERZTISS. Data Structures: Theory and Practice, Second Edition

N. CHRISTOPHIDES. Graph Theory: An Algorithmic Approach

ALBERT NIJENHUIS AND HERBERT S. WILF. Combinatorial Algorithms

In preparation

AZRIEL ROSENFELD AND AVINASH C. KAK. Digital Picture Processing

A 5
B 6
C 7
D 8
E 9
F 0
G 1
H 2
I 3
J 4